'The Scum of The Earth'

'The Scum of The Earth'

WHAT HAPPENED TO THE REAL BRITISH HEROES OF WATERLOO?

COLIN BROWN

First published 2015

by Spellmount, an imprint of The History Press
The Mill, Brimscombe Port
Stroud, Gloucestershire, GL5 2QG
www.thehistorypress.co.uk

British Library Cataloguing in Publication Data.
A catalogue record for this book is available from the British Library.

ISBN 978 0 7509 6185 1

Typeset in Bembo 11/13.5pt by The History Press
Printed in India

CONTENTS

FOREWORD

The Duke of Wellington called his men 'the scum of the earth' in anger. But it went deeper than that. It was a patrician view of the world that left him on the wrong side of history in the early part of the nineteenth century that he, perhaps more than anybody else apart from Napoleon Bonaparte, had helped to shape.

But when the soldiers returned home from battle they found Britain at war with itself. For them, the forgotten heroes, Waterloo was not the end – it was only the beginning.

With the bicentenary of Waterloo approaching, I thought it was time to follow 'the scum of the earth' and find out what happened to them.

I approached this book as an investigative journalist with some trepidation. Historians have churned up the ground of Waterloo for 200 years and there is a minefield of disputed 'facts' surrounding it. There is still a dispute about the time it started. I apologise in advance if I have stumbled on the odd mine.

Colin Brown
Blackheath, England

ACKNOWLEDGEMENTS

On the Internet there is now a wealth of primary source material about Waterloo and the men who fought there. It is readily accessible if you know where to look. Google Books and the American and Canadian libraries deserve praise for making a vast archive of previously rare antiquarian books available free on the Internet, including *The Creevey Papers; Notes of Conversations with the Duke of Wellington* by Earl Stanhope; Dalton's *Waterloo Roll Call*, with notes on the officers, and the many entertaining memoirs of veterans of the battle. You can read the Parliamentary debates of the period in the online *Hansard* through the Parliamentary web portal. Like many heir hunters researching Waterloo, I discovered I had a family connection – Lieutenant Colonel Basil Jackson is my wife's (three-times) great uncle and wrote one of the most entertaining accounts of riding freely about the battlefield without orders because his boss, De Lancey, had been mortally wounded. Wellington's letters are online in the *Despatches*, and the University of Southampton is also placing more of the Wellington Archive catalogue online, though you still have to visit the excellent Hartley Library to see the originals. Project Hougoumont and Waterloo200 have uploaded vast amounts of valuable new research onto the Internet. The military archives are split between the National Archives in Kew and the various regimental archives, many of which are preserved by unpaid volunteers, such as Major Casanove at the Coldstream Guards. They deserve more than thanks – they deserve financial support. I am grateful to experts such as Gareth Glover and Andrew Field, in addition to many academics, who were generous with their time.

I have many to thank. They include:

Marianne Smith, College Librarian, The Royal College of Surgeons of Edinburgh

Christine Drummond, Senior Local Studies and Archives Assistant

Oldham Local Studies and Archives

Michael Powell, Chief Librarian, Chethams Library, Manchester

The Reverend David and Helen Pitcher of the Rectory, Framlingham

Justin Cavernelis-Frost, Archivist at the Rothschild Archive, New Court

Mark Beswick, Archive Information Officer, Met Office, National Meteorological Archive

David Helsden of Great Yarmouth Borough Council

David Thornburn of the Hougoumont Project, who kindly showed me around

Mark Smith at the Royal Artillery Museum, Woolwich

Pip Dodd, Senior Collections Content Curator, National Army Museum

Barry Sheerman MP

David Dykes, John Clare Cottage Museum

Michael Farrar, my expert Waterloo guide

Gregory O'Connor, National Archives, Dublin

Karen Robson, Archivist, Hartley Library – Wellington Archive, Southampton University

Dr Michael Rowe, Senior Lecturer in Modern European History at King's College London

Dr Julian Burton, Clinical Lecturer in Histopathology, Sheffield University

Paul Johnson, Consultant Forensic Pathologist and Home Office Pathologist at the Royal Liverpool University Hospital

Andrew Field, author of *Waterloo – the French Perspective*

Gareth Glover, author and editor of many expert books on Waterloo

Amanda Goodrich, Lecturer in Eighteenth Century History, Open University

Martin Hillman, who acted as my guide in Edinburgh

Derek Glen for help on Bull's Troop

And of course my chief researcher, and my wife, Amanda Brown

Newcastle July 2d 1835

My Dear Lord

I enclose the copy of a letter from the Governor of
Victoria which shews how our Men are going on
in that neighbourhood. These Men are restless hands
from the different Regts of the Army who were sent
to Victoria, after the Battle, each under Officers, in
order to collect the wounded and their stores & accoutrements. It is quite impossible for me or any other
Man to command a British army under the laxity
by them. We have in the service the scum of the earth
as common soldiers, and of late years we have been
doing every thing in our power both by law and by

The Earl Bathurst   his Excellency

To Earl Bathurst, Huarte, 2nd July, 1813

My Dear Lord,

I enclose the copy of a letter from the Governor of Vitoria which shows how our men are going on in that neighbourhood. These men are detachments from the different regiments of the army who were sent to Vitoria the day after the battle, each under officers, in order to collect the wounded and their arms and accoutrements. It is quite impossible for me or any other man to command a British army under the existing system. We have in the service the scum of the earth as common soldiers; and of late years we have been doing everything in our power, both by the law and by publications, to relax the discipline by which alone such men can be kept in order. The officers of the lower ranks will not perform the duty required from them for the purpose of keeping their soldiers in order; and it is next to impossible to punish any officer for neglects of this description. As to the non-commissioned officers, as I have repeatedly stated, they are as bad as the men, and too near them, in point of pay and situation, by the regulations of late years, for us to expect them to do anything to keep the men in order. It is really a disgrace to have anything to say to such men as some of our soldiers are ...

Believe me, etc Wellington.

THE EAGLE
HAS LANDED

The Duke of Wellington's victory at Waterloo was so utterly complete, and so swift that it is almost totally forgotten today that in the spring of 1815 there were many who were against plunging Britain into a fresh war against Napoleon. Astonishingly, the anti-war faction included the Duke of Wellington's elder brother, Richard, the Marquess of Wellesley.

It is easy to see why many were against a new war. Napoleon had been exiled to the safety of Elba, a Mediterranean island off the coast of Tuscany, in 1814. People all over Europe were beginning to enjoy the fruits of the peace. For the first time in a decade, Britons were free to travel to the Continent without the risk of being imprisoned as spies. Thomas Creevey, a Radical MP, his wife – a widow called Eleanor Ord and her children by an earlier marriage – had celebrated the peace in the autumn of 1814 like many new middle-class British families by decamping to the Continent.

The Creeveys – the redoubtable Mrs Creevey had a private income – rented a house in the centre of Brussels, where her daughters, the Ord sisters, and her son, enjoyed a social round of balls, banquets and walks in the central park. They joined the throngs, admiring the formal Dutch gardens, the smartly dressed officers, and the gossip.

But in the spring of 1815 Napoleon escaped and the Creeveys found themselves suddenly caught up like characters in Thackeray's novel, *Vanity Fair*, in the excitement of a city preparing for war, though there was no let-up in the social round of balls, banquets and walks in the central park.

As the city busied itself for war, Creevey received a letter from his close friend and ally, Henry Grey Bennet, one of the most talented Radical MPs in Parliament. It was full of the latest Westminster gossip about who was for war,

Perhaps a less flattering medal portrait of 'Old Hookey' than the one of Napoleon in the colour section. He was known at home as the Iron Duke not because of his military prowess but because of the iron shutters he had installed to prevent protestors from breaking the windows of his home. (From *Napoleon's Medals* by Richard A. Todd)

There's two sides to every story (and every conflict). 'The Treaty of Amiens Broken by England' (1803), an English leopard/lion/bulldog tears up the treaty; engraved by Romain-Vincent Jeuffroy at the *Monnai des Medailles* in Paris. (From *Napoleon's Medals* by Richard A. Todd)

Napoleon dragged off to Elba by the devil in 1814 – 'inseparable friends'. The matter was not settled. (From *Napoleon's Medals* by Richard A. Todd)

and who was against; and the doubts, Bennet claimed, reached right into the Cabinet of Lord Liverpool, the Tory prime minister:

Lord Greville [William Greville, ex-prime minister 'of all the talents'] started furious for war or at least declaring there was no way of avoiding it. A correspondence has taken place between him and Grey [a reformer and ex-Cabinet minister in Greville's government] ... and now he declares his opinions are not made up ...

Lord Spencer [Whig MP] and the Carringtons are for peace and what is more amusing is that Yarmouth who preaches peace at the corners of all the streets and is in open war with Papa and Mama [Lord Hertford, the Lord Chamberlain of the Household and his wife, Isabella, mistress of the Prince Regent] upon that subject.

Prinny [the Prince Regent] of course is for war. As for the Cabinet, Liverpool [the prime minister] and Lord Sidmouth [Home Secretary] are for peace; they say the Chancellor [Sir Nicholas Vansittart] is not so violent the other way. But Bathurst [Secretary of State for War and the Colonies] and Castlereagh [Foreign Secretary] are red hot ...

Bennet, a member of the Whig opposition, undoubtedly exaggerated the opposition to war but there were many who harboured serious doubts about whether Britain should go to war against Napoleon.

Radicals like Bennet and Creevey were reluctant for Britain to meddle in France's affairs to restore a despised Bourbon king, Louis XVIII, while they were dealing with the excesses of their own despised Prince Regent at home.

There was a sullen mood among the Radical MPs against a fresh war with Napoleon in 1815 that was similar to the feeling in the Commons in 2013 when Labour, Lib Dem and Tory MPs voted against military intervention over Syria. They had had enough of war. Britain had spent more than twenty years engaged in wars against the French, first in the Revolutionary Wars and then after a year's respite, the Napoleonic Wars. The country was exhausted by war, and it had its own troubles nearer home – poverty, unemployment, and social unrest.

I discovered that Wellington's older brother Richard was worried about another more serious consequence of two decades of war: Britain was also broke. Napoleon funded his campaigns with plunder. Britain paid for its wars with debt. National debt had rocketed to levels that would make Britain's 'debt crisis' after the 2008 bail-out of the banks look modest. Britain's national debt reached 75 per cent of its gross domestic product (GDP) in 2010. In 1816 it soared to more than 230 per cent of GDP. A few days before the Battle of Waterloo, the Chancellor asked Parliament to support an increase in borrowing to pay for the new war of £6m. Prime Minister William Pitt had introduced income tax as a temporary measure to reduce the debt from the French wars with a sinking fund but it could not keep pace with the colossal cost of war.

The Treasury had raised money to finance the war against France – and subsidise Spain and Portugal – by issuing government stocks and bonds, known as Consuls and Omnium. Wellington also obtained money for his army by issuing bills like IOUs, which could be sold on by traders or redeemed at the Bank of England. Because he was so often short of money on his campaigns, he had to sell these bills to foreign suppliers at a discount, adding more to the burden of government debt. Britain was also going through a slump at home, and Parliament had passed a bill in 1815 to fix the price of grain at 80s (today something over £200) a quarter (about 219kg) to stop cheap imports of grain flooding into Britain as a bonus of the peace.

This crude piece of protectionism was aimed at protecting the profits of the farmers and the livelihoods of farm labourers but it had the effect of putting up the price of bread. As most of the land in Britain was held by members of the small aristocratic elite who effectively ran the country, Parliament was accused with some justification of passing the Corn Laws to help the very richest in the land at the expense of the poor. It was not entirely as simple as that – farm workers were being forced to turn to the workhouse, because the farmers laid them off. But that meant nothing to the poor flooding into London's overcrowded slums trying to keep food on the table.

In 1815, as Britain sent troops to Belgium to do battle against Napoleon, there were food riots on the streets of London. While Wellington's regiments gathered around Brussels, the redcoats were mobilised to throw a ring of bright bayonets around Parliament to protect MPs and peers from a mob protesting against the passage of the Corn Laws legislation.

Opposition MPs were afraid the government was about to impose martial law by deploying troops on the streets around the Palace of Westminster. A government supporter, William Vesey Fitzgerald, assured MPs in the Commons debate in March 1815, the soldiers ringed the Commons 'not to overawe its proceedings but to defend its members from violence'. John Wilson Croker, the Admiralty Secretary, had been 'rudely treated' outside Parliament on his way to the debate, said Fitzgerald, and was only rescued with difficulty from the mob, while other MPs were 'collared, dragged about' and challenged about how they were going to vote. Despite the threats, after a long and rowdy debate, the bill went through unamended, fuelling the anger of the mob outside who had no vote in Parliamentary elections.

Britain was becoming almost ungovernable as it prepared for war. And then on 4 April, Napoleon tossed a diplomatic hand grenade into the laps of the allies to exploit their divisions: he secretly sent an 'overture' to Castlereagh, the British Foreign Secretary and European heads of government, seeking peace. It was sent from Paris by Napoleon's foreign minister, the Duke of Vicence, Marquis de Caulaincourt:

> The Emperor has appeared, the Royal Throne has fallen, and the Bourbon Family have quitted our territory, without one drop of blood being shed for their defence.
>
> Borne upon the arms of his people, His Majesty [Napoleon] has traversed France, from the point of the coast at which he at first touched the ground, as far as the centre of his capital, even that residence which is now again, as are all French hearts, filled with our dearest remembrances ...

This was cleverly crafted to press all the danger points of Britain's troubles at home, starting with the fact that thanks to a wilful Prince Regent, the monarchy in England was increasingly despised. Then he offered peace:

> He has no other wish than to repay such affections no longer by the trophies of vain ambition, but by all the advantages of an honourable repose and by all the blessings of a happy tranquility. It is to the duration of peace that the Emperor looks forward for the accomplishment of his noblest intentions.

Napoleon's secret peace offer was at first denied by the government, but when Whig MPs discovered its existence, the government's handling of the affair caused outrage in the Commons. Reading the Hansard report of the debate on 28 April 1815[1] in the Commons, as Whig MPs attacked Castlereagh and Wellington for marching Britain into war, reminded me strongly of the debates I covered for the *Independent* before the Iraq war in 2003. The protests against the Blair government in the spring of 2003 were a pure echo of Whig MPs in the spring of 1815. The Whig MPs accused the government of Lord Liverpool, and the Duke of Wellington, of declaring war not against a country but against a man, just as Labour rebels had accused Tony Blair of going to war against Iraq to seek 'regime change' over Saddam Hussein. They were furious that Wellington, as Britain's leading diplomat at the Congress of Vienna, which was taking place when Napoleon inconveniently landed in France on 1 March, had signed a declaration on 13 March making Bonaparte an outlaw. It said: 'Napoleon Bonaparte has placed himself without the pale of civil and social relations; and that, as an enemy and disturber of the tranquillity of the world, he has rendered himself liable to public vengeance ...'

It seems remarkable now, but at that time the Radicals were outraged at the idea Britain could be seeking a fresh war to topple Napoleon if the French people wanted him. They said the reference in the declaration to 'public vengeance' was an invitation to assassinate the emperor. The most outspoken Radical MP, Sam Whitbread, a Jacobin sympathiser, accused Castlereagh of 'deluding the House and the country' by 'holding forth the possibility of an alternative to war and the wish to adopt a pacific resolution, when in truth it had been already decided (by the Privy Council) that hostilities should be commenced. Such was the delusion practiced upon Parliament and country.' Whitbread argued that the restoration of the reviled French monarchy had never been a ground for Britain going to war, just as Labour MPs argued it was illegal for Blair to pursue war to change the leader of a foreign power. It was to answer that charge that Blair came up with the dossier on 'weapons of mass destruction' to try to prove that Saddam posed a threat to Britain and its assets abroad. Whitbread said both Pitt (the late prime minister) and the Crown, the Prince Regent, had disavowed war simply to bring about a change in the French government: 'For the first time in the history of the world, war [is being] proclaimed against one man for the demolition of his power,' Whitbread thundered. 'What is his power? His people: and the conclusion therefore is inevitable, that hostilities are to be renewed for the desperate and bloody enterprise of destroying a whole nation.'

But by then the die was cast. Wellington had replaced Castlereagh in early 1815 at the Congress of Vienna, which was busy carving up the map of Europe when Napoleon escaped. From the moment Wellington put his signature to the declaration there could be no accommodation with Napoleon, said the Whig MPs: it meant war.

Whitbread said he felt ashamed that the name of Wellington had been attached to the Vienna declaration outlawing Napoleon: 'While they proclaimed death to Buonaparté and vindicated assassination, by their own abandonment of treaties, they were the direct authors of this new war.' He accused Wellington and Liverpool of 'plunging Great Britain into a war that, if not otherwise terminated, must, in the opinion of all thinking men, be soon abandoned, from a deficiency in our very physical resources'. Hansard, the official Parliamentary report, records other Whig MPs shouted 'hear hear!' after Whitbread said he wished the Commons and the county would weigh the alternatives, before plunging into a new war.

Sam Whitbread was the handsome son of the founder of the brewery. He bore a striking resemblance to Jane Austen's dashing Mr Darcy but would soon suffer a bloody end. He was unusually outspoken but few of his friends, like Creevey, knew he was also deeply depressed by debts of more than £25,000 on the Drury Lane Theatre. It all became too much for him. On 6 July, less than a month after Bonaparte's final defeat at Waterloo, Whitbread committed suicide by slashing his own throat with a razor.

But Sam Whitbread had not been a lone voice. Whitbread did not know it, but Wellington's older brother, the Marquess of Wellesley, was privately airing his misgivings about the prospect of war. And they were cogent, practical reasons why Britain should not go to war against the resurgent Bonaparte. Wellesley had advanced Arthur's military career in India when Richard was its governor-general. He had been the Foreign Secretary in the government of Spencer Perceval. But when Perceval was shot dead in the Commons – the only British prime minister to be assassinated – by a deranged businessman nursing a grudge over his debts, Wellesley refused to serve in the Cabinet of Perceval's successor, Lord Liverpool.

Liverpool – Britain's most underestimated prime minister (Disraeli called him an 'arch mediocrity') – remained in office until 1827 and held the Tory Party together throughout one of the most turbulent times in Britain's long history. This curtailed Richard's ministerial career and reduced his influence over both Liverpool and his brother. Even so, it was a remarkable fact that he secretly lobbied against the war. His reasons were more practical than the Whig MPs'.

I stumbled across Richard Wellesley's opposition to the war in a long-forgotten memorandum attached to the Ninth Volume of the Duke of Wellington's despatches after his death by the Duke's son, Arthur Richard Wellesley, the 2nd Duke of Wellington. The 2nd Duke revealed that in 1815 Prime Minister Lord Liverpool had told the Duke of Wellington he had information, upon which he could rely, that the French nation was decidedly against Bonaparte, and that he was only supported by a military conspiracy, which might easily be put down if the allies mounted an immediate attack on him. The Marquess of Wellesley bluntly told Liverpool – and his brother the Duke – this 'was a fallacy' and even if it were true, it would take at least three months for the Duke to get his army ready. In the meantime, said the Marquess, they ought to look for a negotiated way out:

> Three months of military inactivity must inevitably take place on our side, and it is unwise to forego the possible advantage of negotiation in that interval, if it had no other object than to ascertain the real inclination of the French people, and whether they might not be disposed to choose a government, with or without Bonaparte, which would be agreeable to themselves and promise tranquillity to Europe …

A far bigger objection to war, said Wellesley, was the state of Britain's finances. His greatest objection 'to plunging into a new war, independently of the exhausted situation of this country', was that he could not foresee any benefit that could be expected by England, 'even in the event of complete success.'

Wellesley warned that a military victory would leave Britain having to keep
an occupying force in France for months, perhaps years to come, in order to
keep King Louis XVIII on the throne. Britain could ill-afford the bill for such
a victory, he said. In that, he was proved right. But the victory at Waterloo was
so complete that many have forgotten there were doubters before the battle.
Professor Michael Rowe, Senior Lecturer in European History at King's
College, London, told me:

> With the benefit of hindsight, the outcome of the Waterloo campaign of
> 1815 looks like a foregone conclusion.
>
> However, it is worth bearing in mind that such an outcome was by no
> means obvious to statesmen in the weeks following Napoleon's daring
> escape from Elba and triumphal return to Paris in March 1815.
>
> The challenges confronting the new anti-Napoleonic coalition that
> quickly came into being were formidable. Not least of these was the fact
> that the largest coalition armies – the Austrian and Russian – would take
> a considerable time to deploy, thereby affording Napoleon time to strike
> pre-emptively at the weaker British and Prussian forces available in the
> Low Countries …
>
> The memorandum also points to the wider problems that would arise
> even in the event of a military victory over Napoleon. Not least of these
> was the probability that the Bourbons could only be re-imposed on the
> French people through the long-term commitment of considerable mili-
> tary force by the coalition, a scenario that according to Wellesley was hardly
> in the interests of a war-weary Britain.

It is all remarkably similar to the problems that faced the Americans and
their allies after the invasions of Iraq and Afghanistan in the early twenty-
first century. And it proved to be highly prescient. Britain had to pay for an
occupying force to remain in Paris to shore up the French Crown. However,
Richard Wellesley and the Whig critics of the war had not calculated on his
brother securing such an utterly decisive victory over Napoleon that it would
bring an end to the new Napoleonic war in a day.

At 46, Wellington had never expected to have to climb back into the saddle
to go to war again against Napoleon. He had been enjoying a comfortable
life as a revered war hero, a respected diplomat, and a supporter of the Tory
government under Lord Liverpool with a seat in the House of Lords.

Wellington had returned to Britain in 1814 as a national hero after a final
victory against Marshal Soult at Toulouse. Napoleon was forced into exile on
the mountainous Mediterranean island of Elba. It was near his native Corsica
and he was allowed to preside over it and its people with the laughable title

of 'Emperor of Elba'. It seems astonishingly naïve that the allied governments believed the conqueror of Europe would settle for life as the emperor of an island that at one point is only 2½ miles across, but there was no attempt to imprison Napoleon on the island under lock and key. The island was patrolled by the Royal Navy and a British Army officer, Sir Neil Campbell, was ordered to keep an eye on him, but was away from the island – possibly visiting his mistress on mainland Italy – while Napoleon sailed away with his personal bodyguards. Campbell had a long list of battle honours behind his name, including the capture of Martinique and Guadeloupe, the Siege of Ciudad Rodrigo, the Battle of Salamanca, and was severely wounded in a cavalry charge in France in 1814 by a Russian hussar who mistook him for the enemy. He commanded the 54th West Norfolk Regiment of Foot at Waterloo but inevitably became known as 'the man who let Boney go'. He was rewarded in the way that the army knows how: he was sent to the 'white man's grave' of Sierra Leone in 1826, where he died a year later – causing indignant fury in the press.

While Napoleon secretly plotted his return, Wellington basked in the after-glow of a long, successful military career that seemed over in 1814. He was garlanded with honours and financial rewards for ending Napoleon's tyranny and liberating Portugal and Spain from France. He was lionised in London, feted at banquets and balls in his honour, and showered with glittering prizes by Britain's grateful allies. Capping them all, the Prince Regent bestowed on Sir Arthur Wellesley a title that was grander than the five he already possessed: he was made the 1st Duke of Wellington.* Fashionable Regency ladies flocked to his court. They included Frances, Lady Shelley, an excitable 27-year-old married heiress, who kept a gossipy journal about the sayings of the great and not-so-good. She confided to her journal she was so overwhelmed to be in the Duke's presence, she was struck dumb: 'I must admit that my enthusiasm for this great soldier was so great that I could not utter a word; and it was with the greatest difficulty that I restrained my tears.'

Whatever attracted the ladies, it was not the Duke's sparkling wit. He set about conquering a woman like a military campaign. He paid 100 guineas to an intermediary for an introduction to Harriette Wilson, a high-class Regency courtesan and suggested another 100 guineas for Harriette if he was 'successful' in breaking down her defences. She took the money but com-plained about his lack of charm in her 'kiss-and-tell' memoirs:

---

* His brother William chose Wellington because the family could trace their roots to the nearby Wellesley in Somerset in 1104. The Duke approved but Lady Wellington did not, saying, 'it recalls nothing'. (Wellington Despatches viii 148, Raglan Papers, 13 September 1809)

Most punctual to my appointment, Wellington made his appearance. He bowed first, then said, 'How do you do?' then thanked me for having given him permission to call on me; and then wanted to take hold of my hand. 'Really,' said I, withdrawing my hand, 'for such a renowned hero you have very little to say for yourself. I understood you came here to try to make yourself agreeable?' 'What child!' retorted the Duke. 'Do you think that I have nothing better to do than to make speeches to please ladies?'

Despite this awkward introduction, Wellington stayed, paid her bills, and remained one of her part-time lovers for many years. Frances, Lady Shelley felt that a light had gone out of London society when the Duke accepted the offer of a plum diplomatic post as the British Ambassador in Paris, in the autumn of 1814, but several of his female admirers followed him to the French capital.

Wellington took over the Paris house of Pauline Borghese, Napoleon's sister, rumoured to be another of his conquests, as the British Embassy. He paid her 870,000 francs on behalf of the British taxpayer, for the Hotel de Charost in the rue du Faubourg St Honoré that today, with its great couture houses, is said to be the most fashionable street in the world. It is still the official residence of the British Ambassador, and the equally elegant house next door, No. 35, with French windows opening onto tree-shaded gardens, was added in 1947, and is now the British Embassy, used for hosting more public events. They are shielded from the outside world by discreet black doors on the narrow street, which give no clue to the graceful houses and gardens beyond, to which I can testify, having been there to cover a visit by Tony Blair for a British 'cool Britannia' trade fair.

Throughout his life, Wellington liked to give dinners for a large number of guests (it was a custom, he said, that had been acquired with his officers in the army), and he was soon surrounded by beautiful female admirers at banquets, balls, the theatre, and riding in the boulevards of Paris. His Irish aristocratic wife Kitty, Catherine Packenham (the family name of the Longfords), had never loved the limelight and though devoted to Arthur, found it impossible to play the role of the grand society hostess he wanted; she had captivated him as a young man, but as his star rose, she shrank into the background and they became estranged.

In London, Wellington was lampooned for his sexual liaisons by the great Georgian satirical cartoonists such as Isaac Robert Cruikshank. One showed him sitting astride a cannon to the alarm of two ladies – one says: 'What a spanker! I hope he won't fire it at me.' Her friend says: 'It can't do any harm … he has fired it so often it is nearly worn out.'[2]

Soon the real cannons would be firing again.

The Master of the Ordnance Exercising his Hobby!

Wellington lampooned for his womanising: *The Master of Ordnance Exercising his Hobby* by Robert Cruikshank (© Trustees of the British Museum)

In Paris in December 1814 there was growing unrest among the Bonapartists at the emperor's exile, while Wellington's presence at the head of the foreign occupying force became a cause of worry back in Whitehall. Lord Liverpool became increasingly alarmed for the Duke's safety and looked for something that would get him away from Paris. The prime minister offered Wellington the command of the British forces in North America, where Britain was engaged in a war against the newly independent United States of America (it was called the War of 1812, although it dragged on into 1815). It was a colonialist campaign ostensibly to protect Britain's possessions in Canada, but it developed into a bitter struggle over sea power mixed with a desire for revenge for the loss of Britain's American possessions. In 1814 the British carried out a punitive raid on Washington, the only attack in history on the American capital by a foreign power. Redcoats torched the White House as the President, James Madison and his wife, fled to safety. British troops burned down both houses of Congress, the State Department, the War Office, and the Treasury. The British forces there included some of Wellington's battle-hardened regiments from the Peninsular campaign in Portugal and Spain, but with poor leadership they had suffered a number of reverses.

Wellington wisely turned down the offer to lead his old regiments again – the war with America was practically over and a peace deal was signed a month later.* Instead of heading to America, Wellington agreed to go to Vienna to replace Castlereagh at the Congress, where the brilliant Austrian diplomat Metternich was acting as the Maitre d' of the talks with the four major powers – Britain, Austria, Russia, Prussia – and Bourbon France, represented by the sinuous Charles Maurice Talleyrand, to put flesh on the bones of the 1814 Treaty of Paris. This restored the throne to Louis XVIII and broadly returned France to the lands it held in 1792, before the French Revolutionary and Napoleonic wars began.

It was not a conventional conference, and never met in plenary session. The horse-trading was done by the delegations in separate state-rooms of an Austrian palace. The Russian Tsar, Alexander, was using the post-Napoleon peace talks to annex most of Poland for Russia (a strategic ambition that was realised by Stalin in 1945 at the end of the Second World War). Britain formed a secret alliance with Austria and France (Talleyrand wheedled his way in) against Russian expansionism over Poland, short of war against the Tsar – Earl Bathurst, the Secretary of State for War, wrote to Castlereagh on 27 November 1814, to warn him that the Prince Regent did not want to spark a new Continental conflict against Russia.

When Wellington arrived in Vienna in January 1815 and asked what had been achieved, Prince Metternich bluntly said, 'Nothing'. It probably suited Wellington. The Duke and Metternich were both against radical reform and shared a belief that after the turmoil of the Napoleonic Wars, what Europe needed was a return to stability and the status quo ante – the restoration of the legitimate monarchs of Europe to their thrones, and the old balance of power in Europe maintained, as if the turmoil caused by the upstart Napoleon Bonaparte had never happened.

France was stripped back to its pre-1792 possessions, the Netherlands gained Belgium, Prussia gained Saxony, Russia swallowed part of Poland (though Wellington and Metternich prevented it swallowing it all), and Metternich created the German confederation under Austrian influence (sowing the seeds for a future war with Prussia). Meanwhile, Britain emerged with an enlarged empire and the lucrative colonies in the Cape, South Africa, Ceylon, and Tobago.

The Congress was criticised for being too conservative with its redrawn map of Europe, but it was another ninety-nine years before a British soldier was called upon to fire a gun in anger on the Continent, when the Kaiser launched an attack on France through Belgium, a few miles down the road from Waterloo.

---

*   General Andrew Jackson defeated the English under Packenham (brother-in-law of Wellington) at the Battle of New Orleans in January 1815 before news of the peace deal at Ghent had arrived.

Wellington's approach to diplomacy was rather like his approach to women: he wanted to tackle it head-on. He was uncomfortable with the duplicity of diplomacy as practised by the scheming French foreign minister, Prince Talleyrand,* who had survived the Terror of the French Revolution, the Empire of Bonaparte, and the Restoration of the Bourbon monarchy.

The negotiating tables of the Congress were kicked over on 7 March, when Wellington received a secret despatch from Lord Bathurst saying Bonaparte had escaped. The Russian Tsar Alexander laid his hand on the Duke's shoulder and told him: 'It is for you to save the world again.'

Wellington wrote to Castlereagh on 12 March. I found his original letter in the Wellington archive. He wrote:

> My Lord, we received on the 7th March a despatch from Lord Bathurst giving an account that Bonaparte had quitted the island of Elba with all his infantry officers and about 1,200 troops on the 26th February. I immediately communicated this account to the Emperors of Austria and Russia and the King of Prussia and the ministers of the different Powers and I found one sentiment – to unite their efforts to support the system established by the Peace of Paris [the restoration of the Bourbon Monarchy to the Throne]. The sovereigns and all the persons appointed here are impressed with the importance of the crisis which this circumstance occasions in the affairs of the world.[3]

Wellington asked the arch-plotter Talleyrand, who knew Napoleon, what he thought Bonaparte would do next. Talleyrand told Wellington: 'He'll go anywhere you like to mention, except France.'

Talleyrand was brilliant at political intrigue but he was no military genius. Napoleon – the imperial eagle – had landed in France a week earlier, on 1 March, on the beach at Golfe-Juan, and was already marching north to Grenoble through the mountains of Provence.** When he reached the town of Gap on 5 March, he promised his followers: 'The Eagle with the national colours, shall fly from steeple to steeple until it reaches the towers of Notre Dame!'

The emperor promised to bring back *La Gloire*, the glory days, to France in a ringing declaration:

---

*   On hearing about the death of Talleyrand, Metternich said: 'What did he mean by that?'

**   *La Route Napoleon*, a 350km section of national road N85 through the Alpes-Maritimes to Grenoble, is celebrated by the French with gilded imperial eagles by the roadside.

Soldiers! We have not been conquered. Two men, raised from our ranks, betrayed our laurels, their country, their prince, their benefactor …[*] In my exile I have heard your voice. I have come back in spite of all obstacles, and all dangers. Your general, called to the throne by the choice of the people, and raised on your shields, is restored to you; come and join him. Mount the tricoloured cockade; you wore it in the days of our greatness. We must never forget that we have been the masters of nations; but we must not suffer any to intermeddle with our affairs. Who would pretend to be master over us? Who would have the power? Resume those eagles which you had at Ulm, at Austerlitz, at Jena …Victory shall march at a charging step.

It was a masterpiece of political chutzpah, given his recent fall. And in a passage that echoed Shakespeare's *Henry V* oration to his troops before the Battle of Agincourt, he added:

In your old age, surrounded and honoured by your fellow-citizens, you shall be heard with respect when you recount your high deeds. You shall then say with pride – 'I also was one of that great army which entered twice within the walls of Vienna, which took Rome, and Berlin, and Madrid, and Moscow – and which delivered Paris from the stain which treason and the presence of the enemy imprinted upon it.'

This demonstrated the politician's gift of a short memory: Moscow was a catastrophe that cost him an estimated 300,000 men and it had been Ney who had covered his back as he retreated through the snow. Napoleon was calculating on the army backing him against the despised Bourbons, and the foreigners who occupied their capital and squabbled over the future shape of Europe in Vienna. The soldiers gave him power, and if he could win them back to his eagle standards, he knew the people would follow. As he had promised his followers, Napoleon returned when the violets were in bloom. Violets were worn by Bonapartists in Paris that spring as a symbol of hope.

The emperor showed a combination of personal bravery and a flair for pure theatre: when a royalist force intercepted his forward guard near Grenoble, Napoleon marched to the head of his men, threw open his cape, showing the star of the Legion of Honour on his breast, and said: 'If there be among you a soldier who desires to kill his general – his emperor – let him do it now. Here I am.' He was greeted with the old battle cry, 'Vive l'Empereur!' It would soon reverberate across Europe.

---

[*]   He blamed the Duke of Castiglione for surrendering Lyons without a fight, and the Duke of Ragusa for surrendering Paris to save the city.

He expected his marshals to rally round but Marshal Louis Alexandre Berthier, his elderly chief of staff, refused. Soon after, Berthier fell out of a window to his death, arousing suspicions that he was murdered, though Wellington remained convinced it was an accident, telling a private dinner years later that Berthier was standing by a high window, and having just 'eaten a hearty breakfast, became giddy, and lost his balance'. Either way, you had to be brave to say 'no' to Napoleon. Berthier was replaced by Marshal Soult who, though a capable field commander, was crucially not as effective as a chief of staff. Berthier was sorely missed by Napoleon at Waterloo.

The red-headed Marshal Michel Ney, one of the emperor's most trusted generals before he too capitulated in 1814, had gone over to the Bourbon Crown and boasted to King Louis XVIII he would bring Bonaparte back like a bird in a cage. The king retorted: 'Je n'aimerais pas un tel oiseau dans ma chambre!' (I do not want such a bird in my room!)

Napoleon, who always had a personal touch with his men, sent Ney a personal note praising him as the 'bravest of the brave' for his rearguard action in the retreat from Moscow. When Ney intercepted Napoleon with a royalist force at Auxerre, one of the largest towns in the Burgundy region, about 91 miles south of Paris, his troops switched sides and Ney joined them in the emperor's growing army.

The Duke of Wellington penned another note to Castlereagh from Vienna on 12 March that I found in the Wellington Archive. It was marked 'private'. The Duke said the heads of Europe were pledging three corps to fight Napoleon – 150,000 Austrians who were in Italy; an additional 200,000 Austrians, Bavarians; and the troops of the Lower Rhine with the Prussian Corps, together with the British and Hanoverians in Flanders. Wellington shared the view expressed by Lord Liverpool that had been rejected by his brother Richard:

> It is my opinion that Bonaparte has acted upon false or no information and that the King will destroy him without difficulty and in a short time … If he does not, the affair will be a serious one and a great and immediate effort must be made which will be successful … It will remain for the British Government to determine how far they will act themselves …I now recommend to you to put all your force in the Netherlands at the disposition of the King of France if you can trust the officers at the head of it. I will go and join it, if you like it, or do anything else that the Government chooses.[4]

On 24 March Wellington wrote to his younger brother Sir Henry Wellesley saying: 'You will have seen what a breeze Bonaparte has started up in France.

And in the course of about six weeks there will not be fewer than 700,000 men on the French border. I am going to take command of the army in the Netherlands.' In fact, only a fraction of that number of troops ever arrived to face Napoleon. Captain William Siborne, in his history of the campaign published in the Victorian era, said France resembled a nation buckling on its armour – Napoleon had ordered up to 800,000 men to be mobilised. The *Armee du Nord* that had been hurriedly reconstituted in the north of France amounted to 116,000 men with up to 350 guns.

The emperor had decided to strike before Wellington and Blücher's Prussians could invade France. Unsure of Napoleon's intentions, Wellington rented a house as his headquarters in the fashionable centre of Brussels (the owner retreated to the top floor) and continued on a round of social engagements, balls, banquets, riding out on his favourite warhorse, Copenhagen, often with his society lady friends, to show how unconcerned he was by the threat of war. He remained convinced that the French people did not want Napoleon back in power.

Creevey was better informed. A young British Army officer, Major Hamilton, who was engaged to one of the Ord sisters and was trying to ingratiate himself into Creevey's good books, wrote to Creevey on 18 March promising to give him the latest news from Paris providing he did not 'blab' about the source of the leak. Hamilton, aide-de-camp (ADC) to General Barnes, the Adjutant General of the Army in Brussels, wrote:

> My dear Mr Creevey,
> If you will not blab, you shall hear all the news I can pick up, bad and good as it comes. I am sorry to tell you bad news today. General Fagal writes from Paris to say that Bonaparte may be in that Capital ere many days. His army increases hourly, and as fast as a regiment is brought up to the neighbourhood of Lyons, it goes over to its old master.

The day after Hamilton penned his letter (19 March), Louis XVIII fled the Tuileries palace in the middle of the night, while Napoleon slept at the chateau of Fontainebleau. The white cockade of the Bourbon monarchy was trampled underfoot, and the next day, Napoleon re-entered Paris and thus began The Hundred Days – the time between his arrival on 20 March and the restoration of Louis XVIII on 28 June.

Lord Bathurst appointed Henry Paget, the Earl of Uxbridge (later Marquess of Anglesey) as Wellington's second in command for the Waterloo campaign. This seemed astonishing to Wellington's friends because, during the Peninsular War, Uxbridge had cuckolded Wellington's brother Henry and ran off with his wife, Lady Charlotte. Uxbridge wangled the post now because he was a friend of the Prince Regent. Wellington insisted he did not give a damn and gave short shrift to a friend who said it would cause a scandal:

'Your grace cannot have forgotten the affair with Lady Charlotte?'
'Oh no! I have not forgotten that.'
'That is not the only case, I am afraid. At any rate, Lord Uxbridge has the reputation of running away with everybody he can.'
'I'll take good care he don't run away with me. I don't care about anybody else.'

Wellington regarded the press and 'public relations' with contempt, and treated the scandal sheets with haughty disdain. This was particularly true about his own affairs, which is just as well, because the gossips had a field day when he moved from Paris to Brussels, where he was surrounded by Regency ladies drawn to the city by the excitement of war, the brilliant uniforms, and the dashing commander-in-chief, who, even at 46, was nicknamed by Creevey 'The Beau'. When one of Harriette Wilson's male friends later tried to blackmail him with her memoirs, he famously said: 'Publish and be damned.'

The Duke's list of admirers included the lovely Lady Frances Webster, 21, who clearly captivated Wellington from the moment they first met in Brussels. Lady Frances was the wife of James Webster-Wedderburn, a Regency rake who once foolishly boasted to the Romantic poet, Lord Byron, that women were fair game, but his pious wife could be trusted with any man. He was wrong. Annoyed by Webster-Wedderburn's boasts about his wife's virtue, Byron, like a character in the bad plot of an Italian opera, set out to prove him wrong by seducing her. He described in a letter to Lady Melbourne, a grande dame of Whig society in Whitehall, how he easily succeeded. Lady Frances returned his ardent love when Byron cornered her in the billiard room of her home, but it was an offer he was too afraid to consummate because he feared it could have led to a duel with his friend.

In his letter to Lady Melbourne in October 1813, Byron revealed: 'I have made love – & if I am to believe mere words (for there we have hitherto stopped) it is returned. – I must tell you the place of declaration however – a billiard room!' At 6 p.m. he added a postscript to his letter: 'This business is growing serious – & I think Platonism in some peril – There has been very nearly a scene – almost an hysteric & really without cause for I was conducting myself with (to me) very irksome decorum – her expressions astonish me – so young & cold as she appeared …'

Rebuffed by Byron, Lady Frances went on a few months later to ensnare her greater prize in Brussels. A young subaltern became curious at seeing the Duke of Wellington arrive at the central park, and slip behind some trees.

Soon afterwards, a carriage arrived and he recognised Lady Frances as she 'descended into a hollow where the trees completely screened them'.

It is unclear whether Wellington consummated their affair in the hollow or anywhere else – Lady Frances was more than four months pregnant – but there is little doubt that he was in love with her (paternally or otherwise). He found time to pen notes to Lady Frances in the precious hours on the morning of the Battle of Waterloo and the morning after it.

Rumours of their affair caused a scandal after the battle. While Wellington and his allied army occupied Paris, Lady Frances gave birth to a son in the city on 18 August 1815; he was christened Charles Byron (her husband clearly still counted the poet among his friends). But Wellington was drawn into a scandal in November 1815 over claims in a gossip sheet, the *St James's Chronicle*, that her husband was going to sue Wellington for 'criminal conversation' – the legal expression at the time for extra-marital sex and grounds for divorce – with his wife. Rather than suing the victor of Waterloo, Webster-Wedderburn sued the publisher for libel. He was awarded £2,000. The scandal ended Wellington's fascination with Lady Frances and she passed out of his life, but there were many other female admirers in Brussels and, later, Paris.

Wellington attended a party of Brussels high society on Saturday 22 April 1815, hosted by Lady Charlotte Greville, another from his list of lovers and wife of one of his officers, Colonel Charles Greville, a soldier-politician who supported the Tories. The Duke confidently assured Lady Charlotte's guests that Bonaparte was likely to be killed by a stiletto-wielding assassin in Paris before he could wage war again.

The Duke approached Creevey at the party with a show of such bonhomie that the MP thought the Duke must be drunk. Creevey had metaphorically crossed swords with Wellington at Westminster – he opposed a £2,000-a-year annuity granted by the Prince Regent to Wellington as a reward from a grateful nation for his victory at Vitoria, which freed Spain of the French occupying army. Creevey was flattered by the Duke's attentions to him but not impressed by what he had to say: 'My Lord would have it that Bonaparte would be done up out of hand in Paris,' Creevey shared with his journal. 'I thought several times he must be drunk. But drunk or sober, he had not the least appearance of being a clever man.' Though Creevey conceded: 'Our conversation was mightily amicable and good, considering our former various sparring bouts in the House of Commons ...' Wellington may have believed his assassination theory, but it is more likely he was putting on a brave show to avoid panic spreading in Brussels.

On 15 June Wellington, his ladies, and his senior officers, took part in one of the most celebrated balls in history. It was thrown by the Duke and Duchess of Richmond in the cavernous coach house – it was 150ft long by 54ft wide and decorated with wallpaper of trellis and roses – in the *Rue de la Blanchisserie* at the back of their rented house in *Rue des Cendres*, near the Botanical Gardens in the centre of Brussels.* The guests at Lady Richmond's ball included Lady Frances Wedderburn-Webster, with whom Wellington was already rumoured to be having an affair, and the highly volatile Lady Caroline Lamb – Lady Melbourne's daughter-in-law and Byron's notorious mistress – who claimed she coined the description of the Romantic poet as 'mad bad and dangerous to know'. It could have applied equally to herself.

As the fears about Napoleon gripped the city, the Duchess anxiously asked the Commander-in-Chief whether she should postpone the ball. He calmly assured her the ball would not be interrupted by Napoleon: 'Duchess, you may give your ball with the greatest safety, without fear of interruption.' Wellington undoubtedly wanted to put on a show of confidence at the ball because he did not want to fan the panic that was already growing in the city. Wellington was receiving reports two days before the ball about the French deployment close to the border from Major General Sir Hussey Vivian, commander of the 6th Brigade of cavalry, who had received intelligence from a French deserter. Wellington refused to react until he knew more clearly what Napoleon planned. The first contact came early on 15 June – the morning of the Duchess of Richmond's ball – when the French skirmishers clashed with Prussian picquets inside the Belgian border south of Charleroi, only 37 miles from Brussels.

Bonaparte's aim was to try to force a wedge between Wellington's combined allied force of around 112,000 men and 200 guns and the 130,000-strong Prussian Army under the old Prussian warhorse, Gebhard Leberecht von Blücher known as 'Marshal Vorwarts' (Forwards).

Wellington had perhaps lulled himself into a false sense of security because he believed Napoleon would stand a far better chance of frustrating the Allied armies by fighting a clever defensive war within the French border as he had in 1814. Napoleon instead went for a bold move: strike first and trust to fortune. It was to be the biggest gamble of his life. Wellington heard of clashes with Napoleon's forces from the Prince of Orange at 3 p.m. and at 7.30 p.m. that the Prussians' I Corps under von Zieten was under attack at Thuin near Charleroi. Wellington insisted on attending the ball regardless of Napoleon's manoeuvres, and watched the officers and their ladies twirling to the music until supper was served after 10 p.m. As more reports came in of the clashes with the French, the guests who included most of Wellington's staff officers, brigade commanders, and allied chiefs became more agitated. They watched

---

★   It has long since been replaced by a multistorey car park and boring blocks of grey offices and flats.

the Gordon Highlanders nimbly dancing jigs and reels in their kilts to the sound of bagpipes: 'I well remember the Gordon Highlanders dancing reels at the ball,' recalled Louisa, one of the Duchess of Richmond's daughters:

> My mother thought it would interest foreigners to see them, which it did …
> I remember hearing that some of the poor men who danced in our house died at Waterloo. There was quite a crowd to look at the Scotch dancers.

The foreign dignitaries were amazed to see men in skirts, but in twenty-four hours many were lying dead in the fields near a cross roads at a place called Quatre Bras.

There are still heated disputes about the extent to which Wellington was caught out. Wellington was undoubtedly surprised by the speed of Napoleon's rapid advance but nursed a worry that Napoleon's thrust towards Brussels was a feint, and the real attack would be through Mons to cut him off from the coast. Indeed, he all but admitted it in his famous Waterloo Despatch to Bathurst on 19 June, when he said he ordered his troops to 'march … as soon as I had intelligence from other quarters to prove that the enemy's movement upon Charleroi was the *real* attack …'

As the band played on, around midnight, he was told that the area in front of Mons was clear of enemy troops and ordered his officers to concentrate their men in support of the Dutch forces who were holding Quatre Bras, the strategic crossroads where the main Charleroi–Brussels is intersected by the west–east Nivelles–Namur road. By holding the crossroads, Wellington could keep in contact with Blücher a few miles to the east at Ligny.

The effect on the ball was compared to kicking a bees' nest. Officers in dress uniform dashed for the exit, and hurriedly bade farewell to their dancing partners to join their regiments. Lady Caroline Lamb described its romantic poignancy: 'There never was such a Ball – so fine and so sad. All the young men who appeared there shot dead a few days later.' The injured included her own brother, a dashing cavalry officer, Sir Frederick Cavendish Ponsonby, who was one of the luckiest men to be alive after the battle. Her ex-lover Lord Byron eclipsed her words in a newly-added Third Canto to his epic poem, *Childe Harold's Pilgrimage* although he was not at the ball:

> Ah! then and there was hurrying to and fro,
> And gathering tears, and tremblings of distress,
> And cheeks all pale, which but an hour ago
> Blushed at the praise of their own loveliness;
> And there were sudden partings, such as press
> The life from out young hearts, and choking sighs

Which ne'er might be repeated; who could guess
If ever more should meet those mutual eyes,
Since upon night so sweet such awful morn could rise!

The 'sudden partings' included one of Wellington's ADCs, the Honourable Henry Percy, who pocketed a ladie's velvet handkerchief purse given him as a keepsake by an admirer. The purse was to play a part in the history of the battle and its aftermath. Like his fellow officers, Percy dashed off to war, still wearing the dress uniform he wore at the ball.

The Duke whispered to his old friend, Charles Lennox, the Duke of Richmond, that he needed to see a good map. Richmond took Wellington into his dressing-room and unfolded a map for him on a table. Wellington shut the door and said, 'Napoleon has humbugged me, by God; he has gained twenty-four hours' march on me … I have ordered the army to concentrate at Quatre Bras; but we shall not stop him there, and if so I must fight him there.' According to Richmond, he made a mark on the map with his thumb-nail. It was over a crossroads on the main road into Brussels. It was about 9 miles to the south of the city on the Charleroi road at a hamlet called Mont Saint Jean.[*] Soon the world would know it as Waterloo.

Notes

1. Hansard Report, 28 April 1915.
2. 'The Master of the Ordnance Exercising his Hobby', etching by Robert Cruikshank, British Museum, 1935,0522.11.159.
3. WP 1/453/7, Wellington Archive, Southampton University.
4. WP 1/453/8, Wellington Archive, Southampton University.

---

[*]   The map with Wellington's thumbnail mark was lost. Richmond took it with him to British North America (Canada) when he was made its Governor General, but his map was mislaid after his sudden death there in 1819. While touring the province, he was bitten by a pet fox and died in agony of rabies.

1

THE SCUM OF
THE EARTH

Thomas Creevey was strolling through the Parc de Bruxelles with his step-daughters, the Ord sisters, shortly before the Battle of Waterloo, when they were joined by Creevey's newfound friend, the Duke of Wellington. Creevey had just received the newspapers from London containing reports of the debate in the Commons raising doubts about war, and the MP wanted to ask the Duke himself whether he thought he could win. Creevey noted in his journal:

> He stopt, and said in the most natural manner:—'By God! I think Blücher and myself can do the thing.'—'Do you calculate,' I asked, 'upon any desertion in Bonaparte's army?'—'Not upon a man,' he said, 'from the colonel to the private in a regiment—both inclusive. We may pick up a marshal or two, perhaps; but not worth a damn.'—'Do you reckon,' I asked, 'upon any support from the French King's troops at Alost?'—'Oh!' said he, 'don't mention such fellows! No: I think Blücher and I can do the business.'—Then, seeing a private soldier of one of our infantry regiments enter the park, gaping about at the statues and images:—'There,' he said, pointing at the soldier, 'it all depends upon that article whether we do the business or not. Give me enough of it, and I am sure.'

'That article' was the ordinary British soldier, the anonymous figure in a redcoat that Wellington later christened 'Tommy Atkins'. These were the men on whom the outcome of the battle – and the future of Europe – would rest.

They were men like the self-confessed Irish rogue, Private Charles O'Neil of the 'Slashers', the 28th Regiment. O'Neil, 22, was a serial deserter with no pretentions to heroism. O'Neil was typical of many Irish farm boys who took the 'King's Shilling' – though his bounty was considerably more than 12 pence – because of youthful naïvety and poverty in rural Ireland. He was the youngest of eleven children, including six brothers, born in Dundalk in County Louth, halfway between Belfast and Dublin, in what is now the Republic of Ireland.

Ireland was a prime recruiting area for the British Army. More than 30 per cent of the English county regiments were actually made up with Irish recruits. Not even the threat of being killed put off raw recruits like O'Neil. O'Neil's eldest brother enlisted in the Navy, joined HMS *Terrible* and was killed by a cannon ball a few months later. A second brother joined Wellington's army in the Peninsular campaign, and was killed at Talavera.

O'Neil defied his parents' entreaties and fell for the slick talk of the recruiting officer and the paradiddles of a drummer boy putting on a show from a covered cart in the bustling centre of Belfast:

> We eagerly pushed our way through the crowd, which we had some difficulty in doing; but the eagle eye of the officer soon rested on us, and, perceiving our eagerness, he called out, 'Make way, make way there, my lads! That's right, that's right – fine soldiers you'll be, my hearties, I warrant!'

O'Neil was a simple farm boy when he signed up to the 8th Regiment of Foot in Belfast for the government 'bounty' of 18 guineas, but the money soon ran out – there were deductions for the recruiting sergeant, and the drummer, and O'Neil's uniform, and ribbons for the officer's wife. He did not like army discipline and deserted after just twelve days, disguised as a tramp. Fearing capture and a flogging, he then joined the 64th Regiment of Foot at Navan and was paid a second bounty of 18 guineas but deserted again. He became a wanted man, so to escape arrest joined a militia unit bound for Dublin, and was paid bounty for a third time. In Dublin he was horrified to hear that his new militia unit was to be joined by one of the regiments from which he had deserted, so, to escape again, he offered himself for service abroad, and transferred into the 28th Regiment of Foot, for which he was paid the bounty a fourth time. That is how he ended up in Spain, fighting under Sir Arthur Wellesley, in the Peninsular campaign, and at Waterloo.

O'Neil wrote a lively account of his exploits long after the battle, and reading between the lines of O'Neil's colourful memoir you get the impression that, like a character from a *Flashman* novel by George MacDonald Fraser, O'Neil shrewdly kept his head down and left the heroics to others. O'Neil survived the horror of Badajoz by spending most of his time skirmishing in the mountains against the guerrillas, killing pigs and stealing wine. In Vitoria,

O'Neil and his friends found a couple of wine barrels in a cellar and, intending to get drunk, borrowed an axe from a soldier in the pioneer corps to smash them open. The first barrel contained nothing more intoxicating than butter; they were so furious that they smashed open a second and it spewed out a stream of gold coins, which had been hidden in the butter. O'Neil promptly stuffed a plug of the coins in his knapsack. The French abandoned everything, including the women of Jérôme's travelling brothel and the army's pay in gold coins that had just arrived before the battle. Jérôme left behind his own carriage, and boxes containing the priceless treasures he had looted from Spain and Portugal on the battlefield, worth an estimated £100 million today. Much of the bullion in coins went into men's pockets. A fortnight after O'Neil and his comrades enjoyed their night of bacchanalia in Vitoria, Wellington gave vent to his fury in his letter to Lord Bathurst, the Secretary of State for War and the Colonies.

6

I am in a small room in the Hartley Library at Southampton University with a sheaf of Wellington's original letters on a desk. He wrote his letters with a quill pen in black ink on sturdy cloth or linen-based hand-made paper of varying sizes from folio to smaller sheets, and folded them with a seal, without envelopes. The address was written on the back. Wellington's letter is date-lined Huarte, 2 July 1813 — now a suburb of Pamplona in the Basque region of Spain, near the French border. You can clearly see where he broke off to refill his quill, because the handwriting fades and suddenly darkens where he dipped his quill into the ink. It reads as though he dipped it in venom:

> It is quite impossible for me or any other man to command a British army
> under the existing system. We have in the service the scum of the earth as
> common soldiers; and of late years we have been doing everything in our
> power, both by the law and by publications, to relax the discipline by which
> alone such men can be kept in order.

Even after 200 years, the anger is palpable. Wellington had good reason to be angry with his men after Vitoria. While O'Neil and his comrades had gone on a drunken looting spree after their victory, they had allowed 55,000 French troops under Joseph-Napoleon, Bonaparte's elder brother, to escape over the Pyrenees into France. Wellington went on to complain in the same letter about the desertions from his ranks — in less than a month, he had lost 2,733 men to 'irregularities' including 'straggling and plunder'. The 'existing system' to which he referred was the British preference for a 'voluntary' army.

This was in truth, a lie. While men of the officer classes bought their commissions in the army for the honour and excitement it might bring, the ordinary men in the ranks usually had to be coerced into joining the army. The army was a hard and brutal life in the ranks and boys had to be desperate to volunteer to serve in it; as a result, Wellington believed they recruited the 'scum of the earth' like O'Neil.[1]

Napoleon by contrast had a conscript army, which brought in the sons of what was left of the noblemen after the attentions of the guillotine, as well as the common man. In Britain conscription had been tried and abandoned. The 1803 Additional Forces Act created a new army of reserve, conscripted by a local county ballot. It meant that if your name came out in the ballot, you had to go into a county militia. Those dragged away from their farms included a young shepherd from Dorset called Benjamin Harris who had to leave his old, white-haired father to tend the sheep. Benjamin was too ill after the disastrous Walcheren campaign to serve at Waterloo, but eked out a living in old age as a shoemaker – a trade he picked up in the army – and dictating his memoirs: the 'Recollections of Rifleman Harris' to Lieutenant Henry Curlew (Harris may have been illiterate). As a result, he left us a vivid insight of what life was like in the ranks. Harris was 'a fair sample of the unconquerable British private', said W.H. Fitchett, who republished Harris's memoirs in 1900 – 'stocky, stubborn, untaught and primitive in nature …His endurance is wonderful. Laden like a donkey, with ill-fitting boots and half-filled stomach, he can splash along muddy Spanish roads, under the falling rain, or sweat beneath the Spanish midsummer heats, from grey dawn to gathering dusk …' Harris's vision was narrow … 'it is almost filled up by his right and left-hand files, it never goes beyond the battalion.' But Harris was speaking for the 'common soldiers', the men Wellington called 'the scum of the earth'.

The draft was unpopular and ineffective (large numbers sent substitutes to do service for them) and was quietly dropped after 1805, leaving Wellington to rely on so-called 'volunteers'. Some naïve farm boys joined for adventure, far horizons, and the prospect of drink, plunder and women. Many were running away from something – poverty, prison, or paternity and sometimes all three. Some were the dregs of humanity; they had to be, to join the army. They could be turned into a professional killing machine, but in Wellington's view, this class of soldier needed discipline or he would rebel. O'Neil's fears about being caught as a deserter were well founded. Rifleman Harris was part of a firing squad that executed a young rogue like O'Neil who deserted and enlisted sixteen times for the 'King's Shilling'. He was handcuffed and shot by Harris's firing squad in front of 15,000 men at Portadown Hill, near Hilsea Barracks in Portsmouth, as an example of what could happen to men who deserted. 'His hands waved for a few moments like the fins of a fish … four of our party immediately stepped up to the prostrate body and placing their muzzles to the head, fired and put him out of his misery.'[2]

A shilling a day was the usual pay for an English soldier and the acceptance of a shilling was taken as a symbolic contract between the government and an enlisted soldier. Recruiting sergeants got their unwary targets drunk before slipping them the shilling while they were in their cups. The legend was said to be the reason why pewter mugs were made with glass bottoms, so the unwary could see the shilling in their drink.

Volunteers also joined to escape punishment by the courts – sentences could be commuted to a life in the army by the magistrates; others from Ireland and the Highlands of Scotland were driven by starvation and poverty to seek adventure and a soldier's daily ration of 1½lbs of bread; 1lb of beef or mutton; and half a pint of wine or a third of a pint of rum.

In England, the army had relied on recruits from the rural areas. Around 25 per cent of the Royal Artillery recruits (who needed skill with horses) gave their trade as farm labourer in the twenty years to 1779, but when Wellington led his army to Waterloo, the textile workers outnumbered the farm hands in the ranks of the Royal Artillery. The change was brought about by the dramatic shift in Britain from farms to factories as the populations of the textile towns suddenly expanded. One of the paradoxes of the Regency period is that as the textile industry boomed, more spinners and weavers were put out of work in the old rural cottage looms by the new machines in the mills. One of the recruits was a young lad from Oldham, a rapidly expanding cotton mill town near Manchester, called John Lees. As a Royal Artillery driver, his job was to look after the horses drive the wagons, and haul the supplies for Bull's battery of heavy 5½-in howitzers. The foot regiments had their own batteries, and the army's wagon drivers had to carry everything for an army on the move – animal fodder, camp kettles and kitchens, ammunition, stores of beef, beer and bread, women camp followers who hitched a lift on the carts on top of the baggage, and when times were good, looted goods and plunder from defeated armies. Lees also had to carry ammunition to the gunners in his wagon, which at Waterloo was a perilous job.

Recruits from the industrial towns like John Lees were smaller than men from the country because they were less well fed than farmers' boys, and some regiments established a rule that they would take no men shorter than 5ft 7ins.

John Graham, an Irishman from County Monaghan, was discharged 'for being undersize' in 1817 (after Waterloo), although his size had not mattered before; he may have been one of the few who survived the carnage inside the 27th Inniskilling Regiment's hollow square at Waterloo, when they were cut to pieces by French artillery.

O'Neil was among the few who could read and write in the ranks. Illiteracy is the reason most of the early histories were written by officers, not the men, and it limited a man's chances of promotion to NCO rank; it almost certainly would have barred men from the ranks rising to become officers. In a detailed study of the 27th Inniskilling regiment, Mark Bois[3] estimated 30 per cent of its 700 men were illiterate, although men did learn to read and write in the army, and some units had regimental schools.

The Duke did not only refer to his men as the 'scum of the earth' in anger. He returned to the subject twenty years after the Battle of Waterloo, when he was reminiscing about his wars over dinner at Walmer Castle on the Kent Coast, when he was Lord Warden of the Cinq ports. His loyal friend Earl Stanhope faithfully noted down the Duke's words in his journal. Wellington and his hosts were discussing flogging in the army when his view about the 'scum of the earth' came up. The Duke made it clear to his dinner hosts that he regarded flogging as a necessary evil to try to stop his soldiers and the camp followers, including their wives, from plundering their way across cities like Vitoria in Spain, which would have alienated the local people from his army.

Napoleon's army may have survived on plunder in the countries it occupied, but Wellington paid for his provisions to win the support of the local people (see Chapter Eight). Stopping looting was vital to his strategy but it was an annoying inconvenience for his men. Captain Alexander Cavalié Mercer, who tried to match 'the beau ideal' required for horses in the Peninsular War[4], complained Wellington wanted it both ways – he harshly criticised Mercer for failing to keep his horses in prime condition, but put him on a charge for 'borrowing' forage from the French farmers without paying for it. Wellington took an unusually strict view of looting because he knew he could not liberate Spain and Portugal if he had to fight a guerrilla war with its hostile inhabitants as an occupying army at the same time as fighting the French. Thirty lashes for his miscreants were a small price to pay for keeping the local population content.

However, the brutality of flogging had been criticised at home by Radical writers such as William Cobbett, who had spent time in Newgate prison for writing an attack on flogging in the army in his popular *Weekly Political Register*, and there was a growing campaign in Parliament to have flogging banned, at least for women. The Duke did not agree with such a relaxation of army custom and practice.

The Duke said the only way of tackling plundering by his own army 'is to have plenty of provosts to hang and flog them without mercy, the devils incarnate'. He told Lady Salisbury: 'It is well known that in all armies the Women are at least as bad, if not worse than men as Plunderers! And the exemption of the Ladies would have encouraged Plunder!' Women could expect thirty vigorous and painful lashes on the bare backside when they were caught. The Duke said the army needed to retain flogging, if only as a reserve so that officers could impose milder punishments on their men such as 'billing up' – confining to barracks which he had suffered as a young officer – without the risk of the officers being defied.

Stanhope then asked the great man if the French Army beat their men. 'Oh, they bang them about very much with ramrods and that sort of thing, and then they shoot them,' said Wellington cheerfully. 'Besides a French army is composed very differently to ours. The conscription calls out a share of every class – no matter whether your son or my son, all must march – but our friends, I may say this in this room, are the scum of the earth.'

He went on in a matter-of-fact way: 'People talk of their enlisting for their fine military feeling – all stuff – no such thing. Some of our men enlist for having got bastard children – some for minor offences – many more for drink; but you can hardly conceive such a set brought together, and it really is wonderful that we should have made them the fine fellows they are.'

Wellington's army of defenders have quoted this qualification – that the army transformed the 'scum of the earth' into fighting men – to show that he actually respected his men. That is true, but only up to a point. They may have become 'fine fellows' with army discipline, but Wellington was viscerally opposed to the idea of promoting some of the 'scum' from the ranks to become officers. And in his next breath at the dinner, he explained why: they could not hold their drink. The Duke firmly supported the system by which gentlemen could get their 'step' – obtain promotion – with cash, by buying commissions in the army, which he clearly felt kept out the riff-raff. 'I am all for it – of having gentlemen for officers.' He did not believe in promoting men from the ranks as officers. 'I have never known officers raised from the ranks turn out well, nor the system answer; they cannot stand drink.' Drink was a serious problem in maintaining discipline in the ranks. He said after Oporto: 'The army behave terribly ill. They are a rabble who cannot bear success any more than Sir John Moore's army could bear failure. I am endeavouring to tame them ….'

It has never been medically proved that the sons of aristocrats are any better at holding their drink than the sons of farmer labourers, and it is easy to see why Wellington never excited the love that Napoleon did in his men (despite adopting the trappings of monarchy) and the Duke would not have wanted it. The Victorian military historian W.H. Fitchett said the Duke had 'about his men as little human feeling as a good chess player for his pawns'.[5] That is harsh on the Duke – he took care to protect his men from Napoleon's cannon; Napoleon was far more ready to sacrifice his men than Wellington. But Frances, Lady Shelley, recorded in her journal the Duke's distaste for the cheering of his men under orders. As she rode alongside the Duke reviewing his troops in Paris after Waterloo, Wellington turned to her and said: 'I hate that cheering. If you allow soldiers once to express an opinion, they may on some future occasion, hiss instead of cheer …'[6]

Wellington's biographer, Elizabeth Longford, a member of his wife's family, excused the Duke for his outburst against his own men like a respected but slightly batty grandfather. She said that when he used phrases like 'scum of the earth' or 'very worst members of society' he was not being vindictive or descriptive: he was merely stating the harsh sociological facts as he saw them. He had once used the same phrase to describe the Duke of York's mistress when it was discovered she was selling commissions to supplement the income the prince was giving her.

Longford conceded he was wrong in one respect … not nearly such a large proportion of the army was 'scum' as he implied. She was probably right about that. The late Richard Holmes, the military historian, reckoned that the proportion of 'incorrigibles' – the men who could not be forced to obey the rules by flogging or locking up – was only about 10 per cent of the army.

I believe Wellington's view about his men went deeper and it would put him at odds with the men he had once led when they demanded social reform to which he was implacably opposed. It would end in Wellington's own Waterloo (Chapter Eleven). As a High Tory, Wellington believed fundamentally in the natural order of things – the rich man in his manor house, and the poor man at his gate; and that the monarchy was at the centre of an ordered system that operated as naturally as the planets circled the sun. Being a patrician conservative meant respecting the poor man, and when necessary providing poor relief, and charity (though not too much to breed idleness), but the poor man had to know his place; it certainly did not mean inviting the poor man to have a say in how he ran his manor.

Wellington refused to countenance the 'scum of the earth' being in charge of their own destinies: he would never surrender them the vote. Wellington's great fear, shared by the Tory prime minister, Lord Liverpool, and most of his Cabinet, was that the plague of Jacobin revolution would be carried across the Channel from France, even after the defeat of the French at the Battle of Waterloo and the second abdication of their champion, Napoleon.

As he prepared to do battle against Bonaparte, Wellington was acutely aware there was social unrest leading to mobs, street riots and civil disorder at home. Men in England prided themselves on being free; Magna Carta gave them the same rights as kings under the law; and yet the vast majority – around 97 per cent, 7.8 million people[7] – did not have a vote on how their lives were run. Britain over the centuries had replaced the absolute rule of the monarch but the country was now run by a tiny aristocratic elite of families such as the dukes of Norfolk with hereditary seats in the House of Lords and by the privileged sons of peers or well-connected allies who had seats in the House of Commons. Powerful landowners like the Norfolks had a number of seats in their gift, called 'pocket boroughs' – the Norfolks had eleven seats under their control – often with more sheep than voters.

It is perhaps ironic that Thomas Creevey, a campaigner for the common man, had got his seat in Parliament for Thetford, Norfolk, in 1802 as a result of his patronage by the Duke of Norfolk. Thetford was the home of Tom Paine, author of the revolutionary *Rights of Man*, but the town was in the Duke's pocket (today it is more famous for its forest than its people – it still only has a population of 22,000). That did not stop Creevey pressing for reform, but Wellington, Lord Liverpool and Lord Sidmouth, the Home Secretary, saw demands for the vote by the common man (women were not even considered) as a sign that the revolution was spreading. Faced with legitimate demands for representation in Parliament from the rapidly expanding industrial towns of the north of England, Wellington and the government had a choice: reform or repression. They opted for repression. But that was for later. Right now, Wellington had a rag-tag army to pull together and a battle to fight.

Notes

1. W1P/373, Wellington Archive, Hartley Library, Southampton University.
2. W.H. Fitchett (ed.), *Wellington's Men: Some Soldier Autobiographies* [online book] (London: George Bell and Sons, 1900) <www.openlibrary.org>, p. 146.
3. Mark Bois, 'The Inniskillings at Waterloo' (www.napoleon-series.org, November 2007).
4. General Cavalié Mercer, *Journal of the Waterloo Campaign* (William Blackwood and Sons, London, 1870), p. 164.
5. W.H. Fitchett (ed.), *Wellington's Men* (1900), p. 19.
6. Richard Edgcumbe (ed.), *The Diary of Frances Lady Shelley* [online book] (London: John Murray, 1913) <www.openlibrary.org>, p. 113.
7. Nationalarchives.gov.uk.

2

WATERLOO

The story of Waterloo starts with an explosion 7,000 miles away.

The sun was setting over the Bali sea on 5 April 1815, when the long dormant Mount Tambora on the remote Indonesian island of Sumbawa exploded, throwing millions of tons of ash 18 miles into the stratosphere. It was heard by Thomas Stamford Raffles, the colourful British governor of Java, 800 miles away. He thought the distant rumbling was the sound of naval gunfire, but when it rained ash in Java, Raffles realised that a volcano had exploded somewhere in Indonesia.

The eruptions rumbled on for a month, spewing pumice into the sea, but there was an even more violent explosion at about 7 p.m. on 10 April that blew the top off the mountain. The 4,300m Tambora peak disappeared, leaving a crater 7km across. Volcanologists calculate it was the biggest eruption in recorded history, greater than Krakatoa, in 1883, and Vesuvius that buried Pompeii and turned its people into pumice stone in the year AD 79.

Within twenty-four hours an ash cloud 2,600 miles across, roughly the size of Australia, spread from Tambora, affecting weather patterns across the globe. The ash cloud from Tambora is estimated to be 1,000 times greater than the Eyjafjallajökull volcano in Iceland, which grounded civil airlines in 2010. Around the archipelago of Indonesia, the ash cloud eclipsed the sun, turning day into night. Crops in fields 100 miles away were covered in ash 8 to 10in deep.

But that was only its local impact. The eruption was to have a far wider impact around Planet Earth. The blast ejected an estimated 55 million tons of sulphur-dioxide gas into the middle of the stratosphere, where it formed an aerosol cloud of sulphuric acid. The gas was picked up by the jet streams

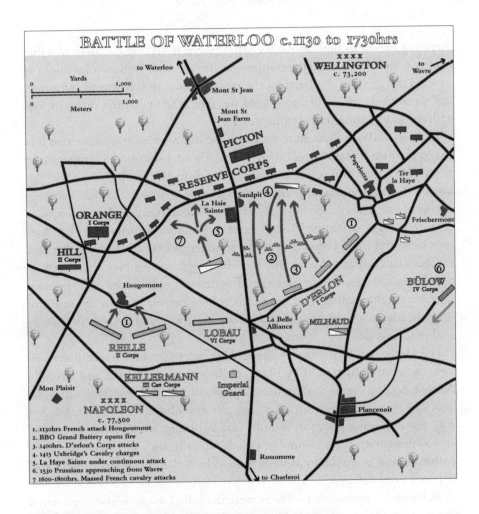

BATTLE OF WATERLOO c.1130 to 1730hrs

to Waterloo

XXXX WELLINGTON c. 73,200

to Wavre

Mont St Jean

Mont St Jean Farm

PICTON

RESERVE CORPS

Papelotte

Ter la Haye

Sandpit ④

La Haie Sainte

Frischermont

ORANGE I Corps

① ②

HILL II Corps

⑦ ⑤

③

D'ERLON I Corps

BÜLOW IV Corps ⑥

Hougomont

La Belle Alliance

MILHAUD

REILLE II Corps ①

LOBAU VI Corps

Yards 0 1,000
Meters 0 1,000

Mon Plaisir

KELLERMANN III Cav Corps

Imperial Guard

Plancenoit

XXXX NAPOLEON c. 77,500

1. 1130hrs French attack Hougoumont
2. BBO Grand Battery opens fire
3. 1400hrs. D'erlon's Corps attacks
4. 1415 Uxbridge's Cavalry charges
5. La Haye Sainte under continuous attack
6. 1530 Prussians approaching from Wavre
7 1600-1800hrs. Massed French cavalry attacks

Rossomme

to Charleroi

Plaster model of the lion on top of the monument by J-L Van Geel. (Musée d'Art Ancien, Brussels)

that cross the earth high above the atmosphere, reflecting the sun's rays like a mirror, and reducing temperatures on the ground. Within a fortnight it covered the girth of the Earth at the equator, then slowly spread out north and south to the poles, bringing cold weather as temperatures dropped, and with the low pressure, cataclysmic storms.

Tambora today is thought to be the cause of even worse weather that followed in 1816. It was the so-called 'year without a summer' – temperatures plummeted, hail stones like canister shot fell in July, crops failed, and the weather brought misery to people across Europe, who were already living on the bread line. The decade from 1810 to 1819 was to become the coldest since the bitter 1690s, when the Thames froze in London. In Britain the bad harvests increased social unrest. But in the summer of 1815 the bad weather that Tambora had unleashed across the world brought rain – heavy, sheeting, torrential rain. On Saturday, 17 June 1815 thunderstorms driven by a low pressure system brought slashing rain across the rolling countryside to the south of Brussels, where around quarter of a million men were lining up to do bloody battle the next day.

The Horse Artillery officer, Captain Alexander Cavalié Mercer, described how the clouds turned 'inky black, their lower edges hard and strongly defined, lagging down, as if momentarily about to burst, involving our position and everything in it in deep and gloomy obscurity'. They exploded with the deafening boom of thunder and lightning. Meteorologists believe he was describing cumulo-nimbus clouds typically associated with thundery outbreaks and unstable conditions pushed by a cold front sweeping across Belgium from the west.[1]

Wellington's bedraggled soldiers were drenched, hungry, and tired when they squelched through the fields and up the hill to the ridge at Mont St Jean, where the Duke of Wellington had decided to fight.

On Friday 16 June, Napoleon had attacked Blücher at Ligny, while his left wing, under the red-headed Marshal Ney, attacked the Prince of Orange's forces, supported by Wellington's hurriedly assembled force, at the Quatre Bras crossroads. Had Marshal Ney attacked in the morning, when he had 18,000 men against the Dutch holding force of 8,000 infantry, the Allied force would have been badly mauled, but he delayed until the afternoon, when Wellington's troops arrived. Wellington's men suffered – the Highlanders were decimated after being run down by cavalry in a field of tall corn – but they held the position overnight. At daybreak on Saturday 17 June, Wellington sent his chief ADC, Sir Alexander Gordon, with a troop of cavalry to find out how Blücher had fared. He had warned Blücher's staff when he rode over to Ligny before the battle that Blücher was leaving his men dangerously exposed on a hill in full view of Napoleon's guns. Gordon returned about 7 a.m. with the grim news that Blücher's army had been mauled just as Wellington had feared. Blücher, 72, had been unhorsed and ridden over twice by enemy cavalry, and was only saved by a quick-thinking aide who threw a coat over him to hide his medals. Blücher had fallen back to Wavre but there was one piece of good news – the indefatigable Prussian field marshal had promised Gordon he would stay in close contact and join Wellington's forces in battle against Napoleon. Wellington ordered a planned withdrawal to the ridge at the hamlet called Mont St Jean on the Charleroi–Brussels road.

Torrential rain storms began to sweep across the fields on Saturday afternoon, as the allied army fell back, and the rain became Wellington's ally. The curtains of rain and low black cloud shrouded his army's retreat and slowed the heavy French 12-pounders, which sank up to their axles; it took a superhuman effort for Napoleon's gunners to heave them through the mud.

William Wheeler, a private in the 51st Regiment of Foot, described the retreat from Quatre Bras in Wagnerian terms in a letter home:

> The rain beating with violence, the guns roaring, repeated bright flashes of lightning attended with tremendous volleys of Thunder that shook the earth … the night came on, we were wet to the skin … It would be impossible for any one to form an opinion of what we endured that night. Being close to the enemy we could not use our blankets, the ground was too wet to lie down, we sat on our knapsacks until daylight without fires, there was no shelter against the weather – the water ran in streams from the cuffs of our jackets. In short we were as wet as if we had been plunged over head in a river.

When they reached the wet slopes of the ridge, many collapsed where they stood. Sixteen-year-old Ensign George Keppel, of the 3rd Battalion of the 14th Regiment of Foot, said: 'It was like lying in a mountain torrent.' But before settling down, Keppel had piled up his arms with his comrades and lined up for a regimental gin ration: 'Every officer and man was, in turn, presented with a little tin-pot full. No fermented liquor that has since passed my lips could vie with that delicious Schnapps.' It could not stop the rain but it helped to ease the discomfort.

As night closed in, Wellington and his staff officers commandeered beds in the inn and nearby cottages in the village of Waterloo, but most of his senior officers shared the misery of the men in the fields, farms, and primitive houses around Mont St Jean. The rain ran in torrents along ditches, down banks, and trickled into their boots. The rain turned sunken roads into small rivers and the rich grey Belgian earth into a cloying mud, just as it had almost exactly 400 years before at the battle of Agincourt; only this was worse.

Waterloo literally means, 'Wet meadow' according to the guide to the official celebrations for Waterloo 200, but muddy meadows and hollows of the gently rolling hills around Mont St Jean had rarely been this wet. The rain relented before sunset but it came on with more violence after nightfall. The rain drenched everything – men, horses, cannon, and muskets. Men grabbed what shelter they could under hedgerows, in roadside ditches, under fruit trees in the orchards at Hougoumont. Some held their rough woollen pitching blankets over their heads to form makeshift tents. In the orchard at the farm of Mont St Jean, Captain Mercer sheltered by the 6-pounder guns of his G Troop of the Horse Artillery, under his trusty umbrella, ignoring Wellington's order banning brolleys from the battlefield as 'unmilitary' and enjoyed a cigar before trying to get some sleep.

As Keppel and his battalion tried to find shelter on the slopes, they heard the thunder of guns in the dark from below their position. It was part of the rearguard action from Quatre Bras. Keppel recalled:

Looking to the south, in the direction of the ground we had lately traversed, we heard heavy firing to our left. This proceeded from La Haye Sainte [a farm 200yds below them] where Picton had ordered two brigades of artillery to play upon the French infantry, which was pressing upon the Anglo-Allied forces in retreat upon Waterloo from Quatre Bras. It was probably then that Napoleon, who was with this portion of his army first understood that Wellington was in position, and prepared to receive him on the morrow.

The gunfire in the dark told the emperor what he wanted to know. He halted his men on a slope facing Wellington's rain-sodden army, barely a mile from their front line. Here, near an inn called La Belle Alliance, he established his grand battery of eighty guns. Napoleon, now knowing where Wellington intended to fight, retired for the night to a farm house called Le Caillou, 2 miles back along the Charleroi road, confident of victory in the morning.

Keppel, later to become a Whig MP and 6th Earl of Albermarle, slept soundly – helped by the gin – until two in the morning when he was shaken awake by his soldier servant, Bill Moles. Moles – *Baldrick* to Keppel's *Blackadder* – had scouted out some drier quarters, in a small cottage in the village at Merbe-Braine, near a ravine just north of Hougoumont. They trudged through the dark to the cottage and found three officers there drying themselves in front of a blazing fire with their coats hanging up to dry on the backs of their chairs. They were burning bits of furniture, tables, broken window frames and doors, which had been smashed up for firewood. The officers squeezed up to make room for the young Ensign and his grubby servant, and they spent the rest of the night dry and warm. In the morning, the young Ensign realised he had been sharing the space with some of Wellington's most distinguished officers, including Colonel Sir John Colborne, the six-foot-three-tall commander of the 52nd Light Infantry. Colborne offered to share his breakfast with the sixteen-year-old Ensign but Keppel was over-awed and politely declined before walking back to the ridge with Moles, looking for the rest of his soaking-wet battalion of the Buckinghamshire Regiment of Foot. The next day, Keppel was nearly killed when he was stroking the face of a horse to calm it down and a cannon ball smashed into the mare's head. Keppel, who was inside a defensive hollow square of infantry waiting to be attacked by cavalry, was pitched head over heels on the ground with the drum. The horse plunged about in agony but was killed by his comrades with their bayonets.

Along the ridge, bivouacking in village buildings, Captain Hastings Brudenel Forbes complained to his friend and fellow-officer, Ensign Charles Lake of the Third Guards, that his servant had forgotten his cloak and he was getting soaked. Forbes asked Lake to let him share a corner of his large cloak and they sheltered together under it. 'Poor fellow!' said Lake. 'It was his last sleep for he was shot through the breast early on the morning of the eighteenth.' The Ensign found a miniature portrait concealed on his friend's body the next day. It was 'of the lady to whom he was engaged' and whom Lake had seen dancing with Forbes only a few days before at the Brussels balls.

Close to where Lake and Forbes grabbed what cover they could from the rain, General John Byng, commander of the 2nd Guards Brigade, 'slept covered with nothing but straw and bellowed lustily at one of our officers accidentally treading on him'.

Some older veterans who had fought with Wellington through Portugal and Spain recalled over spluttering fires that there had been just such a terrible storm the night before the Battle of Salamanca on 22 July 1812, and Wellington had won a great victory over the French the next day.[2] If that did not lift the dampened spirits of the men, they also had gin. Private Wheeler wrote he and his friends were 'wet and comfortable' after sharing a bottle of gin in torrential rain. When they landed at Ostend with their horses and guns, the men had found that gin was far cheaper than in London, to the consternation of their officers. 'Gin here is so cheap that we are obliged to keep a very sharp look out to keep our men,' Lieutenant George Hussey Pack wrote home to his father in Manchester Square, London after disembarking at the port. 'What they charge in England 1/- you get here for a penny; my man has got drunk once since he has been here and I think myself pretty lucky he is not drunk day and night.'[3] Drink was the curse of a fighting army, but that night before the battle it helped the men blot out the pain, and the thoughts of what greater horrors the morning would bring.

In the fields to the south of the bucolic ancient farmhouse and chateau called Hougoumont, covering Wellington's right flank, the Coldstream Guards could hear the French moving around during the night, barely 300yds away. They had the solace of knowing at least their enemy was suffering just as much discomfort as they were.

Charles O'Neil, the roguish Irish private in the 28th Regiment of Foot, was jolted awake by a fellow Irishman who said he had a premonition he was going to be killed in the morning and wished to make an arrangement with O'Neil to tell his parents how he died. He offered to do the same for O'Neil, if he was killed:

> We then exchanged the last letters we had received from home, so that each should have the address of the other's parents. I endeavoured to conceal my own feelings, and cheer his, by reminding him that it was far better to die on the field with glory than from fear; but he turned away from me, and with a burst of tears that spoke the deep feelings of his heart, he said, 'My mother!' The familiar sound of this precious name, and the sight of his sorrow, completely overcame my attempts at concealment, and we wept together.

His friend's foreboding was justified. 'We had not been in action 25 minutes when he was shot down by my side.' O'Neil was injured but survived to keep his promise and tell his friend's parents how he died.[4]

There were tens of thousands of horses on the two hillsides, from thorough-bred cavalry mounts to cart horses, and they were terrified by the thunder and lightning. Some horses bolted down the hill from the allied lines to the farm at Hougoumont, 500yds in front of Wellington's lines, and they had to be chased and caught by the soaking men in the steepling rain. Infantry were also spooked, as they bivouacked in the open fields, by the commotion in the dark into thinking they were under attack.

Ensign Charles Short, aged 16, of the Coldstream Guards 2nd Battalion recalled, 'We formed a hollow square and prepared to receive Cavalry twice but found it was a false alarm both times.' He added:

> We were under arms the whole night, expecting the attack and it rained to that degree that the field where we were was half-way up our legs in mud; nobody, of course, could lie down. The ague got hold of some of the men. I with another officer had a blanket and with a little more gin we kept up very well. We had only one fire, and you cannot conceive the state we were in.

At Hougoumont, Private Matthew Clay was soaking wet and muddy, after slipping into a water-filled ditch that he had tried to jump across in the dark:

slimy ground and the increased weight of my wet blanket made me slip and being neck-deep in the ditch, I found it very difficult to get out.' When dawn broke, damp and drizzling rain across the fields, some had more gin to lift their spirits for breakfast. Ensign Short wrote to his mother: 'Soon after daylight, the Company sent up with the greatest difficulty some gin, and we found an old cart full of wet Rye loaves which we breakfasted upon. Everybody was in high spirits ...'

Private Clay, like many soldiers that morning, had more mundane matters on his mind. He checked the flintlock of his musket to see if it would still fire. Muskets were notorious for misfiring when it was wet: 'The flint musket then in use was a sad bore from the effects of the wet,' Clay later noted in his pay book. 'The springs of the lock became wood-bound and would not act correctly and when in action the clumsy flints also became useless.'

As the rain eased, Clay bit off the end from a paper cartridge, opened the frizzen, poured some dry powder into the pan, rammed the rest of the powder and the ball down the muzzle, cocked the hammer, and fired at an object he had put on a bank of earth. 'The ball embedded in the bank where I had purposely placed it as a target.'

The Land Pattern Musket had been in service since 1722 and it had helped Britain win the empire, but, despite being affectionately known as 'Brown Bess', ballistic tests have shown that it was inaccurate over more than 100yds. In fact, muskets like those carried at Waterloo were inferior in range, accuracy and rate of fire to the longbow that Henry V's archers used to defeat the superior French force at Agincourt, 100 miles away, on 25 October 1415. Muskets were deadly when fired in volleys at close range but that would test the discipline of the men Wellington had called 'the scum of the earth'.

Specialist sharp shooters, including Sir John Kincaid's[*] green-jacketed rifle brigade carried variants of the Baker rifle developed by a London gun-smith, Ezekiel Baker. It had grooves down the barrel that could spin the shot through the air, making it far more stable, and more accurate than the stand-ard musket. It was still muzzle-loaded, and slower than the musket because wadding had to be placed around the ball to make a tight fit. A well-trained soldier could fire about two shots a minute with a Baker rifle, compared to four-a-minute with the musket – but a marksman could drop a man over 300 paces with a Baker rifle. That was an important advantage when defend-ing the farms at La Haye Sainte and Hougoumont, where the defenders were vastly outnumbered.

---

[*]   Captain Johnny Kincaid was a real-life version of Richard Sharpe, but the author of the Sharpe novels, Bernard Cornwell, denies he was the inspiration for his fictional hero.

Wellington awoke at around 3 a.m. at the Brabant inn in Waterloo, which he had made his headquarters, and dealt with some paperwork. It is remarkable that he found the time to write a hurried note to Lady Frances Webster in Brussels to reassure her she would be safe:

> My dear Lady Frances. We fought a desperate battle on Friday (Quatre Bras) in which I was successful though I had but very few troops. The Prussians were very roughly handled and retired last night which obliged me to do the same to this place yesterday. The course of the operations may oblige me to uncover Bruxelles for a moment for which reason I recommend that you and your family should be prepared to move to Antwerp at a moment's notice. I will give you the earliest information of any danger that may come to my knowledge; at present I know of none.

The reference to leaving Brussels 'uncovered' is significant. He clearly still feared a flanking attack on Brussels by Napoleon through Mons but he may also have had a contingency plan – as many suspected – to fall back to the coast, through Hal, where he had stationed 15,500 troops, if he failed to hold Bonaparte at Waterloo, leaving Brussels at the mercy of the French. This also suggests that he was not as confident of victory as he had led Creevey to believe. Whatever his doubts, he kept them to himself.

After dealing with his mail, he breakfasted lightly on tea and toast at the inn, assuring the landlady that she would be safe, and then rode out on his chestnut charger, Copenhagen, at the head of a cavalcade of about forty of his staff officers, foreign liaison officers and their aides.

Copenhagen was 15.1 hands high, and had two great attributes for a war horse: he was unflinching under fire, and had stamina. He would need both that Sunday. Copenhagen was sired by a famous racehorse, Meteor, but never quite made the grade, though he was fast enough to win a couple of races. His dam was called Lady Catherine, which had been sired by 'John Bull', winner of the 1792 Epsom Derby. Colonel Thomas Grosvenor of the 65th Foot took the mare with him to Copenhagen in 1807 for a brutally effective campaign led by Wellington to stop the Danish fleet falling into French hands. When his mare gave birth to a leggy chestnut foal, Grosvenor named the colt after the action. Grosvenor sold him as a mount for the army to General Sir Charles Stewart, then Adjutant General to Wellington in Spain. When Stewart was invalided back to Britain in 1812, he offered Copenhagen to Wellington, who bought him for 400 guineas: 'There may have been many faster horses, no doubt many handsomer, but for bottom and endurance, I never saw his fellow,' said Wellington. It was a partnership that was to endure through roundshot and riot for the next twenty-four years.

Wellington was dressed for battle as a gentleman should be – not in a bright scarlet uniform, but in civilian clothes that he habitually wore as Commander-in-Chief of the allied forces: a cocked hat (worn fore and aft), white cravat, dark-blue coat with a cape against the rain, white leather breeches, and hessian boots. He wore a black English cockade with three small cockades about an inch in diameter, for Spain, Portugal and the Netherlands, as a token of holding rank in their armies.

As he rode out past the soaking wet bivouacs of his men, he had the air of a huntsmen off to find the fox, with his personal staff, including Lord FitzRoy Somerset, his military secretary, and eight ADCs.

Wellington's ADCs were a band of dashing young blades, a privileged elite, drawn from the nobility and the Guards regiments. They were his 'family', and acted as his 'eyes and ears', riding across the battlefield carrying his urgent orders, as well as standing by Wellington as the shot and shell flew past. They were expected to show *sang froid* under fire to inspire confidence among the troops, and two would be killed that day.

In addition to FitzRoy Somerset, his military secretary, later Lord Raglan, who had been the Duke's right-hand man in Portugal, Wellington had five ADCs on the army pay. They were all well-connected, as well as being well-heeled: his chief ADC, Sir Alexander Gordon, 29, was the third son of Lord Haddo, and his brother was the Tory Lord Aberdeen, a diplomat who had been with Wellington at the Congress of Vienna and would become prime minister; John Fremantle had been given the honour of bringing home the despatch from Vitoria and laying war trophies at the feet of the Prince Regent (his uncle William was an MP and close friend of Lord Buckingham, the Army Paymaster General); Charles Fox Canning was the first cousin of the future prime minister George Canning and brother of the diplomat Stratford Canning, who had personally asked Wellington to take Charles on his staff for Waterloo; Lord George Lennox was the second son of the Duke of Richmond, an old friend and army veteran who had taught the Duke drilling in Ireland when he was a young officer; and the Prince of Nassau, the young son of Duke Bernard of Nassau, who paid for his inclusion by sending a contingent of Nassau troops to fight at Waterloo.

Wellington had a further three extra ADCs who were added at his own expense: the Honourable Henry Percy, son of the Earl of Beverley, Lord Arthur Hill – later Lord Sandys, and George Cathcart, son of a viscount who was later killed in the Crimea at the Battle of Inkerman.

They were joined by the Prince of Orange and his six ADCs; staff officers including Adjutant and Quartermaster Generals, each with a suite of half-a-dozen officers; the commanding officers of engineers and artillery; and liaison officers embedded in Wellington's headquarters, Baron von Müffling,

the Prussian liaison officer; the Spanish aristocrat, Ricardo Álava; and Louis
XVIII's trusted aide, Pozzo di Borgo. As they rode jangling the mile or so from
Waterloo to the front line, Captain Rees Howell Gronow, a Welsh Grenadier
Guards Officer, thought the 'glittering staff seemed as gay and unconcerned as
if they were riding to meet the hounds in some quiet English country.'

Captain Mercer, drying himself out in the orchard at Mont St Jean, noticed
bizarrely there were three civilians, who rode past his gun troop to the front
line. They including the Duke of Richmond, whose wife had thrown the
glittering Brussels ball on the eve of Quatre Bras. Richmond, a seasoned
soldier who had been Wellington's secretary in Ireland, had wanted a post
in the army but Wellington turned him down. Instead he decided to go as
a spectator. He galloped after Wellington's cavalcade with two young sons,
including 15-year-old, William, who had an arm and an eye bandaged up – he
had broken his arm and been blinded in one eye in a fall from his horse in
the park at Brussels a few days before. The boy had been taken on by General
Sir Peregrine Maitland, commander of two battalions of Grenadier Guards,
as an extra ADC, probably as a favour to his father. When Wellington saw the
boy all bandaged up, he acted with fatherly concern: 'William you ought to
be in bed.' He told the boy's father: 'Duke, you have no business here.' Father
and son ignored his order and stayed on the field of battle as spectators until
about 5 p.m. Richmond had two older sons who were in the thick of it: Lord
George Lennox on Wellington's staff and Charles Gordon-Lennox, ADC to
the Prince of Orange, who became the 5th Duke of Richmond.

At *Le Caillou*, about 3 miles from Wellington's lines, Napoleon was served
breakfast off silver salvers with his marshals. He was confident of beating
Wellington because he was sure that Blücher and the Prussians could not
come to his aid, but Napoleon was testy over the eggs and bacon. General
Maximilien Foy felt he had a duty to tell him – 'as an old soldier' – 'you are
now in front of an infantry, which, during the whole of the Spanish war,
I never saw give way.'[5]

Marshal Soult supported Foy and urged Bonaparte to recall the 33,000
troops who had been sent east towards the town of Wavre under Grouchy to
hold back the Prussians. Napoleon ridiculed him: 'Just because you have been
beaten by Wellington, you think he's a good general. I tell you, Wellington is
a bad general, the English are bad troops and this affair is nothing more than
l'affaire d'un dejeuner [a picnic].'

Bonaparte turned to Marshal Honoré Reille, another of his generals who
had been defeated by Wellington in the Peninsular War, and asked him what
he thought of Wellington's army. With remarkable candour, Reille told the
emperor it was well-posted as Wellington knew how: 'Attacked from the front,
I consider the English infantry to be impregnable owing to its calm tenacity

and its superior aim in firing.' Before Napoleon could react, the emperor's younger brother, Jérôme Bonaparte, arrived at the farmhouse with disturbing rumours that Wellington had met up the night before with Blücher and got a promise that the Prussians would support him. In fact, the promise was given by Blücher to Wellington's ADC, Sir Alexander Gordon. Napoleon dismissed his brother's report: 'Nonsense – the Prussians and the English cannot possibly link up for another two days after such a battle [Ligny].'

It was so nearly true. Napoleon assumed the Prussians would retreat east to Liege, after their beating at Ligny, while Ney attacked Wellington's forces at Quatre Bras. In fact, that had been the strong view of Blücher's chief of staff, von Gneisenau. Wellington's liaison officer in Blücher's camp, Lieutenant Colonel Sir Henry Hardinge heard the row as he was lying in pain on straw in Blücher's ante-room, after having had his left hand amputated. His hand had been smashed by shot at Ligny and he lay listening to Blücher and his generals arguing as they passed by. Hardinge recalled:

> Blücher sent for me, calling me Lieber Freund etc and embracing me, I per-
> ceived he smelt most strongly of gin and rhubarb. He said to me, 'Ich stinke
> etwas', that he had been obliged to take medicine, having been twice rode
> over by the cavalry, but that he should be quite satisfied if in conjunction
> with the Duke of Wellington he was able now to defeat his old enemy.[6]

Hardinge added:

> I was told there had been a great discussion that night in his rooms and that
> Blücher and Grolmann [Karl Ludwig von Grolmann] had carried the day
> for remaining in communication with the English army, but that Gneisenau
> had great doubts as to whether they ought not to fall back to Liege and
> secure their own communication with Luxembourg. They thought that if
> the English should be defeated, they themselves would be utterly destroyed.[7]

Wellington described it as 'the decisive moment of the century', though he played down the importance of the Prussians to the outcome.

Napoleon had planned to begin the battle shortly after daybreak with a ferocious two-hour barrage from his grand battery of cannon to smash Wellington's centre. The emperor delayed because his bedraggled troops were still arriving on the battlefield. He was also concerned about the rain, which was continuing though it had now slowed to a soaking drizzle from the torrential downpours during the night. As a former gunnery officer, Napoleon knew the lethal power of his guns to destroy Wellington's infantry would be reduced by the soft ground; cannon balls would get stuck in the mud, rather

than ricocheting through Wellington's ranks. He concurred with Antoine
Drouot, his artillery commander: the mud would require enormous effort for
his men to wheel their guns around the battlefield into position. Confident
that Blücher was out of the picture for a day or more, the emperor decided to
let the ground dry out. He ordered that the main barrage should be delayed
until 12 noon. It was a fatal mistake. By delaying the onslaught, he gave
Blücher more time at the end of the day to join Wellington, as he had promised. Napoleon made other errors that day that contributed to his defeat, but
the weather was to become an important factor in Wellington's great victory.

The logs of Royal Navy warships, HMS *Alert*, *Erebus*, *Foxhound*, *Sharpshooter*,
Swan and *Wrangler* all reported the atrocious weather conditions.[*] Low pressure was recorded across England and the Low Countries on 17 June, which
was dominated by a cold front advancing from the west, causing heavy overnight rain. Force-6 winds of 24 knots in the Channel were reduced to little
more than a gentle breeze across the battlefield, but the thick low cloud
caused 'murky' conditions with poor visibility even after the rain stopped. It
may have been the brightening skyline in the west, after the worst of the rain
storms had passed, that may have encouraged Napoleon to accede to Drouot's
request for a delay to allow the ground to dry out. The weather was a factor
in determining the outcome of the battle, according to two meteorologists,
Dennis Wheeler and Gaston Demaree, who reconstructed the weather of
16–18 June for a paper for the Royal Meteorological Society, though it was
not the only reason Napoleon lost.[8]

A respected British geologist, the late Kenneth Spink linked the rain storms
over Waterloo that weekend to the Tambora eruption. Spink told a conference at Warwick University in 1996 less than 3 inches of rain normally would
be expected in the month of June: 'Enormous rainstorms developed before
and during the series of battles leading to the major conflict at Waterloo. With
the benefit of hindsight, it can be seen that these were caused by the eruption
of Tambora … This bad weather was almost entirely to Wellington's advantage.'[9] Victor Hugo lamented, 'Had it not rained in the night 17–18 June 1815,
the future of Europe might have been different. A few drops of water, more
or less, were what determined Napoleon's fate.' The writer claimed: 'Had the
ground been dry, so that the artillery could move the battle would have begun
at six in the morning; it would have been over and done with by two, three
hours before the Prussians could turn the scales.'

The writer was excusing the emperor's mistakes by heaping the blame on
the weather. In 1816, far worse weather was to shape events across the globe.
The ash spread around the earth, reflecting sunlight, causing the climate to

---

[*]   The Met Office was not created until 1854.

change by lowering temperatures. In London, people witnessed remarkable sunsets, because the volcanic dust was acting like a curtain on the sun's dying rays. The year after Waterloo, 1816, 'the year without a summer', deepened the distress and unrest in Britain while it was still celebrating victory; unseasonal rain ruined the crops and made the crushing poverty even harder to endure. When Wellington's 'scum of the earth' returned home, they found their country at war with itself.

But first they had a battle to fight.

Notes

1. Dennis Wheeler and Gaston Demaree, *Weather*, Royal Meteorological Society, June 2005, vol. 60, no. 6.
2. Julian Paget and Derek Saunders, *Hougoumont Waterloo* (Battleground Books), p. 32.
3. Gareth Glover (ed.), *The Waterloo Archive Vol. IV: British Sources* (Barnsley: Frontline Books, 1999), p. 98.
4. Charles O'Neil, *Private O'Neil: The Recollections of an Irish Rogue* (Leonaur Books, 1997).
5. Andrew Roberts, *Waterloo – Napoleons Last Gamble* (London: Harper Perennial, 2005), p.41.
6. Ibid., p. 110.
7. Ibid.
8. Dennis Wheeler and Gaston Demaree, *Weather*, Royal Meteorological Society, June 2005, vol. 60, no. 6.
9. K. Sping, 'Geological Constraints at the Battle of Waterloo', Applied Geoscience Conference, 15–18 April 1996, Warwick University.

3

THE BATTLE

The National Army Museum in Chelsea has a finely detailed model of the battlefield by the army expert topographer and historian Captain William Siborne. As I tried to work out the lie of the land on Siborne's model, I over-heard a conversation between two young army officer types: 'Have you ever been to the battlefield, Henry?'

'Oh yah,' drawled his friend. 'It's boring.' Henry missed the point. It is the banality of the bucolic landscape today, the farms, the gently rolling fields with neatly planted rows of corn, which makes the carnage that happened within the compass of about 8 square miles truly shocking.

The battle had five key phases: 11.20 a.m. the first shots of the battle were fired over Hougoumont and went on all day, almost in isolation from the main action: 12–1.30 p.m. – Napoleon softens up Wellington's centre by unleashing an artillery bombardment on the ridge that was so deafening it could be heard in Brussels and, allegedly, Dover; 1.30–2 p.m. Ney follows up the bombardment by launching a frontal assault on the ridge with the Comte d'Erlon's infantry in columns – they are repulsed by allied infantry and a cavalry charge; 4 p.m. Ney (thinking Wellington's infantry is in retreat when they are pulled back from the cannon fire on the ridge) launches massive charges by forty-three squadrons of cavalry, 12,000 horses – the allied infantry form defensive hollow squares on the plains, holding their bayonets out like porcupines – and lacking sufficient artillery support, the French cavalry are again repulsed; 7.30 p.m. Napoleon launches the Imperial Guard against Wellington's exhausted lines.

Arguments still rage over whether the arrival of Blücher's Prussians turned the tide of the battle. Siborne infuriated Wellington by including 40,000 Prussian troops on the original model. Wellington's secretary wrote to Siborne protesting 'those who see the work will deduce from it that the result of the Battle was not so much owing to British Valour, and the great Generalship of the Chief of the English Army, as to the flank Movements of the Prussians'. Siborne was summoned to Bathurst's War Office at the corner of Downing Street to be told he was 'mistaken' and must have the Prussians removed. Wellington mounted a whispering campaign to discredit Siborne, insisting to friends he had won the battle before Blücher's troops arrived. Frances, Lady Shelley noted in her journal: 'The Duke himself told me in Paris that the battle was won before the Prussians arrived.'

There could only be one winner between Wellington and the low-ranking army surveyor – Siborne's model today has only a token force of Prussians, although there is good evidence Siborne was right. As a journalist, I see Siborne as one of the largely forgotten heroes of the battle (although he arrived in Paris after it was over): he spent eight months on the battlefield at La Haye Sainte doing painstaking research and gathered a unique archive of 700 letters from the main participants to piece together the story of the battle for his model. He discovered the uncomfortable truth that the Prussians arrived in force after 4 p.m. – three hours before Wellington admitted – and when he wrote his history of the battle, Siborne stood by his evidence. The army refused to pay for Siborne's model so he put it on private show. Although it was over twenty years after the event, it caused a sensation – it was seen by 100,000 people paying a shilling a head at the Egyptian Hall, Piccadilly in 1838. But he never got the proceeds and went broke. He gained a sinecure at the Royal Hospital, Chelsea, to see out his old age in relative comfort, and died aged 51 in 1849. He is buried at Brompton Cemetery.

Standing at the crossroads on the ridge at Mont St Jean today, the battlefield seems horrifyingly small given the slaughter that happened here. On this patch of lush green fields, about 4 miles (6.5kms) by 2 miles (3.5kms), an estimated 47,000 men were killed or injured in about twelve hours.

The opposing slopes where Wellington and Napoleon marshalled their men are (according to Siborne's measurements) only 2,500yds apart, with undulating fields and a shallow valley running east–west between them, covered in clover and ripening waist-high rye. Wellington must have been able to see Napoleon, although he said years later, 'No I could not – the day was dark, there was a great deal of rain in the air.' Wellington must have been turning a Nelsonian blind eye to the emperor. Sir John Kincaid, stationed with his rifle regiment in the sand pit opposite the farm of La Haye Sainte, clearly saw Napoleon on his white mare, Desiree:

The formation of the French lines was scarcely completed when the magnificent and animating spectacle which they presented was heightened in an

extraordinary degree by the passing of the Emperor along them, attended
by numerous and brilliant staff. The troops hailed him with loud and fervent
acclamations.

The Duke much later admitted to Frances, Lady Shelley, he:

> saw an officer ride along the French line and heard a tremendous cheer
> which was kept up during that officer's progress. The Duke felt sure it was
> none other than Bonaparte himself. It was probably the moment when
> Bonaparte pointed his finger in the direction of Brussels and promised his
> troops the plunder of that city.

Sunday, 18 June 1815 was the first time Napoleon and Wellington had faced
each other on a battlefield. Wellington was extraordinarily single-minded; to
force himself to focus on a military career, he gave up gambling at cards and
burned his beloved violin as a young man of 24 (his father Garret Wesley,
a musical prodigy, was professor of music at Dublin University). Napoleon,
a genius of offensive war, would meet his defensive match in Wellington.
Crucially, Wellington used three farms on the battlefield – Hougoumont on
the extreme right of his lines, La Haye Sainte in the left-centre, and Papellotte
on his far left – as breakwaters against the waves of French columns, to limit
the emperor's ability to move his troops on the field of battle.

Napoleon's plan was astonishingly simple, as described by Victor Hugo in
Les Miserables:

> To go straight to the centre of the Allies' line, to make a breach in the enemy,
> to cut them in two, to drive the British half back on Hal, and the Prussian
> half on Tongres, to make two shattered fragments of Wellington and
> Blücher, to carry Mont-Saint-Jean, to seize Brussels, to hurl the German
> into the Rhine and the Englishman into the sea.

There were striking similarities between the two men: they were both the
same age, 46, and both had learned their trade at a French military school
(where the Duke learned to speak fluent French). But the two commanders
were on very different form that day.

Wellington was in his prime, slim and fit and every eyewitness said 'Nosey'
seemed to be everywhere. With a long, boney nose like a raptor's beak,
Wellington truly watched the battlefield like a hawk through a portable brass
field telescope from his vantage point sitting on Copenhagen under an elm
tree at the Mont St Jean crossroads. He restlessly patrolled the ridge, keeping a
grip on his lines, issuing orders through his ADCs (who acted like messengers),

riding to crisis points, cajoling, steadying, ordering Maitland's guards to lie down to save them in the final attack, and finally ordering them to stand and fire, before waving his hat in the air to signal the general advance. Lieutenant Colonel Basil Jackson, a staff officer attached to the deputy Quartermaster General Sir William De Lancey, recalled years later:

> As I looked over my saddle, I could see the outlines of the Duke and his horse amidst the smoke, standing very near to the Highlanders of Picton's division bearing a resemblance to the statue in Hyde Park when partially shrouded by fog, while the balls – and they came thickly – hissed harmlessly over our heads.

Jackson added, 'It was a time of intense anxiety for had the Duke fallen, heaven only knows what might have been the result of the fight!' The Duke, who had no time for false modesty, would have agreed with Jackson. The ADCs had been warned to stay back, but Jackson spotted one ADC still with him – Lord Arthur Hill 'the most portly young man in the army' who was known at Military College as 'fat Hill'.

Napoleon in contrast was decidedly past his best, flabby after putting on weight in exile on Elba and suffering from piles that made him irritable and riding difficult. His Equerry, Jardin Aine said he rode through the lines and gave orders to make certain that every detail was executed promptly but returned often to Le Caillou on horseback. 'There he dismounted and, seating himself in a chair which was brought to him, he placed his head between his hands and rested his elbows on his knees. He remained thus absorbed sometimes for half-an-hour, and then rising up suddenly would peer through his glasses on all sides to see what was happening. At three o'clock an Aide-de-Camp from the right wing came to tell him that they were repulsed and that the artillery was insufficient ...'[1] He spent two hours away from the battlefield in the afternoon, leaving Marshal Ney in charge of the battle at a crucial time.

Napoleon was under 5ft 7in tall, thick about the shoulders and neck, with grey eyes that, to Lieutenant Colonel Jackson, who accompanied him later to exile in St Helena, appeared 'wholly devoid of expression'. Napoleon habitually wore a green cut-away military coat, white waistcoat, breeches, and silk stockings, a cocked hat, worn square on, with a tricolour cockade and the star of the Legion d'Honneur. Jackson, no fan of Bonaparte, said he was vain about his physique, often given to using coarse expressions, mistrustful and on his guard, apt to talk too much and then withdraw what he had said; he could not tolerate being contradicted, disliked the wealthy but revered *la noblesse*, and had a horrid habit of spitting, even in bed, whether it hit the carpet or the bed-curtains. Flattery failed towards him, but probity and diligence succeeded. His decision to attack the Allied armies instead of waging a defensive campaign inside France had been a great gamble, but he confessed much later that he felt as though he had lost his winning touch. During his exile on St Helena, he said:

> I sensed that Fortune was abandoning me. I no longer had in me the feeling of ultimate success, and if one is not prepared to take risks when the time is ripe, one ends up doing nothing – and, of course, one should never take a risk without being sure that one will be lucky.

Wellington rated Napoleon as a field commander, saying he was worth 40,000 men in boosting the morale of his troops, but Napoleon underrated Wellington. He dismissed the Duke as a 'sepoy' general, a reference to his rise in India under the patronage of his older brother Richard, the governor-general, fighting the armies of the maharajas. It was obviously a barb that stung the Duke. Colonel Daniel Mackinnon, the Coldstreams' historian, said when the Duke's Spanish friend and military attache, Don Miguel de Álava arrived at Mont St Jean from Brussels, he found Wellington in a tree observing the French deployments. Wellington said: 'How are you Álava. Bonaparte shall see today how a General of Sepoys shall defend a position!' The Duke had used the experience he had gained in India and the Peninsula to scout out the perfect place for a defensive position, a ridge with a 'reverse slope', which could protect his troops from Bonaparte's famous artillery.

In the weeks before the battle, the Duke ordered his engineers to draw up a detailed topographical map of a wide area to the south of Brussels. Ten Royal Engineer Officers, under the command of Lieutenant Colonel Carmichael Smyth and Brigade Major Oldfield, rode for miles, mapping every hill and dale. I found their map at the Royal Engineers Museum in Chatham, Kent, largely ignored by most visitors, who were drawn to the strange Heath Robinson contraptions for allowing armies to cross rivers or scale heights. The map shows that Wellington's engineers did not have a clue precisely where he intended to make his stand. James Scott, deputy curator of the museum, told me they produced ten sheets covering 120 square miles at 4 inches to the mile that were stitched together to make one vast map 135cms x 95cms. The contours of the gently rolling farm fields are picked out in coloured shading in grey and green wash and red pigment like a modern Ordnance Survey map. Oddly, the greatest detail is around Hal, well behind his front lines. Here Wellington controversially stationed 15,500 troops to protect his escape route to the coast, or to prevent Napoleon outflanking him to the west – a manoeuvre never contemplated by Bonaparte because it would have pushed Wellington towards the Prussian army on the east. The reserves at Hal never fired a shot, although they were sorely needed in the battle, but the map for Hal gives a clue to its importance in the Duke's thinking: it is drawn on better paper than the rest of the map, with more detailing showing tree lines and hill shading. The engineers clearly thought this area was going to be the focus of his action, and, perhaps, so did Wellington. The actual battlefield, before the ridge at Mont St Jean, a little over a mile south of Waterloo, is in the extreme right hand corner of the map and on inferior brown paper with less detail, suggesting it was hurriedly added at a later stage as an afterthought. Three prominent farms are labelled, 'Chateau Goumont' for Hougoumont, La Haye Sainte, and La Belle Alliance. If you look carefully you can see a faint loop around Mont St Jean in grey pencil. This is the pencil mark left by Wellington's own hand. The faint grey swirl of pencil is the closest you can get to Wellington's careful planning for defeating Napoleon.

He circled the ridge probably as he stood at Quatre Bras to show De Lancey exactly where wanted his forces concentrated after receiving the news carried by his ADC Sir Alexander Gordon that the Prussian field marshal Blücher had been forced to fall back on Wavre, about 8 miles to the east of Mont St Jean. De Lancey, as Wellington's Quartermaster General, folded up the map and carried it through the battle until around 3 p.m., when he was mortally wounded as he spoke to the Duke on horseback. De Lancey was hit in the back by a bouncing cannon ball and was pitched over the head of his horse onto the ground. He tried to get up – Wellington said he bounced up like a 'struck pheasant' – but collapsed with terrible internal injuries. Wellington, who had been warned by his ADCs to take care of the roundshot, dismounted and went to him:

> A ball came bounding along en-richochet as it is called and, striking him on the back, sent him many yards over the head of his horse. He fell on his face and bounded upwards and fell again. All the staff dismounted and ran to him and when I came up he said, 'Pray tell them to leave me and let me die in peace.' I had him conveyed to the rear …

De Lancey, 37, the American-born son of a Huguenot family, was carried away in a blanket, but before doing so, the precious map was recovered by Brigade Major Oldfield and passed to Lieutenant Colonel Carmichael Smyth, commander of the Royal Engineer Officers on Wellington's staff. Carmichael Smyth later kept it safe at home until his death in 1860. It was then lost but it resurfaced at a London bookseller's in a job lot of maps in 1910. The book-seller recognised its importance and tipped off the Royal Engineers Museum. Fortunately, a curator at the Museum bought it with his own money, and rescued it. It was painstakingly restored and at the time of writing was being prepared for representing with an inter-active display at the Chatham museum in 2015 for the bicentenary of Waterloo. It is one of the most telling relics of the battle because it gives us a window on Wellington's mind.

Wellington had carefully scouted out the land to the south of Brussels in the weeks before the battle, and had found what he was looking for at Mont St Jean – a ridge with a reverse slope. There was a forward slope to give him the advantage over the emperor's feared columns, but the reverse slope back towards the farm at Mont St Jean enabled the allied commander to shield his troops from direct sight by Napoleon's beloved 12-pounders, which the emperor called 'my beautiful daughters'. Wellington may have identified this position a year before. 'In the summer of last year (1814), his Grace went there on his way to Paris, and on that occasion took a military view of it,' said one of his aides. 'He then declared, that if ever it should be his fortune to defend Brussels, Waterloo would be the position he would occupy.' This could be true – he often played a game guessing at what lay out of sight, over the crest of a hill to test his skills at topography. And Mont St Jean lay on the main route into Brussels from Charleroi and the French border. If Napoleon was to be stopped, it would have to be here.

At the top of the ridge today, on the west side of the Charleroi–Brussels crossroads, there is a bus stop shaded by a stand of towering elms. This is where the distinctive figure of Wellington could be seen by his men, scanning the battlefield mounted on Copenhagen. Today the battlefield is little changed, apart from the Lion Mound, which dominates the skyline on Wellington's ridge like a monumental piece of Belgian surrealist art. It is as if someone has dropped the Great Pyramid of Egypt on Belgium, painted it bright green and stuck a lion on top as a joke.

The Lion Mound is 141ft high and was created on the orders of King William of Orange to mark the spot where his son, the Prince of Orange, was hit in the shoulder by a musket ball. Being hit by a musket ball was often fatal. The Duke of Brunswick had been killed two days earlier at Quatre Bras by a musket ball that went through his bridle-hand and hit his liver: 'He fell, and breathed his last in ten minutes.' And with the lack of modern medicine, a musket ball did not need to hit a vital organ to kill.

However, given the general slaughter all around, it seems odd that this huge mound was produced to celebrate the prince's recovery from a shoulder wound. Of course, it is nothing of the kind. The Lion Mound was a monument to hubris. Belgium, split between French speakers in the Walloon area in the south – including Waterloo – and the Dutch-speaking Flemish area in the north, had been annexed by the First French Republic ending Austrian rule. The Mound was a very visible reminder to the French-speaking Belgians that after Waterloo, they were firmly under the rule of the House of Orange as part of the Netherlands. It did not work. Within four years of the Mound being completed in 1826, the Belgians revolted and secured their independence.

Wellington was understandably furious when he first saw the Mound. Victor Hugo wrote that he complained: 'They have altered my battlefield.' If Hugo is right, he was being diplomatic in his language. It was created by scraping 10 million cubic tons of Belgian earth from the ridge and wiped away one of the most important features to understanding the battle and Wellington's strategy; it removed the steep ridge that protected his men, and virtually obliterated the steep banks surrounding a 'sunken' road running east to west along the ridge at Mont St Jean.

It is difficult today to visualise just how steep the slope and the bank of the sunken road was. The slope made the climb through fields churned to mud a real slog for the French infantry. It also meant they would have been unable to see their enemy until the last moment, because they were in a dip, and when Maitland's Guards stood up it looked as though they were rising out of the Belgian soil. The psychological shock effect was enormous even before the musket balls struck flesh, sinew and bone.

Soil sampling and GPS computer modelling have confirmed that the ridge was a far more prominent feature before the thousands of tons of earth were piled up to make the Mound. The Gordon monument, erected by the family of Wellington's chief ADC, Sir Alexander Gordon in 1817, is a good guide to just how high the ridge was; the base is the old height of the land before the construction of the Lion Mound and it is reached by a flight of twenty-three stone steps.

The opposing armies presented a spectacular sight before the slaughter started. Before the days of camouflage, every regiment strutted like peacocks in bright colours. The British infantry famously wore scarlet but many regiments wore more gaudy outfits to 'outdo' each other and some wore elaborate plumed hats like Ladies' Day at Ascot. The French cavalry were magnificent to the eye, according to a contemporary account:

> chasseurs in green and purple and yellow; hussars with dolmans and shakos of all tints – sky-blue, scarlet, green and red; dragoons with turban-helmets of tiger skin; carabineers – giants of six feet, clad in white – with breast-plates of gold and lofty helmets with red plumes; grenadiers in blue, faced with scarlet, yellow epaulettes and high bearskin caps; the red lancers – red breeched, red-capped with floating white plumes half a yard long ...[2]

The cavalry was notorious for being style-conscious. The Royals and the Life Guards wore tight scarlet tunics with blue facings and gold lace; the Horse

Guards and the Dragoon Guards wore blue with scarlet facings and gold lace; the Inniskilling Dragoons wore scarlet with yellow facings and gold lace; while the Hussars wore blue with white facings and silver lace. Captain Rees Howell Gronow, a Regency dandy who had decided to leave London and join Wellington's army of his own volition, observed:

> You discovered at a distance what appeared to be an overwhelming, long moving line, which, ever advancing, glittered like a stormy wave of the sea when it catches the sunlight. On they came until they got near enough, whilst the very earth seemed to vibrate beneath the thundering tramp of the mounted host. One might suppose that nothing could have resisted the shock of this terrible moving mass.[3]

Despite the smart uniforms, Wellington's army was a far cry from the seasoned, battle-hardened fighting machine he had left in Toulouse in 1814, when Napoleon was first forced to abdicate. The Duke was contemptuous of it: 'On the whole our army was an infamously bad one,' he said two decades later, 'and the enemy knew it.' The overwhelming majority of Wellington's force at Waterloo, 64 per cent, was drawn from Continental Europe. Just 35 per cent of Wellington's army was British. Wellington fielded 67,665 men and 156 guns but by the time he got to Waterloo, Colonel Daniel MacKinnon, the Coldstream's historian, who was there, reckoned the total force – after losses at Quatre Bras and the reserve of 15,500 men held at Hal – was no more than 55,000 against Napoleon's 68,900 men and 246 guns. The exact numbers are still a contentious issue. I have used the detailed returns gathered for Captain Siborne's *History of the War in France and Belgium in 1815* (first published in 1848 by T. and W. Boone of London). The British contingent comprised 15,181 infantry, 5,843 cavalry, 2,967 artillery and 78 guns – a total force of 23,991 British troops. The majority of his forces (38 per cent) were from the German states thanks to the links with Britain's Hanoverian king, George III. They ranged from the Hanoverians from George III's homeland, Brunswickers and the crack King's German Legion, raised in England from German ex-patriots, who fought to the death to defend La Haye Sainte, to Nassauers and 17,000 Dutch-Belgians under the command of the Prince of Orange. Wellington, like his commanders, clearly did not trust some of these Continental forces to stand firm under fire, particularly the French-speaking Belgians, although the 1st Dutch-Belgian Brigade under Colonel Detmers was credited with helping to break the Imperial Middle Guard at the crux of the battle.

There are still heated debates about claims of cowardice or worse, treachery, by the some of the Continental troops that littered the memoirs of British soldiers. Wellington, typically, had no such qualms. Years after the battle, he was still accusing the Nassau troops of being turncoats: 'The next thing I saw of them at Waterloo was them running off, and what is more, firing upon us as they ran!'

The most shocking anti-Belgian propaganda was still being recycled as late as 1890 by Charles Dalton in the foreword to his *Waterloo Roll Call*:

> Of the Nassau, Dutch and Belgian troops, it is only fair to say they were, mostly, utterly useless at Waterloo. The glamour of Napoleon was upon them. They had lately been in his service and had a settled conviction that Wellington would be defeated and his army cut to pieces … the 'Brave Belgians' … retired from the field and carried news of Wellington's defeat to Brussels.

This Victorian jingoism has fuelled one of the most persistent myths about Waterloo: that it was a British – or even more inaccurately, an English – victory. This may also have helped to strengthen the view in Britain about itself: that 'plucky little Albion' has been called upon to rescue Europe from a power-crazed tyrant three times within 200 years. This historic self-view, reinforced by Waterloo, may still have an impact on Britain's attitude towards the European Union. Wellington later told his female admirers he layered the suspect units with the tougher British and German battalions behind them to make sure they did not break. Some of the German and British regiments were battle-hardened after the Peninsular War, but the truth is many of the British troops were also inexperienced. Again there are disputes about the proportion, but some estimates suggest only six of his twenty-five British battalions had served in Spain. As soon as peace was secured in Paris in 1814, some of Wellington's best regiments were sent to fight in America for the War of 1812 and the Anglo-American peace treaty signed in Ghent in January 1815 was too late to bring back more than a handful of units in time to fight Napoleon.

I walk along a track at the traffic lights along the ridge in the direction of the Waterloo golf course, somewhere in the distance. A few yards along the rough track, I find a small metal plaque that at first sight looks like a milestone: 'In memory of the heroic stand by the 27th Inniskilling Regiment of Foot … when of the 747 officers and men who joined battle, 493 were killed or wounded. A noble record of stubborn endurance.'

A social history of the Inniskilling regiment has shown that they were mostly Catholics from Fermanagh, from poor homes, and more than thirty from Galway, Kerry and Donegal could speak only Irish.[4] They were a unit closely knit by their Irish ties, and the next day they were found dead together still 'in square' where they fell. They had been drilled to respond to a cavalry charge by forming a square; so long as they did not break, cavalry found it impenetrable – there were eyewitness accounts of the frustrated French cuirassiers riding up and exchanging insults with the men. But they were horribly vulnerable to artillery in their square formations, and when La Haye Sainte, the farm just below the ridge, fell at about 6.30 p.m., Napoleon pushed forward his field guns and pounded the squares with a murderous fire. Wellington regretted it deeply, remarking at dinner years later: 'We should not have lost La Haye Sainte any more than Hougoumont if there had only been a wicket (a gate) behind to let in ammunition. But the French kept up such a fire on the front that we could not supply it from that quarter.'

Across the track, overlooking the rolling hills south towards La Belle Alliance is another marker stone with a plaque. It says:

> To the gallant memory of Lieutenant General Thomas Picton Commander of the 5th Division and the left wing of the Army at the battle of Waterloo. Born 1758. Died near this spot in the early afternoon of 18 June 1815 leading his men against Count Drouet d'Erlon's advance.

It took nerves of steel to hold steady on the ridge, as more than 16,000 of d'Erlon's infantry, a quarter of Napoleon's army, advanced in columns after the emperor's cannon fell silent; the columns were roughly 150 men across, 24 deep, around 3,600 soldiers in each (though there is a debate about exactly how they were composed). It would have taken them about twenty minutes to cross the muddy fields, wading through the waist-high corn, under fire from roundshot and canister balls as they got closer to the allied guns. But to the 4,000 defenders on the ridge, their steady advance with drums pounding was a frightening, bowel-liquidising sight that had made armies all over Europe crack and run. Historian Richard Holmes said in his BBC *War Walks* series the sight of 20,000 men advancing with fixed bayonets was inclined to make men 'find an urgent engagement somewhere else'.

Lieutenant Colonel Basil Jackson said in his memoirs:

> The system is as old as the Macedonian phalanx … the undisciplined armies of the French Revolution relied on the moral effect of rapidly pushing forward large masses against the weakest parts of an enemy's position – a method that rarely failed of success against continental armies, for, impelled by natural ardour and enthusiasm, they dashed on with the elan for which they have credit and actually frightened the defenders by their rapid and imposing advance.

The only way to stop them in 1815, before the advent of machine guns, was for lines of infantry in two or three ranks to hold firm and, rank by rank, mechanically pour continuous volleys of musket fire into the advancing columns at point-blank range as their officers shouted out the orders: 'present, fire, reload, present, fire, reload'. The allied ranks had been subjected to a terrifying bombardment of roundshot from 12 noon to around 1.30 p.m. that took off men's heads, splashed their comrades with blood and brains, mingling the screams of horses and men, blood and smoke.

D'Erlon's forces, including the 45th – 'the Invincibles' – were hit by roundshot and canister (dozens of large balls in a canister that exploded out of the cannon like giant gunshot rounds) but they tramped remorselessly up the slope, and shouted 'Vive l'Empereur! En avant! En avant!' as their drummers beat out the roll of the 'pas de charge'.

When d'Erlon's men crashed through the hedges at the top of the ridge, von Bijlandt's Dutch-Belgian brigade fell back, running past Lieutenant General Sir Thomas Picton's jeering 5th Division.* The Highlanders – remnants of the regiment that had been decimated defending Quatre Bras – were being pushed back, and d'Erlon's corps was threatening to drive a wedge between Pack and Kempt's brigades to take possession of the ridge.

Picton, hugely experienced, a blood-and-guts leader who had fought all the way through the Peninsular campaign – saw the French columns momentarily pause to spread out so they could fire at the thin red lines on the ridge. He seized the moment and ordered his men to fire a volley from their muskets at point-blank range through the hedge that concealed them. Three thousand muskets in two thin lines fired into the French massed ranks. Almost before the smoke cleared Picton yelled: 'Charge! Charge! Hurrah! Rally the Highlanders!' Picton was on horseback, wearing a top hat and civilian clothes, cursing the French and his own men in his usual fashion. Picton's men burst through the hedge with their bayonets, but as they did so, Picton was shot from his horse and he was dead before he hit the ground. A musket ball had gone through his right temple, leaving a hole through his top hat** and through his brain. The musket ball was later cut out with a razor. It had lodged on the lower and opposite side of his head, where it appeared just breaking through the skin.[5] His corpse was found to be terribly bruised just above the hip with the skin very distended by a mass of coagulated blood. Picton must have been badly injured, possibly by roundshot at Quatre Bras, but had said

---

* Some, including Basil Jackson, said they ran; others say they were carrying out an orderly retreat.

** The hat with the hole of the musket ball is in the National Military Museum, Sandhurst. The top hat he wore in the Peninsular campaign to shield his eyes from the sun is in the National Army Museum, Chelsea.

nothing about the wound to his side, and got his servant to bandage it up. His death came at a moment of great peril for Wellington's line. There were few reserves of infantry immediately behind the lines on the ridge for Wellington to push forward. The Earl of Uxbridge, commanding the cavalry and standing close to Wellington, decided he had to throw in the heavy cavalry to maintain the momentum of Picton's counter-charge.

The 1st Brigade of heavy cavalry, under Major General Lord Edward Somerset, comprised the 1st and 2nd Life Guards, the Royal Horse Guards, known as the Blues, and the 1st Dragoon Guards. The 2nd Brigade was commanded by Major General Sir William Ponsonby. It was known as the Union Brigade because it included Scots, English (the Royals) and Irish (Inniskilling) Dragoons. In total there were over 2,000 horsemen on the reverse slope waiting for the order to charge.

Uxbridge rode up at speed and ordered a double charge of the Heavy Cavalry. He told Ponsonby to attack the infantry and Somerset's cavalry to stop the French cuirassiers, who were riding towards the ridge in support of the infantry. Uxbridge, in his excitement, placed himself in front of Somerset's brigade. The sabres of over 2,000 horsemen were raised, waiting for the order to advance. They paused for a moment, the horses ready, ears pricked. The head of the French column of infantry had crossed the sunken ridge road. Uxbridge's order to advance was repeated down the line by other officers. Major George de Lacy Evans, who had been taken on by Ponsonby as an extra ADC a few weeks before on his return from service in America, waved his hat as a signal to the line to go forward. Uxbridge led Somerset's Brigade slowly at first, at no more than a walk, but gathering pace. Captain Alexander Kennedy Clark of the Royal Dragoons and his Corporal, Francis Stiles, had been standing on the reverse slope at Mont St Jean patiently waiting for their moment, and it was now.

Notes

1. Jardine Aine, *Equerry to the Emperor Napoleon, With Napoleon at Waterloo*, unpublished papers edited by Mackenzie Macbride (London: Francis Griffiths, 1911), p.184.
2. W.H. Fitchett, *Wellington's Men* (1900), p. 16.
3. Captain Rees Howell Gronow, *Reminiscences of Captain Gronow* (London: Smith, Elder and Co, 1862).
4. Mark Bois, 'The Inniskillings at Waterloo' (www.napoleon-series.org, November 2007).
5. John Booth, *Waterloo* (London: 1816, Google Books), p. XXXV.

4

THE MAN WHO CAUGHT AN EAGLE

D'Erlon's leading column was 80yds away when Captain Alexander Kennedy Clark of the 1st Royal Regiment of Dragoons saw the look of panic in their eyes at the sight of the two heavy brigades of cavalry bearing down on them. They 'gave us fire, which brought down about twenty men', and then they turned on their heels and tried to flee back through the two hedges that topped the ridge, he recalled.

The Royals, a wave of scarlet and gold lace, had difficulty keeping up the momentum, as they negotiated a steep drop into the hollow lane on their heavy horses, but when they crossed the obstacle, they plunged into the melee of the French troops, who were caught in confusion. The French tried to escape the slashing sabres while the men behind pressed on:

> We were upon and amongst them before this could be effected ... the whole column getting into one dense mass, the men between the advancing and retiring parts getting so jammed together that the men could not bring down their arms ... We had nothing to do but to continue to press them down the slope.

The Royals were commanded by Lieutenant Colonel Arthur Clifton, and Kennedy Clark was one of four captains. They scythed through the head of the 105th Infantry Regiment, slashing with their long, straight, heavy swords at the massed ranks of blue coats and black shakos. Captain Duthilt of the French 3rd Division of infantry was pushing one of his men back into the ranks when he suddenly saw the man fall at his feet, bleeding from a sabre wound; he turned round and instantly saw the Union cavalry forcing their way into the midst of his men, hacking them to pieces with their sabres:

> In vain our poor fellows stood up and stretched out their arms; they could not reach far enough to bayonet these cavalrymen mounted on powerful horses, and the few shots fired in chaotic melee were just as fatal to our own men as to the English. And so we found ourselves defenceless against a relentless enemy who, in the intoxication of battle, sabred even our drummers and fifers without mercy.

Captain Kennedy Clark had been slashing with his sabre at the massed ranks of d'Erlon's columns for five minutes when he saw the gilded eagle about 40yds in front of him. It glittered on top of the standard of the *105me Regiment d'Infanterie de Ligne*, with their battle honours. It was to his left and surrounded by French colour guards, who were pushing back deeper into their own ranks to protect it.

Captain Kennedy Clark gave the order to his squadron, 'Right shoulders forward, attack the colour,' leading the attack himself with his sword stretched out in his right hand:

> On reaching it, I ran my sword into the officer's right side, a little above the hip joint. He was a little to my left side, and he fell to that side with the eagle across my horse's head. I tried to catch it with my left hand but could only touch the fringe of the flag and it is probable it would have fallen to the ground, had it not been prevented by the neck of Corporal Stiles' horse, who came up close on my left at the instant. Corporal Stiles was Standard Coverer; his post was immediately behind me and his duty to follow wherever I led.

Captain Kennedy Clark shouted, 'Secure the colour, secure the colour, it belongs to me.' The Captain grabbed the staff of the standard and tried to break the golden eagle off the top of the pole with the intention of stuffing it into the breast of his coat, but he could not break it. Captain Kennedy Clark says Corporal Stiles told him, 'Pray sir, do not break it.' The Captain replied, 'Very well, carry it to the rear as fast as you can, it belongs to me.' Stiles rode back to the crest of the ridge with the prize in his hand, cheered by the men as he went.

At least that is the official version of how the eagle was captured.

I found Captain Kennedy Clark's captured eagle on show in a display case at the National Army Museum next door to the Chelsea pensioners' hospital in London. The eagle does not look worth dying for. The gilded bird with its arrogant raptor's head is perched on top of a short pole on a small gold plinth with the number 105 embossed on the base. Its beak is turned to one side, as if it is about to strike at a victim, and it grips a golden spindle in its right talon. It is tarnished but the spotlights in the display case lend a glint to its defiant gaze at passers-by, who glance and move on, not knowing its story. It is not made of precious metal, but it embodied the pride of Napoleon's regiments and was regarded by their enemies as a trophy of priceless worth, more valuable than if it were made of solid gold.

I look closer at the black wooden pole and I can clearly see the cuts, including one deep notch about 2ft below the eagle where Captain Kennedy Clark tried to hack off the eagle with his sabre.

The eagles were a symbol borrowed by Napoleon from the all-conquering legions of Rome to instill pride and solidarity in his regiments. These were the prized possessions of each of Napoleon's regiments and were defended to the death by the standard bearers. The coveted eagles of the old regiments were so potent that they were destroyed on the orders of King Louis XVIII after the emperor's abdication in 1814, but the emperor presented 100 new eagles for his 1815 campaign at a spectacular military review that was called the *Champ de Mai* in Paris though it was actually held on 1 June 1815. One British officer, Captain Scott wrote: 'They glittered over the heads of the vain Parisians, amid cries of Vive L'Empereur.'

Napoleon presented this eagle to his 105th Line Regiment, commanded by Colonel Jean Genty, which formed part of Drouet d'Erlon's 1st Corps with the regimental colours and a list of its battle honours, including Jena, Eylau, Essling and Wagram. Men gave their lives for it, because losing it would bring shame on their regiment. It was mentioned by Wellington in his Waterloo Despatch:

> Lord E. Somerset's brigade, consisting of the Life Guards, the Royal Horse Guards, and 1st Dragoon Guards, highly distinguished themselves, as did that of Major General Sir William Ponsonby, having taken many prisoners and an eagle.

However, a note in the display of the National Army Museum hints at an awkward dispute that arose over its capture and nagged on for years afterwards. The note says: 'Captain Clark was severely wounded at the Battle. When he recovered, he found all the credit of the capture had gone to Corporal Stiles. His part in securing it was officially recognised in 1838.'

Captain Kennedy Clark, in his account of the capture, clearly regrets he left it to Stiles, who took it to the rear. Part of the standard pole that carried it has disappeared with the colours. Lieutenant General W. Scott wrote that when he saw it after the battle, it 'was much defaced with blood and dirt, as if it had been struggled for, and the eagle was also broken off from the pole, as if from the cut of a sabre; but it was nevertheless preserved.' Captain Kennedy Clark staked his claim to the eagle in a series of letters to Captain Siborne when Siborne was doing the painstaking research in the 1830s for his detailed model of the Waterloo battlefield for a new United Services Museum. Captain Kennedy Clark modestly did not mention he was seriously injured after taking the eagle, but his version of the incident was taken as the official account.

Officials at the United Services Museum who first displayed the eagle of the 105th clearly supported Captain Kennedy Clark's version of events. The army is designed to believe in hierarchies – knowing who is in charge makes taking orders much simpler – so it was natural that the army establishment should back the officer. Stiles had his moment of glory but it was fleeting. The corporal was cheered when he galloped back to Brussels and, for a time, became famous as the 'man who captured the eagle'. An official website of the Royal Dragoons says: 'It was probably only because Corporal Stiles was seen removing the eagle by many senior Officers (including Wellington) that it was thought he had captured it.' Infuriatingly for Captain Kennedy Clark, Corporal Stiles appeared in a fanciful Dutch painting of the wounded Prince of Orange and Wellington posing heroically after the battle. The prince is lying pasty-faced from his shoulder injury while the Duke takes the accolades from his troops. Stiles appears in the extreme left of the painting, holding the eagle standard. Captain Kennedy Clark is nowhere to be seen. However, I discovered that Stiles – another example of Wellington's 'scum of the earth' – did not go quietly into oblivion. He was adamant that he deserved the credit for capturing the eagle and refused to be silenced. Stiles felt he had a right to take the glory, because he insisted that *he*, not Captain Kennedy Clark, had run through the colour guard and captured the eagle. His claims clearly caused consternation in the army.

Six months after the battle, when he was stationed in Ipswich, Sergeant Stiles was challenged by his own commanding officer, Lieutenant Colonel Arthur Clifton, to produce a witness who could verify what he was claiming had happened. Stiles wrote a letter from his Ipswich barracks to Lieutenant George Gunning, an officer in Captain C.L. Meredith's D Troop of the First Dragoons, in Cheltenham, on 31 January 1816 asking Gunning to back him up:

Sir,
This day, Colonel Clifton sent for me about taking the Eagle and Colours.
He asked me if I had any person that see me take the Eagle.

I told him that you see me, I believe, as the officer of the French was making away with it. I belonged to your troop at that time and you gave me orders to charge him, which I did, and took it from him. When I stated it to him this day he wants to know the particulars about it, and me to rite to the Colonel as you was the nearest officer to me that day. Sir by so doing you will much oblige. Your most obedient and humble servant,

Francis Stiles,[*] Sergeant 1st Royal Troop.

This letter with its spelling mistakes and grammatical errors represents more than a clash of two men over the eagle. It is also a clash of class, and there could only be one winner in Wellington's day. Stiles was semi-literate judging by his letter, and his word was never going to be taken before that of Captain Alexander Kennedy Clark. The dispute put Gunning on the spot. I have not been able to trace his reply to Stiles, if he wrote one, but there is clear evidence that Gunning did back up Stiles even though this meant challenging the version of events by his superior officer.

In a long forgotten footnote in the *Waterloo Roll Call* written at the turn of the nineteenth century, there is a paragraph on Gunning by the army historian Charles Dalton. It says:

> Lieutenant George Gunning, Eldest son of George Gunning of Finsbury JP ... Commanded his troop at Waterloo in the famous charge, where he was severely wounded. He always claimed that he gave the order to Corporal Stiles to seize the eagle of the 105th French regt. from the officer who held it. Died at Brighton 5th Jan 1849.

Kennedy Clark fought for over twenty years to have his claim to the eagle fully recognised. In 1838, Colonel Kennedy Clark was officially recognised as the man who captured the eagle. He was allowed to include the eagle in his family coat of arms to commemorate his heroism in capturing the French standard, and his regiment was permitted to wear the eagle among its badges. Having settled the matter in Kennedy Clark's favour, the row was eventually brushed under the regimental carpet. Corporal Stiles was given a sergeant's stripes and then an ensigncy for his trouble, and was quietly elbowed out of the official history.

By the time Charles Dalton compiled the *Waterloo Roll Call* in 1904, Stiles was not to be believed. Dalton wrote in a brief sketch of Captain Kennedy Clark:

---

[*] He signed himself 'Stiles'. Siborne spelled his surname as 'Styles', which has caused confusion ever since.

It was this officer and not Corporal Stiles who *personally* captured the French Eagle of the 105th Regiment at Waterloo after a desperate fight in which he was severely wounded and handed it over to Corporal Stiles to carry it to the rear.

The emphasis is Dalton's, who was in effect calling Stiles a liar. But then Stiles was long dead by that time and had no one to speak up for him.

However, seven years earlier, in 1897, the military artist James Princep Beadle blundered into the dispute when he painted his first major battle canvas, choosing the heroic story of the capture of the eagle standard of the 105th for his subject. Instead of Kennedy Clark, he painted Stiles of the Royal Dragoons capturing the standard of the 105th in the centre of his large canvas. Stiles sits on his horse, heroically holding the eagle aloft with the French regiment's colours and battle honours fluttering in the breeze, surrounded by cheering soldiers of the Black Watch and the Gordon Highlanders. Stiles is bare-headed, with ginger hair, sideboards and a square jaw. The painting is called *The Captive Eagle* and there is no sign of Captain Kennedy Clark. It is one of the most heroic images of the battle and by a renowned war artist. You would expect it to be in some regimental museum, but I discovered it on the wall by the entrance to the assembly room in Great Yarmouth Town Hall. Quite why it is there, nobody at Great Yarmouth borough council, who own it, could tell me, but it could be because the army regard it as perpetuating an unfortunate mistake. It is said that every picture tells a story but if the official record is to be believed, *The Captive Eagle* tells a lie.

The fates of the two men could not have been more different after Waterloo. Captain Kennedy Clark was from an old and revered Scottish family – the Clarks of Nunland in Dumfries. His family on his mother's side – the Kennedys of Knockgray – owned a mansion and estate in the nearby grouse-shooting moorlands of Galloway. He succeeded to the Kennedy estate in 1835 and after that, as laird of the manor, he adopted his mother's family name as a surname; he thus became (confusingly) Sir Alexander Kennedy Clark-Kennedy. He married Harriet Randall in December 1816, had a son called John, who became a distinguished officer and was promoted to the post of colonel of the 6th Dragoon Guards and then the 2nd Dragoons. Sir Alexander went on to enjoy a life as a member of the privileged ruling class. He was knighted and elevated to the pinnacle of social respectability in Victorian England by being made an ADC to Queen Victoria. It was a largely ceremonial appointment, started by Queen Victoria to confer on a few high-ranking officers the greatest esteem of the young monarch. Prince William, the current Duke of Cambridge, is an ADC to Queen Elizabeth II. But it meant that Sir Alexander was a palace insider at a time of historic events, including the Crimea War. He also gained immense wealth when he inherited his mother's family estate. He died at the grand age of 82 in 1864 and was buried in the family plot in Dumfries.

Sir Alexander Kennedy Clark-Kennedy lived long enough to have his photograph taken by one of the earliest plate cameras shortly before he died; it was placed in the National Portrait Gallery. He sits in a chair, in full dress uniform, wearing his Waterloo and campaign medals, the Star of the Order of Bath, and a long curved sabre, a plumed hat resting on his right knee. He is white-haired, and looks relatively cheerful. By then he had ensured that he would go down in history as 'the man who captured the Eagle'.

Stiles had joined the 1st Dragoons – the Royals – on 21 May 1804 at the age of 18 or 19. He had been a trooper in the cavalry for eleven years, but he was still only a corporal when he rode after Captain Kennedy Clark down the slope at Waterloo. He certainly could not afford the cost of buying a commission. The best he could hope for was the three sergeant's stripes he got for his supporting role when Captain Kennedy Clark captured the eagle. Stiles did become an officer – he was promoted to Ensign, the lowest commissioned rank, in the 6th West India Regiment as a reward for his undoubted courage in the capture of the eagle – but was quickly discarded by the army: like thousands of other soldiers, the peace meant poverty for Stiles; he was placed on half pay on 28 December 1817, aged 32, and effectively laid off.

He went to live in the East End of London after his discharge from the army, and it is not clear how he made a living, or how he made ends meet, but it must have been a hard life in Clerkenwell, East London. That may explain why he died in 1828 aged just 43. I searched through the parish records to find out more about Stiles, and found a tantalising record of a Francis Stiles getting married in 1818. He would have been 33, and his bride was Mary Ann House. They were married on 29 April 1818, at St James's Church, a Georgian gem in the narrow lanes around Clerkenwell, with the curate T. Thimbleby officiating. Judging by their names, the witnesses were not related to either the bride or groom; perhaps they were friends. However, only ten years later, on a cold winter's day on 17 January 1828, Francis Stiles was buried at the same church. No cause of death was given but cholera and typhoid were a scourge in the overcrowded east end of London and that year a satirical cartoon appeared in the London prints of a woman looking horrified at seeing the monsters in the water in her tea cup through a microscope; it is called 'Monster Soup commonly known as Thames water'. Perhaps Stiles was one of its many victims in London's east end?[*]

---

[*] John Snow pioneered the science of epidemiology in 1854 when he drew up a map of cholera deaths around Broad Street in Soho and deduced they were caused by the public water pump. Disabling it helped to cut the number of deaths. A pub near the site – now called Broadwick Street – is named after him.

St James's Church, Clerkenwell, where Stiles was buried.

The register of deaths shows Stiles went to his grave still claiming he captured the eagle.

By the early nineteenth century Clerkenwell had become fashionable with artisans and professionals, attracted by the large houses. However, it had seriously declined as a place to live by the time Stiles died. It was crime ridden, and overcrowded with terraces in multiple occupation. Spa Fields, where civil unrest broke out on 2 December 1816, was just around the corner, as well as the Clerkenwell House of Correction (prison).

Stiles lived in Gloucester Street, now renamed Gloucester Way. The old Georgian terraces were bomb-damaged in the Second World War, and many were swept away in the 1950s passion for slum clearance, which often did more damage to the urban landscape than the Luftwaffe. Stiles's house went the same way. It was replaced by an uncompromising block of council flats for social housing.

Islington remained rundown until the late twentieth century, when it was rediscovered by the professional classes – particularly the media (and Tony Blair) – and then it began its renaissance. The area where Stiles lived was gentrified, as part of sought-after Islington, handy for the City, with a slightly bohemian feel. Today, a six-bed Georgian terraced house near the street where Stiles lived in Clerkenwell can fetch £4.2 million.

I found the church where Stiles was buried is still there. It had a number of graveyards, but Stiles's headstone, if he had one, has been cleared away. The graveyard around the church has been turned into a rough patch of grass and a playground. Some of the Georgian and Victorian headstones have been used as paving slabs around the edges of the open space, but if his is there, I could not read it. I found one with a barely legible inscription, green with moss and worn beyond recognition by the weather and the tread of feet. Stiles is so completely forgotten, even senior members of the church are unaware that they have a hero buried somewhere in their trendy patch of London.

But I did find the register in which Stiles's burial was recorded. The pages for January 1838 provide an insight into life in Clerkenwell in the new Victorian era (Queen Victoria succeeded to the throne the year before). Several of the dead are in their twenties, and there is a child of two years. Just above Stiles's name is a prisoner who died in jail; we do not know how. His name was Michael Toomy; he died aged 22 and his address was given as the House of Correction. Stiles took his claim to his grave. Below Toomy's entry in the parish register, the curate has written in a flowing hand, 'Francis Stiles captor of an Eagle at the great Battle of Waterloo'.[1]

Notes
1.   Register of Burials, January 1828, St James's Church, Clerkenwell.

5

'SCOTLAND FOREVER!' – ENSIGN EWART

With Uxbridge riding at their head, Lord Edward Somerset's Household Brigade – the Life Guards, Royal Horse Guards (known as the Blues) and the Dragoon Guards – smashed into the cuirassiers with a 'shock like two walls'. Somerset said their sabres clanged on the shiny metal breast-plates (the cuirass) of the French cavalry with a sound 'like braziers at work'. He lost his hat and went bare-headed into the charge, and while looking for it, a cannon ball took off the flap of his coat and killed his horse. Somerset found another mount and a Life Guard's helmet that he wore throughout the rest of the battle.

Sergeant Charles Ewart of the Scots Greys plunged down the slope after Uxbridge and Somerset, and rode into history. Ewart, at 46, was a veteran and one of the most respected men in his regiment, the Royal North British Regiment of Dragoons – known as the Scots Greys because of their insistence on riding grey horses – when it was ordered to Waterloo. Born in Kilmarnock in 1769, on Bedoes farm in Kilmarnock into a family of seven, he was tall and powerfully built, with black hair and a receding hairline. He had become famous in his regiment for training his favourite horse, Jock, to perform tricks in front of the men. Ewart had grown up around horses, which probably led to his decision to join a cavalry regiment. He enlisted in the ranks at the age of 20. Sergeant Major Cotton described Ewart as 'a man of Herculean strength and of more than ordinary stature being six foot four inches and of considerable skill as a swordsman'.

Ewart's party trick was to get Jock to stand on his hind legs while Ewart pushed up its forequarters, making it look as though muscle-bound Ewart was lifting up the horse. This performance on the parade ground won him many admirers, but not his major. Ewart taught Jock to grab hats with his teeth, and could not stop Jock one day making a grab for his major's bearskin. Ewart was also the regimental fencing master and after the Earl of Uxbridge ordered the double charge of the two heavy brigades he put his brilliant skill with a sword to lethal use. The Scots Greys looked magnificently menacing in scarlet tunics with blue facings and gold lace, topped with bearskins and a white plume, but it was the powerful grey horses that Napoleon remembered.

Not far from Sergeant Ewart was another farmer's son from Scotland, John Dickson of the Scots Greys. Dickson, a corporal in Captain Vernor's F troop, was mounted on Rattler and closely followed Ewart. He was from East Lothian – his family were tenants of the landowner, Lord Wemyss, an ancient Scottish family with ancestral lands in Fife. Dickson was described as a 'typical yeoman', of ruddy complexion, brown hair and hazel eyes. He had enlisted in Glasgow when he was barely 18 in 1807, after a wave of patriotism swept Britain in response to Napoleon's growing threat to Britain after the Tilsit peace treaty with Russia and Prussia. Dickson noticed that Major General Sir William Ponsonby, the second son of the Irish peer, Lord Ponsonby of County Cork, was on a bay hack because his groom with his thoroughbred charger could not be found when they saddled up. It was to cost Ponsonby his life. Wearing a long cloak and cocked hat, Ponsonby spurred his bay to the thick hedge at the top of the bank before the sunken road. He was followed by his ADC, Major George de Lacy Evans, a veteran of storming parties in the Peninsular War, who had returned a few weeks earlier from America where, with a small body of infantry, he had captured the Congress House in the punitive raid on Washington when the White House was burned down.

Ponsonby looked down at the fighting below then Dickson saw de Lacy Evans wave his hat as a signal to the brigade to advance. Below them, the Highlanders – the 42nd Black Watch and 92nd Gordon Highlanders – fired at the advancing columns barely 20yds away. Sir Denis Pack, commander of the 9th infantry Brigade of Picton's 5th Division shouted to the Gordon Highlanders: '92nd you must advance!' The Highlanders fixed their bayonets and pushed forward through a holly hedge at the top of the ridge. The Scots Greys were supposed to be in reserve but Lieutenant Colonel James Inglis Hamilton, commander of the regiment, ordered them forward to support the Highlanders, shouting: 'Now then, Scots Greys, charge!' Hamilton was from a humble background – he was the son of a sergeant major called Anderson from Lanarkshire but had been adopted by his father's commanding officer, who brought him up as his own son; he joined the Scots Greys as a Cornet at the age of 15 under his adoptive father's name. Drawing his sword, Dickson said, Hamilton rode straight at the holly hedge near the crest of the ridge and crossed it. A great cheer rose from the ranks of the Greys and they followed

Hamilton. Beyond the first hedge, Dickson said the road was sunk between high, sloping banks, and it was very difficult to descend without falling, but there were few accidents:

> All of us were greatly excited, and began crying 'Hurrah the 92nd! Scotland for ever!' as we crossed the road for we heard the Highland pipers playing among the smoke and firing below … I dug my spur into my brave old Rattler and we were off like the wind. Just then I saw Major Hankin fall wounded. I felt a strange thrill run through me, and I am sure my noble beast felt the same for, after rearing for a moment, she sprang forward, uttering loud neighings and snortings and leapt over the holly-hedge at terrific speed.

Dickson plainly saw his old friend Pipe Major Cameron standing apart on a hillock, coolly playing 'Johnny Cope, are ye wakin' yet?' above all the din of battle. The Highlanders parted for their fellow Scots on horseback and the rousing shout went up: 'Scotland Forever!'

> As we tightened our grip to descend the hillside among the corn, we could make out the feather bonnets of the Highlanders and heard the officers crying out to them to wheel back by sections. A moment more and we were among them.

Some of the Highlanders had no time to get out of the way and were knocked down by the Greys. According to Dickson 'many of the Highlanders grasped our stirrups and in the fiercest excitement dashed with us into the fight'.

Towering above the French infantry, the men on the grey horses powered their way into Donzelot's and Marcognet's infantry, flashing their sabres right and left as the columns marched up the slope to the east of the Charleroi–Brussels road. 'A young officer of the [French] Fusiliers made a slash at me with his sword, but I parried it and broke his arm; the next second we were in the thick of them. We could not see five yards ahead for the smoke,' said Dickson. He saw Armour, a friend from the Ayrshire town of Mauchline, and Sergeant Ewart to his right beside a young officer, Cornet Francis Kinchant. 'I stuck close by Armour; Ewart was now in front.' Ewart recalled: 'We charged through two of their columns, each about 5,000.' The Highlanders and other foot regiments following behind took thousands of prisoners. De Lacy Evans said:

> By the sudden appearance and closing of our cavalry upon them (added to their previous suffering from musketry and grape) they became quite paralysed and incapable of resistance, except occasionally, individually, a little.

Another who took part in the charge said d'Erlon's columns 'fled as a flock of sheep across the valley'. Many of the French were shouting 'Quarter' to surrender. Ewart was about to cut down one French officer when Cornet Kinchant accepted his surrender. Ewart kicked his horse on but heard a shot and looked around to see Kinchant falling from his horse. The French officer who had just surrendered had shot him in the head. Ewart was so enraged that he slashed at the officer, cutting him 'down to the brisket' (the lower chest).

In his fury, Ewart spurred his horse forward to kill more of d'Erlon's men. That is when he saw Napoleon's golden eagle with the standard of the emperor's 45th Ligne. It was surrounded by a colour guard, determined to defend the eagle with their lives. Dickson saw it too, and spurred on Rattler, hard on Ewart's heels. He saw Ewart taking on the colour guard single-handed. Dickson kicked Rattler to give Ewart support: 'I cried to Armour to "Come on!" and we rode at them. Ewart had finished two of them and was in the act of striking a third man who held the eagle; next moment I saw Ewart cut him down and he fell dead.' Ewart said:

> He and I had a hard contest for it. The bearer thrust at my groin. I parried it off and cut him down through the head, after which I was attacked by one of their Lancers, who threw his lance at me, but missed the mark by my throwing it off with my sword by my right side. Then I cut him from the chin upwards, which cut went through his teeth.

Dickson was just in time to thwart a bayonet thrust that was aimed at Ewart's neck. Armour finished another of them. Ewart said, 'Next I was attacked by a foot soldier who, after firing at me, charged me with his bayonet. But he very soon lost the combat for I parried it, and cut him down through the head, so that finished the contest for the eagle.'

Ewart's bloody prowess with a heavy cavalry sabre is a source of some amazement by fencers today. Owen Davis, one of Ewart's descendants, said:

> This feat of arms was nothing short of spectacular and as a sport sabre fencer myself I can appreciate the agility and quick thinking needed, notwithstanding the strength required to cut up through a man's skull and to move from guard with such an unwieldy weapon as the 1796 Heavy Cavalry Pattern Sword.[1]

The pole of the eagle standard had been jammed in the soft ground, while the fight to the death went on around it and Ewart snatched it up before it fell to the ground:

I was about to follow my comrades, eagle and all, but was stopped by the General (Ponsonby) saying, "You brave fellow, take that to the rear; you have done enough till you get quit of it," which I was obliged to do, but with great reluctance.

On the ridge, Ewart watched with increasing horror as one of the greatest cavalry charges in British military history turned into a disaster:

I retired to a height and stood there for upwards of an hour which gave a general view of the field, but I cannot express the horrors I beheld. The bodies of my brave comrades were lying so thick upon the field that it was scarcely possible to pass, the horses innumerable.

Across the battlefield, it was every man for himself. Corporal John Shaw of the Life Guards, one of Ewart's garrison friends, wielded his heavy sabre with skills he had learned from Ewart, slashing through a man's skull so hard that the 'face fell off like a bit of apple'.[*]

Shaw was a celebrated former prize fighter who had been taught by Ewart how to use a sword while they were both in London. Shaw was from farming stock at Wollaton, Nottinghamshire, and built like an ox. He was 6ft 3in tall and weighed 15 stone, and was proud of his powerful physique; he had posed naked for the art classes of the Royal Academy in London including a study by William Etty, now in the Household Cavalry Museum, Horse Guards, Whitehall. In the barracks at London, he had shown Ewart how to box while Ewart showed him how to perfect his sword play. Shaw was fighting on the fields to the east of La Haye Sainte and slashed a 'giant cuirassier' across the neck. Major Waymouth of the Life Guards saw Shaw, in his red tunic, surrounded by assailants, but hacking them down in a fighting frenzy. He said, 'Corporal Shaw was very conspicuous, dealing deadly blows all round him ...' Sergeant Thomas Morris, a Londoner of the 73rd Regiment of Foot, which suffered 225 men killed and wounded – the biggest casualties of any line regiment after the Inniskillings – said Shaw had been at the gin before the battle and was fighting drunk. He saw Shaw 'running a-muck at the enemy, was cut down by them as a madman ...' Like others in the heavy brigades, Shaw rode too far, and when he reined in his horse, he found his way back to the allied lines was cut off. Shaw was last seen:

surrounded by overwhelming numbers of the foe. The contest was a long one and it was only when his sword had been broken in his hand that Shaw's defence was overcome. Hurling the hilt of his weapon among the enemy, he

---

[*]   Shaw so inspired Sir Walter Scott he had a cast made of his skull. A copy is on show at the Horse Guards Museum, Whitehall.

tore off his helmet and struck out right and left with it; but the swords of the cuirassiers ultimately cut him down.[2]

He was left for dead on the ground where he fell. Victor Hugo said that as Shaw lay on the ground, 'a French drummer-boy gave him the coup de grace' but that was artistic licence. Major Waymouth said Shaw 'was probably shot down, near that spot, by a cuirassier who stood rather clear of our left and occupied himself by shooting our people with his carbine, taking very deliberate aim.'[3] Another eyewitness says Shaw dragged his body up the hill on the French side after the battle to one of the houses lining the Charleroi Road:

> After being rendered unconscious by the many wounds he had received, he had crept in pain from the open ground to the protection of the farm buildings at La Belle Alliance. Shaw whispered, 'I am done for'. He then fell back from sheer exhaustion. In the morning, he was found lying dead, as a result of loss of blood.[4]

This too may be another of the myths surrounding his heroic death. Private Thomas Playford of the 2nd Life Guards recalled seeing Shaw's body lying below La Belle Alliance on the field of battle, surrounded by dead French soldiers. Corporal Webster told Playford he recognised Shaw. There was a 'deep wound in his side, near the heart which appears to have been inflicted with either a bayonet or a lance ...'[5]

Shaw's name lived on long after his death. A character in Bleak House by Charles Dickens said: 'Old Shaw, the Life Guardsman! Why he's a model of the whole British army himself. Ladies and gentlemen, I'd give a fifty pound note to be such a figure of a man.'

Ponsonby's brigade charged too far up the opposing slope and reached Napoleon's grand battery, where they madly slashed their sabres at the gunners and their horses. They suddenly realised they had overreached themselves. Dickson and his fellow Scots Greys had continued riding down through the French columns that seemed to open up to let the Greys through. The Scots Greys were riding well to the east of the Charleroi Road and they saw the Royals and Inniskillings clearing the road and hedges at full gallop away to their right. It had all been going so well, until the rout turned to ruin for the men and horses of the heavy brigades: 'It was a grand sight to see the long line of giant grey horses dashing along with the flowing manes and heads down, tearing up the turf about them as they went,' said Dickson:

> The men in their red coats and tall bearskins were cheering loudly and the trumpeters were sounding the Charge.

In five minutes we had cut our way through as many thousands of Frenchmen. My brave Rattler was becoming quite exhausted, but we dashed onwards.

At this moment, Colonel Hamilton rode up to us crying 'Charge! Charge the guns!' and went off like the wind up the hill towards the terrible battery that had made such deadly work among the Highlanders …

It was a mad charge to the grave for many. The heavy cavalry careered on, like Shaw and Lieutenant Colonel Hamilton, slashing all before it, driven either by gin or by the intoxication of war. Hamilton was terribly injured in both arms, but a major saw him going at full speed towards the French guns holding the bridle-reins of his horse in his teeth. Hamilton's body was found on the field, shot through the heart. His sword had gone, but his scabbard and a sash were still intact, and these were taken back to his family.[6]

Napoleon was moved to say, 'These terrible grey horses, how they fight!' He sent in the lancers to cut them to pieces. The Union Brigade's horses including the Greys, like Rattler, were blown, and when the troopers reined in, they saw their retreat was cut off in the muddy bottom of the valley between Hougoumont and La Belle Alliance by the lancers of Baron Jacquinot's 1st Cavalry Division, and Edouard Milhaud's cuirassiers, who had rallied for a counter-charge.

The death of Major General Ponsonby by M. Dubourg after Manskirch, printed 1 January 1817. (Musée Wellington, Waterloo)

Ponsonby was chased into a ploughed-up waterlogged field, where his horse was overtaken and he was speared by a lancer. British accounts say he was surrounded and captured in the mud – after handing a picture and a watch out of his pocket to his ADC to give to his wife – when there was an attempt by three Scots Greys to rescue him. He was brutally speared to death by his captor.

But according to the French Colonel Louis Bro, commander of Napoleon's 4th Lancers, the truth was less romantic. Ponsonby was trying to seize a third French eagle, when his Lancers crashed into the Greys: 'I was lost in a fog of gunsmoke. When it cleared, I saw some English officers surrounding Lieutenant Verrand, the eagle-bearer. Gathering some riders I went to his aid. Sergeant Orban killed General Ponsonby with a blow of his lance. My sabre felled three of his captains. Two others fled.' The French account is probably nearer to the truth: Major De Lacy Evans made no mention of the eagle but admitted he was with Ponsonby in the thick of the action, and had to abandon him to his fate because Ponsonby's horse was blown:

> Everyone saw what must happen. Those whose horses were best or least blown, got away. Some attempted to escape back to our position by going round the left of the French lancers. Sir William Ponsonby was one of that number. All these fell into the hands of the enemy. Others went back straight – among whom myself – receiving a little fire from some French infantry towards the road on our left as we retired.[7]

De Lacy Evans added that 'Poor Sir William' would have got away with his life, but he was on the small bay hack that was blown. He was one of the most senior British officers killed at Waterloo and Ponsonby's wife, Georgiana, gave birth to his son and heir in February, 1816.

In all, more than 2,000 French soldiers were taken prisoner after the charge of the heavy brigades; it was claimed up to forty pieces of cannon were put out of action; and two eagles were captured. D'Erlon's attack was turned by the charge of the heavy cavalry just when it threatened to break Wellington's thin red line. To that extent, it was a success. But the price paid by the two brigades was appalling. Somerset's 1st Brigade, which was led by Uxbridge, lost a total 525 men killed, wounded or missing; Ponsonby's 2nd Brigade posted 533 men killed, wounded or missing, a grand total of 1,058 men out of a total strength on paper of 2,651 horsemen (the actual number who took part in the charge of the two heavy cavalry brigades was slightly less, making the casualty rate worse). This amounted to a casualty rate of 40 per cent.[8] The Scots Greys had 102 killed and 97 injured with 179 horses killed and 47 mounts injured. Ewart's troop fared reasonably well – of 53 officers and men commanded by Captain Robert Vernor, ten were injured – a casualty rate of under 20 per cent.

Across the battlefield, Ponsonby's second cousin, Sir Frederick Cavendish Ponsonby, had also been left for dead. Sir Frederick, commanding two squadrons of the 12th Light Dragoons in Sir John Vandeleur's 4th Brigade, was ordered to cover the retreat of the Union Brigade as it was trying to extricate itself from its charge to the guns, when he was wounded. His Light Dragoons, in blue tunics with yellow facings and silver lace, had charged through a column of French infantry and then upon the right flank of the lancers when he was cut across the head and both arms, and knocked from his horse.

Sir Frederick, brother of the scandalous Lady Caroline Lamb, who nursed him back to health, later gave his graphic account – one of the most remarkable personal stories of the battle – to Frances, Lady Shelley, who passed it on by letter to his mother, Lady Bessborough:

We were attacked in our turn before we could form, by about 300 Polish Lancers, who had come down to their relief—the French artillery pouring in amongst us a heavy fire of grape-shot, which, however, for one of our men killed three of their own. In the melee I was disabled almost instantly in both my arms, and followed by a few of my men who were presently cut down—for no quarter was asked or given—I was carried on by my horse, till receiving a blow on my head from a sabre, I was thrown senseless on my face to the ground. Recovering, I raised myself a little to look round, being I believe at that time in a condition to get up and run away, when a Lancer, passing by, exclaimed :'Tu n'es pas mort, coquin,' ['You're not dead, scoundrel'] and struck his lance through my back. My head dropped, the blood gushed into my mouth; a difficulty of breathing came on, and I thought all was over. Not long afterwards (it was then impossible to measure time, but I must have fallen in less than ten minutes after the charge) a tirailleur came up to plunder me, threatening to take away my life. I told him that he might search me, directing him to a small side pocket, in which he found three dollars, being all I had. He unloosed my stock [high collar], and tore open my waistcoat, then leaving me in a very uneasy posture. He was no sooner gone, than another came up for the same purpose, but assuring him I had been plundered already, he left me. When an officer, bringing on some troops (to which probably the tirailleurs belonged) and halting where I lay, stooped down and addressed me, saying he feared I was badly wounded, I replied that I was, and expressed a wish to be removed into the rear. He said it was against the orders to remove even their own men, but that if they gained the day, as they probably would, for he understood the Duke of Wellington was killed and that six battalions of the English army had surrendered, every attention in his power should be shown me. I complained of thirst, and he held his brandy bottle to my lips, directing one of his men to lay me down on my side, and placed a knapsack under my head. He then passed on into the action, and I shall never know to whose generosity I was indebted, as I conceive, for my life. Of what rank he was I cannot say; he wore a blue great-coat.[*] By-and-bye another tirailleur came, and knelt down and fired over me, loading and firing many times, and conversing with great gaiety all the while. At last he ran off, saying: 'Vous serez bien aise d'entendre que nous allons nous retirer. Bon jour, mon ami.'

Lady Caroline, known as Caro, typically saw romanticism mixed with the horrors of the injured like her brother when they brought him back to Brussels. In a letter to her mother-in-law, Lady Melbourne, Caro wrote:

It is rather a love-making moment, the half-wounded Officers reclining with pretty ladies visiting them … It is rather heart-breaking to be here, however, & one goes blubbering about – seeing such fine people without their legs & arms, some in agony, & some getting better … Lady Conyngham is here—Lady C. Greville—Lady D. Hamilton, Mrs. A. B. Smith, Lady F. Somerset, Lady F. Webster most affected; Lady Mountmorress, who stuck her parasol yesterday into a skull at Waterloo

Frederick later married the daughter of Lord Bathurst, the War Minister, and landed a plum job as governor of Malta. He died suddenly in a pub in Basingstoke in 1837 aged 53.

With such true stories of valour as Cavendish Ponsonby's – the stuff of legend – the charge of the heavy brigades and the capture of the two eagles in a single action was seen as a famous triumph at home and caught the imagination of the Prince Regent, who promptly made himself Captain General of the Life Guards and Blues for their 'brilliant' conduct at Waterloo.

The legend of the cavalry charge was further ornamented for a Victorian audience in a celebrated heroic painting titled *Scotland Forever!* by Lady Elizabeth Butler, which remains one of the most often reproduced images of Waterloo. It shows the Scots Greys in a headlong charge, their sabres raised, their horses' nostrils flared, as if they are about to leap out of the canvas at the viewer. She was one of the few women artists who specialised in military subjects and continued painting to the First World War. Elizabeth Thompson

---

[*]   Ponsonby later met Major de Laussat of the Imperial Guard Dragoons in 1827 and discovered in their conversation that he was the French officer who had helped him.

was married to Lieutenant General Sir William Francis Butler, who is said to have arranged for the Scots Greys to charge past her as she made sketches from life. *Scotland Forever!* was painted in 1881, long after Ewart had died, and included a portrait of the hero bare-headed after losing his bearskin. Her painting of the Scots Greys is scoffed at by some military experts today as inaccurate because they are charging, but she caught the madness in the eyes of the horses and the thrill on the faces of the men, just as Corporal Dickson described it.

Today, the glory of capturing the eagles and turning d'Erlon's attack into a rout still masks the inconvenient truth. Those closer to the action at the time realised the charge of the heavy cavalry ended in a disaster. Captain Rees Howell Gronow, of the 1st Foot Guards claimed:

> The Duke of Wellington was perfectly furious that this arm had been engaged without his orders and lost not a moment in sending them to the rear where they remained during the rest of the day ... I recollect that when his grace was in our square, our soldiers were so mortified at seeing the French deliberately walking their horses between our regiment and those regiments to our right and left that they shouted, 'Where are our cavalry? Why don't they come and pitch into those French fellows?'

Uxbridge shouldered the blame for the losses, saying he had been wrong to lead the charge himself, because he could no longer hope to control it from that position: 'After the overthrow of the cuirassiers I had in vain attempted to stop my people by sounding the rally but neither voice nor trumpet availed ... I committed a great mistake in having myself led the attack.'[9] In his own defence, he said that when he returned to the ridge, Wellington and his whole *corps diplomatique militaire* seemed 'joyous – they thought the battle was over'.

Wellington took the view recklessness was endemic in the British cavalry. Captain Gronow claimed that a few days after his arrival in Paris, the Duke was told by Colonel Felton Hervey, who carried despatches from London, about the Prince Regent's self-appointment as a cavalry Captain General. Wellington, Colonel of the Royal Regiment of Horse Guards, replied, 'Ah, his Royal Highness is our Sovereign and can do what he pleases; but this I will say, the cavalry of other European armies have won victories for their generals, but mine have invariably got me into scrapes ...' Gronow encountered a French officer, Marshal Exelmans, who said the fine horses and riders of the British cavalry were spoiled by their officers:

> who have nothing to recommend them but their dash and sitting well in their saddles ...The British cavalry officer seems to be impressed with the

conviction that he can dash and ride over everything; as if the art of war were precisely the same as that of fox hunting.[10]

When compounded by confused orders, the readiness of British cavalry to make suicidal charges against overwhelming odds was to cause the catastrophe thirty-nine years later at Balaklava, known to history as the Charge of the Light Brigade. On 25 October 1854, the Light Brigade led by the incendiary Lord Cardigan, who had clashed with his commanding officer Lieutenant General Lord Lucan, charged 25,000 Russian troops powerfully defended by artillery. Of the 673 men who rode into the valley at Balaklava, only 195 returned – an attrition rate of 71 per cent. The man who presided over the allied army in the Crimea that day was the one-armed, doddery Lord Raglan, formerly FitzRoy Somerset, Wellington's military secretary at Waterloo, who – like Ewart – had watched in horror as the cavalry rode to their deaths.

Capturing the eagle may have saved Ewart's life. After watching the horror unfold from the ridge, he took the eagle into Brussels 'amid the acclamations of thousands of spectators who saw it.'

In his dotage, Ewart went for a drink with a reporter from the *Observer* in Ayrshire, called James Paterson,[11] in a pub in Kilmarnock called The Monument Inn. Over a few drinks, Ewart told Paterson his life story, and about his capture of the eagle. The old soldier proved a fund of stories for Paterson, who incorporated a brief biography of the hero who captured an eagle in a book of his own reminiscences.

Sergeant Ewart was 46, the same age as Wellington, and, like the Duke, not expecting to go to war in Europe, when Bonaparte escaped from Elba. After Waterloo, Ewart spent some months with the occupying forces in Paris and had a stroke of luck in Calais while he was waiting for embarkation on a packet ship to England. While cooling his heels on the dockside, he met Sir John Sinclair, a friend of the Duke of York, the Commander-in-Chief of the British Army, who had heard about Ewart's fame for capturing the eagle. Sir John said he was so moved by Ewart's 'modesty and valour' that he asked Sergeant Ewart what reward he wanted most in life? Ewart was a very practical Scot: he said if he could be made an Ensign in a veteran battalion, he could retire on an officer's pension.

Sinclair gave Ewart a letter addressed to Major General Sir Henry Torrens (ADC to the Prince Regent) and instructed Ewart to deliver it in person to Torrens at Horse Guards. Sir Henry wrote to Sir John in 1816 confirming that the Prince Regent, under the direction of his brother the Duke of York, 'has been pleased … to appoint Serjeant Ewart of the 2nd Dragoons to an ensigncy in the 3rd Veteran Battalion.'

Ewart's elevation to the officer classes caused a vacancy for a sergeant that was filled by Dickson, who became a sergeant major and served for twenty-seven years in the Scots Greys. Dickson lived to a ripe old age, still regaling locals at a little Fifeshire inn in Crail with his recollections on the anniversary of 18 June. He died on 16 July 1880, aged 90.

Ensign Ewart returned to Britain as a national hero, and on 18 June 1816 he was invited to attend the first Waterloo dinner at the Edinburgh Assembly Rooms. The *Edinburgh Advertiser* reported:

> Nearly 400 noblemen and gentlemen sat down to an elegant dinner in the Assembly Rooms, the Rt Hon William Arbuthnot, Lord Provost of the city, in the chair. After several toasts had been given and duly honoured, Sir Walter (then Mr) Scott proposed a bumper to the health of Ensign Ewart, late of the Scots Greys, whose bravery was so conspicuous where he took a French Eagle and killed with his own hand three of Napoleon's guard. The toast was drunk with great acclamation, and a general expectation prevailed that Ensign Ewart, who was present, would address the company. After a short pause, the Lord Provost rose and, at the request of Mr Ewart, stated how much he felt honoured by this mark of the company's approbation but that he would much rather fight the battle all over again and take another Eagle, than make a speech.

He managed a few words and was given thunderous applause. His fame increased when he was portrayed capturing the eagle in an heroic painting *The Fight for the Standard* by Richard Ansdell (who was born in Liverpool and was even more famous with Victorians for his *Stag at Bay*). It was reproduced as a print, and the popular image was reprinted many times. It shows Ewart about to slice through the neck of the colour-guard with his sabre. The original painting is on show in pride of place in the ancient Great Hall, Edinburgh Castle, near to the Royal Scots Dragoon Guards museum, which has his eagle.

Around 1821, the veterans' battalion[*] was disbanded and Ewart, 52, was finally retired on his Ensign's pension of 5s 10d a day. He went to live in Salford with his wife 'Maggie', Margaret Geddes, who had been with him on some of his campaigns. Ewart supplemented his pension by spending his retirement as a fencing instructor. Fencing and boxing were fashionable pursuits for gentlemen in the Georgian period and Ewart's fame would have gained him a good living. He overcame his fear of public speaking and continued

---

[*]   It is likely he was in the 5th Veteran Regiment, not the 3rd, as mentioned in the Torrens letter.

to tour the country recounting his memories of capturing the eagle into the Victorian era, sometimes with Sir Walter Scott, who became a friend and his unofficial agent. When he was interviewed by Paterson for his *Autobiographical Reminiscences*, the journalist said Ewart, in his seventies, could have passed for a man of 60.

Ewart died at Davyhulme, a suburb of Manchester, on 23 March 1846 at the age of 77. Ensign Ewart was given a hero's funeral and was laid to rest at the New Jerusalem Temple in Bolton Street, Salford. Maggie survived him by ten years but was buried in the Geddes family plot at the east end of the churchyard in nearby Flixton. An inscription at the foot of the Geddes family gravestone read: 'Also Margaret, Relict[*] of Ensign Ewart, late of the Scots Greys.' A local history of Davyhulme[12] published in 1898 complained about Ewart and Maggie being apart in death:

> It is somewhat pitiful that these two worthies who held on to one another through such eventful episodes, should in death be separated. The officers of the Scots Greys, I understand, did, sometime during last year, send an emissary relative to these two graves with the idea of (with other things) re-interring Sergeant Ewart to the grave of his 'Maggie' but the contemplated alterations at the east end of Flixton Church caused the project to remain in abeyance.

That is where Ensign Ewart's story should have ended. But the church and the churchyard where he was buried at Bolton Street became redundant, and his grave was lost beneath the lumber and detritus of a builders' yard. I went to see what had happened to his burial place.

I am standing at the scruffy entrance to a surface car park by the side of the Salford Central railway station. The minicab driver thought I was crazy when I asked for Bolton Street. It is now no more than a short stub, jutting into the side of the car park, with double yellow lines to stop anyone parking here. A fragment of wall blackened by ancient soot is all that remains of the buildings that were once there. The taxi driver gets interested when I tell him the reason I have come here.

It is hard to imagine now, this unlovely and unloved urban corner of Greater Manchester was the last resting place of one of the great heroes of the Battle of Waterloo. The wall is perhaps the last remaining trace of the non-conformist New Jerusalem Temple, a branch of a religious sect based on the beliefs of a Swedish philosopher called Emanuel Swedenborg, mixed

---

[*]   Relict was an ancient term for a widow, though, as they belonged to different churches, they may not have been actually married.

Nearly the last resting place of a hero, a car park in Salford, until Charles Ewart was reburied in Edinburgh. (Author)

with mysticism and spiritualism. A Victorian photograph shows the Temple with three nattily dressed men posing for the camera by the entrance in dark suits with waistcoats. They appear to be wearing top hats. It is a handsome, oblong, Georgian-style building, with a glass lantern in the roof, and five large windows down each side, surrounded by paving slabs, which appear to be shiny and wet, as though it has been raining. It is enclosed by a short brick wall topped by some railings. This could be a fragment of the brick wall that I can see. When it became redundant it was knocked down and the land cleared for the builder's yard. I can find no sign that Ensign Ewart was ever buried here. There is no plaque or headstone. Just cinders, and cars.

The hero's grave remained totally lost and forgotten for ninety-two years, and would have stayed so, but for an inquisitive member of Ewart's regiment called H. Otto, who spent twelve years trying to find his remains in the 1920s and '30s. In 1936 Otto finally found Ewart's bones under the rubble of the builder's yard. Ewart's remains were exhumed two years later and were carried to Edinburgh, the home of the Scots Greys. He was finally laid to rest with full honours on the Esplanade of Edinburgh Castle in 1938 as Britain prepared for the Second World War. *The Scotsman* reported:

> About half the crowd had assembled when a motor hearse, with blinds drawn, appeared on the Esplanade, and came to a stop beside the spot where the hero's remains now rest ... The clock in Crown Square had just struck seven when the unpolished oak coffin was taken from the hearse and borne reverently to the grave. As it passed through the lines of onlookers – among them some women and children – heads were bared and policemen saluted.

A large stone memorial to Ensign Ewart was placed on the Castle Esplanade overlooking the city to ensure his name is not forgotten again.

Owen Davis, who has traced his family tree back to Ewart, said: 'He without a doubt has earned his final resting place on the Esplanade of Edinburgh Castle, the accolades history has showered upon him and above all, the title of "hero".' A pub on the Esplanade at Edinburgh Castle was also renamed in his honour. The Ensign Ewart briefly hit the headlines in 2013, when staff at the pub refused to serve the Royal Navy crew from HMS *Edinburgh* because they were wearing military uniform.[13] The sailors had been on a goodwill visit to their home city, and had taken part in a march with the bands playing up the Esplanade. It was all due to a misunderstanding about local by-laws banning bars from serving military personnel during the Edinburgh Tattoo but it seemed to some that it was a case of life imitating art. In his poem, *Tommy*, Rudyard Kipling anticipated just such an event:

> I went into a public-'ouse to get a pint o' beer,
> The publican 'e up an' sez, 'We serve no red-coats here.'
> The girls be'ind the bar they laughed an' giggled fit to die,
> I outs into the street again an' to myself sez I:
> O it's Tommy this, an' Tommy that, an' 'Tommy, go away';
> But it's 'Thank you, Mister Atkins', when the band begins to play,
> The band begins to play, my boys, the band begins to play,
> O it's 'Thank you, Mister Atkins', when the band begins to play.

Ensign Ewart would raise a glass to that.

Notes

1. Hougoumont Project website, www.projecthougoumont.com.
2. E. Bruce Law, 'Life Guardsman Shaw – A Hero of Waterloo', *With Napoleon at Waterloo* unpublished papers edited by Mackenzie Macbride (London: Francis Griffiths, 1911).

HERE LIES
ENSIGN EWART
ROYAL NORTH BRITISH DRAGOONS

AT WATERLOO AS SERGEANT IN THE ROYAL NORTH BRITISH DRAGOONS
HE CAPTURED THE STANDARD OF THE FRENCH 45TH REGIMENT FROM WHICH
THE EAGLE BADGE NOW WORN BY THE ROYAL SCOTS GREYS IS DERIVED
ERECTED TO HIS MEMORY IN APRIL 1938 BY THE OFFICERS WARRANT OFFICERS
NON COMMISSIONED OFFICERS AND MEN PAST AND PRESENT OF THE ROYAL SCOTS GREYS

Ewart Monument, Castle Esplanade, Edinburgh. (Martin Hillman)

3. Major-Gen H.T. Siborne (ed.), *Waterloo Letters*, (London: Cassell and co., 1891), p. 57.

4. Mackenzie Macbride (ed.), 'A Hero of Waterloo', 'With Napoleon at Waterloo' and other unpublished documents of the Waterloo and Peninsular Campaigns (London: Francis Griffiths, 1911).

5. Gareth Glover (ed.), *The Waterloo Archive Volume 1V: The British Sources* (Barnsley: Frontline Books, 1999).

6. Charles Dalton, *Waterloo Roll Call* (London: Eyre and Spottiswoode, 1904).

7. Major-Gen H.T. Siborne (ed.), *Waterloo Letters*, p. 69.

8. Return of killed, wounded and missing. Captain W. Siborne, *History of the Waterloo Campaign* (First published 1848; London: Greenhill Books, 1990), Appendix XXXVl.

9. Major-Gen H.T. Siborne (ed.), *Waterloo Letters*, p. 19.

10. Captain Rees Howell Gronow, *Reminiscences of Captain Gronow* (London: Smith, Elder and Co., 1862).

11. James Paterson, *Autobiographical Reminiscences* (Glasgow: Maurice Ogle, 1871, American Libraries), pp. 205–13.

12. Richard Lawson, *A History of Flixton, Urmston and Davyhulme* (Urmston: Richard Lawson, 1898), p. 115.

13. STV News, 24 May 2013, www.news.stv.tv.

6

GUTS AND GLORY

Shortly after 3 a.m. on the morning after the battle, Monday, 19 June 1815, Wellington's Scottish surgeon, Dr John Robert Hume, climbed the stairs to the room on the first floor at the wagoners' inn in Waterloo, where the Duke was sleeping on a rough mattress on the floor. Hume was reluctant to wake the Duke because he went to bed exhausted and had only had three hours' sleep, but Sir Charles Broke, De Lancey's replacement as Quartermaster General, had arrived seeking orders for the movement of the army at dawn from the Commander-in-Chief. Worse, Hume was dreading breaking the news to him that his chief ADC, Sir Alexander Gordon, had just died in the surgeon's arms. Hume recorded Wellington's reaction in his medical notes, which are in the archive at the Royal Society of Surgeons, Edinburgh:

I went upstairs and tapped gently at the door, when he (Wellington) told me to come in. He had as usual taken off his clothes but had not washed himself.

As I entered, he sat up in bed, his face covered in the dust and sweat of the previous day, and extended his hand to me, which I took and held in mine, whilst I told him of Gordon's death, and of such of the casualties as had come to my knowledge. He was much affected.

I felt tears dropping fast upon my hand and looking towards him, saw them chasing one another in furrows over his dusty cheeks. He brushed them suddenly away with his left hand, and said to me in a voice tremulous with emotion, 'Well, thank God, I don't know what it is to lose a battle; but certainly nothing can be more painful than to gain one with the loss of so many of one's friends.'

Two of Sir Charles Bell's watercolours of the Waterloo wounded. Bell's own description of the injured:
Left: 'A Sabre Wound … The soldier belonged to the 1st Dragoons. He could not speak and stooped languidly with a vacant and indifferent expression of countenance.'
Below: 'Arm carried off by cannon shot close to shoulder joint. Patient is Sergeant Anthony Tuittmeyer 2nd Line Battalion King's German Legion. He rode 15 miles into Brussels after being wounded.' (From *Wellington's Doctors* by Dr Martin Howard, courtesy of The Army Medical Services Museum)

Wellington went in to see Gordon's body lying in his cot. He returned bitterly upset. Gordon, 29, was Wellington's favourite among the elite band of young Guards officers on his staff, having been with him since the Peninsular Campaign. He had been hit by a musket ball in the thigh, late in the battle, as he tried to rally the wavering allied ranks when Napoleon threw the Imperial Guard against their lines.

The use of the Imperial Guard – the Immortals – was the emperor's last throw of the dice. They had never been beaten; they marched through the fields with one intention – to smash the faltering allied lines on the ridge. For the defenders on the ridge, the 'Immortals' seemed like giants in their bearskins topped by red plumes, as they climbed up the muddy slope, with ported arms, their officers waving their swords, 'as if on a field day', and pressed on by the insistent thumping of the drummer boys, 'rum dum, rum dum, rummadum dummadum, dum dum'. Ney himself led his men, his face blackened by smoke.

Around 3,000 veterans of the Middle Guard tramped up the slopes to the west of La Haye Sainte (towards the ridge where the Lion Mound now stands) and formed three attack forces. Two battalions of French Grenadiers pushed back the first line of British, Brunswick and Nassau troops. Gordon and Lieutenant Colonel Charles Fox Canning, another of Wellington's ADCs, were hit by musket balls – Gordon in the thigh, Canning in the stomach – as they tried to rally the young and largely inexperienced recruits from the city of Brunswick and the Nassau regiment on the ridge. Canning crumpled and bled to death on the battlefield, cradled by the Earl of March, another of Wellington's ADCs and one of the two sons of the Duke of Richmond who were in the battle that day. It was in the same desperate action that the Prince of Orange was hit by a ball in the shoulder (now the site of the Lion Mound).

Wellington had ordered two battalions of more than 1,600 1st Foot Guards commanded by General Sir Peregrine Maitland to lie down behind the ridge so they could not be seen until the last moment. It was a tactic he had used before in the Peninsular War. They were attacked by two battalions of Chasseurs in the second prong of the Imperial Guard attack. Wellington shouted the order: 'Stand up Guards!' They rose up as if from the Belgian soil, and the men in the first of four ranks of muskets fired at point-blank range into the mass of blue coats; then the second, third, and fourth ranks fired in turn: 'The French columns appeared staggered … and convulsed,' said Lieutenant Colonel J.P. Dirom of the 1st Foot Guards.[1]

Captain H.W. Powell of the 1st Foot Guards wrote:

Those who from a distance and more on the flank could see the affair, tell us that the effect of our fire seemed to force the head of the column bodily back. Whether it was from the sudden and unexpected appearance of a corps so near them which must have seemed as starting out of the ground, or the tremendously heavy fire we threw into them, La Garde, who had never before failed in an attack suddenly stopped.

The third force of the Imperial Guard, a fresh Chaasseur battalion, came up to push the assault forward, but they were stopped by a surprise attack organised on their flank by Sir John Colborne – the officer who had squeezed up to let the young Ensign Keppel and his muddy servant warm themselves the night before. Colborne used his own initiative to bring his men of the 52nd Foot to the left side of the French column. Now he ordered his men to fire into the flanks of the Immortals, as they recoiled from the volleys in their front. The emperor's 'invincible' Imperial Guard tottered under the shock of musket fire, and for the first time in their lives, they wavered. Wellington shouted: 'Now Maitland … now's your time.' As the Imperial Guard turned and fled, Maitland's Guards Brigade charged after them, down past Hougoumont with their bayonets. For the first time in their history, the Imperial Guard ran in confusion shouting: '*La Garde Recule*' ('The Guard Retreat'). With a wave of his hat, Wellington signalled the general advance. The defenders of Hougoumont only then realised that the battle was won.

Gordon was stretchered off the battlefield after 7.30 p.m. on a door scavenged from Mont St Jean by a sergeant major. He was in excruciating pain and had lost a lot of blood when they reached Dr Hume at the farm, where he was using the barn as a field hospital. The surgeon slashed away Gordon's uniform trousers and quickly inspected the wound. Dr Hume noted the musket ball had entered on the inside of Gordon's left thigh and had wounded the femoral artery a little above where it pierces the biceps muscle. Going downwards, the ball had shattered the femur in several pieces, lodging in the knee near the surface of the integument. Dr Hume thought Gordon would 'suffer torture' if he was stretchered down to Waterloo, over a mile away, along a road crowded by the chaos of war. There was also the added risk that carrying him further with broken bones moving in his thigh would sever an artery and he would bleed to death. Dr Hume decided he must operate immediately and called over Assistant Surgeon Kenny of the Artillery regiment to assist him. Using a knife and a saw that had seen plenty of work that afternoon, Dr Hume sawed off Gordon's left leg high above the thigh. He later noted:

Notwithstanding it was necessary to take off the thigh very high up, he bore the operation well and though weak was in tolerable spirits asking me several questions about different officers whom he had seen carried from the field wounded and requesting me to tell him how soon I thought he would get well, whether he should not be able to ride …[2]

Gordon told Dr Hume through his pain he felt easy and asked to be carried to Wellington's headquarters at the inn a mile down the road. Dr Hume went with him, but said he unfortunately entered the inn 'at the moment when Mr Sunning was in the act of amputating Lord FitzRoy Somerset's arm'. FitzRoy Somerset, who later commanded the army in the Crimea as Lord Raglan, had been wounded by a musket ball when he was riding alongside the Duke near La Haye Sainte, after it fell to the French. Wellington felt sure it had been fired from the roof of the farm. The ball smashed his right elbow. FitzRoy Somerset walked back to a room by the inn in Waterloo used as a field hospital and showed remarkable *sang froid* while having his arm sawn off. The Prince of Orange, lying wounded in the shoulder in the same room, was unaware that an operation had been performed until FitzRoy Somerset's arm was tossed onto a growing pile of severed arms and legs outside and FitzRoy Somerset called out, 'Hey bring my arm back. There's a ring my wife gave me on the finger.'

Dr Hume, who was clearly worried he would be blamed for Gordon's death, said he was convinced that the sight of FitzRoy Somerset's bloody stump had a fatal psychological impact on Gordon's condition. He noted:

> From that instant, he became very restless and uneasy, sighing frequently and begging for a little wine. I gave him a small quantity with water and as soon as Lord FitzRoy and the Prince of Orange (injured by a shot in the arm) set out for Brussels, I had him put to bed and gave him a few drops of Laudanum with a little wine.

Gordon was in such pain that he sent for Dr Hume at 10 p.m., but the doctor was busy again.

One of the Earl of Uxbridge's young ADCs, 24-year-old Captain Horace Beauchamp Seymour, rode back to the inn and told him the Earl had been badly wounded in the leg with one of the last shots of the battle. He told Hume Uxbridge was being carried to him in a gig, a small carriage. Dr Hume went out into the road to meet the gig, but he recalled there were so many wounded men that he felt obliged to deal with them first:

> I had hardly got to the end of the town when his lordship made his appearance in a gig or Tilbury supported by some of his aides-de-camp.

> I followed him to his quarters and found on inspection that a grape shot [canister] had struck him on the right knee close to the lower edge of the Patella [knee cap] and entered on the inside of the ligament, and having torn open the capsular ligament, had made its exit behind, externally fracturing the head of the tibia and cutting the outer hamstring in two.

The Duke and the Earl of Uxbridge were riding in pursuit of the routed French army across the fields below La Haye Sainte when a ball from canister fired by a French battery passed over Wellington's horse and smashed into Uxbridge's knee, shattering the knee joint. Uxbridge exclaimed, 'I've got it at last!' Wellington replied, 'No? Have you by God?'* Wellington, who had been looking at the battery that fired the canister, snapped shut his telescope and held Uxbridge up in the saddle until he was helped down by other officers from his horse. Then the Duke spurred Copenhagen on towards the French gun that had fired the shot, shouting an order to Major General Frederick Adam in command of the 3rd British Brigade of foot soldiers, 'Adam – you must dislodge those fellows.'

A worried aide urged him to be careful but Wellington said: 'Never mind. Let them fire away. The battle's gained. My life's of no consequence now.'[3]

Wellington's famously laconic exchange with Uxbridge is often seen as the ultimate example of the British 'stiff upper lip' and proof that Wellington was cold hearted. Uxbridge emphasised in a letter years later to historian Captain William Siborne that the Duke 'throughout was invariably concilia-tory and confiding', but he was clearly being diplomatic. There was bad blood between Wellington and Uxbridge going back to Uxbridge's cuckolding of Wellington's brother. Uxbridge's sister, Lady Caroline Capel, gave vent to her outrage at Wellington, when the Duke gave scant credit to her brother for the victory in his Waterloo Despatch. She called it 'odious'.

Hume was amazed to find Uxbridge 'perfectly cool, his pulse was calm and regular as if he had just risen from his bed in the morning'. Indeed, the surgeon said Uxbridge showed 'excessive composure' though his suffering must have been extreme. He was not 'heated' and did not show the least agita-tion, despite the pain or his exertions at being in the saddle all day, and taking part in many cavalry charges. Dr Hume decided to operate in Uxbridge's quarters, a small cottage in Waterloo, but he clearly felt nervous about operat-ing on the second most senior man in the British Army. He wrote that he felt he owed a duty to Uxbridge's family to do nothing until 'evincing to all the world' that amputation was not only necessary but unavoidable. He went out to collect as many medical officers as he could to assist him and confirm his diagnosis. He met with several surgeons of Artillery who accompanied him, and he borrowed a knife from one of them because his own knife had 'been a good deal employed during the day' – it was blunt.

He was preparing to operate with the other surgeons standing by when a young assistant 'pushed himself forward' and told Uxbridge without

---

*   This exchange is famously reported as Uxbridge: 'By God! I've lost my leg.' Wellington: 'Have you by God?' But Croker claims the true exchange is quoted above and it was given to him by Lord Anglesey himself in 1816.

consulting Dr Hume that he would save the leg. The unnamed assistant said: 'My Lord, this is a very nasty wound. It may be long of getting well, but a stiff joint will be the only consequence, there will be no need for taking off the limb.' Dr Hume was furious: 'I never felt myself so completely confounded and taken aback, however restraining myself, I said: "Sir, you have not examined the wound. When you have it will be time enough to give your opinion".' They then had an argument over the patient. Dr Hume angrily told the pushy young assistant:

> You see that the ball has passed through the centre of the joint, that the head of the tibia is smashed to pieces and that the capsular ligament which is torn open is filled with fragments of bone and cartilage from the middle external condyle of the femur, the outer hamstring is also divided: even were the capsular ligament simply punctured with a sword, my own opinion would be against risking the life of the patient under all the circumstances.

Uxbridge remained unruffled by the argument among the surgeons over his body. He told Dr Hume:

> I put myself under your charge and I resign myself entirely to your decision … whilst I observe to you that I feel as any other man would naturally do, anxious to save my limb, yet my life being of infinitely more consequence to my numerous family … I request that you will … act in such a way as to the best of your judgment is most calculated to preserve that.

Dr Hume said: 'Certainly my Lord, but …' Uxbridge interrupted: 'Why any buts – are you not the Chief? It is you I consult on this occasion.' He told Uxbridge that it was better to operate sooner rather than later. 'Very well,' Uxbridge replied, 'I am ready.' Having applied a tourniquet, probably a leather strap tightened around the thigh to snapping point to cut down the loss of blood, Dr Hume took up the knife in his hand. Uxbridge was lucky – the knife was sharp, because (unlike the knife he had used on Gordon) it was new. Lord Uxbridge said, 'Tell me when you are going to begin.' Dr Hume replied: 'Now my Lord.' Uxbridge laid his head on a pillow, put his hand up to his eyes and said, 'Whenever you please.'

The surgeon recorded the operation in eye-watering detail that made me wince when I read it:

> I began my incision … with one stroke of the knife I divided the muscles all round down to the bone and having retracted them on both sides I took

the saw.[*] I had sawed nearly through the femur, but the person who held the leg, being over apprehensive of splintering the bone, raised up the limb, so that the saw being confined, could not be pushed forwards or backwards. I did not perceive what was the cause and said angrily, 'Damn the saw' when Lord Uxbridge said with a smile, 'What is the matter?' These were the only words he spoke and during the whole of the operation he neither uttered a groan or complaint, nor gave any sign of impatience or uneasiness.[4]

Dr Hume noted he gave Uxbridge a very small quantity of weak wine and water and checked his pulse – it was only 66 beats per minute. 'I am quite certain had anyone entered the room they would have enquired of him where the wounded man was ...'

Uxbridge (later made the Marquis of Anglesey by the Prince Regent) interred his leg in a 'grave' at the cottage, which became a bizarre tourist attraction. In the Victorian period, tourists armed with their edition of *Baedeker's Belgium* were told:

The garden of a peasant (a few paces to the N of the church) contains an absurd monument to the leg of the Marquis of Anglesey ... the proprietor of the ground who uses all his powers of persuasion to induce travellers to visit the spot, derives considerable income from this source.

The false leg that he later wore became a model for army prosthetics and is on show at the Horse Guards Museum, Whitehall. It is said he went back to the cottage with his sons, found the table on which he had his leg amputated and had his dinner off it. But today you cannot see the cottage opposite the inn where Uxbridge had his leg removed. It was recently demolished for flats.

While Dr Hume was in the middle of the operation on Uxbridge, he had a message from Gordon's bedside to say that his stump was bleeding and Gordon was very uneasy. He sent a surgeon from the 15th Hussars called Carter to see Gordon. Carter brought back word that Gordon was very restless, although nothing appeared amiss with the stump.

As soon as he finished with Uxbridge, Dr Hume went to inspect Gordon's wound:

I found the ligatures on the arteries all perfectly secure but there was a very considerable venous oozing all over the surface of the stump and particularly from the great femoral vein round which I had put a ligature, cleaning away

---

[*] The saw is on display in the National Army Museum, Chelsea, with a glove belonging to his ADC, Captain Thomas Wildman and a sabretache, both soaked in Uxbridge's blood.

about eight or 10 ounces of clotted blood which had collected about the
ends of the muscles and the integument. I again did up the stump carefully
moistening the bandage with cold water and I repeated the anodyne draught.

Surgeons like Hume are among the forgotten heroes of Waterloo. They had
to operate in primitive conditions, with war raging all around them and no
anaesthetic apart from weak wine or laudanum. It is hardly surprising that it
was reckoned that one in three patients died from shock after amputations.

Surgeon Samuel Good of the 3rd Foot Guards and Matthias Kenny, a
second assistant surgeon with the Ordnance Medical Department, were also
at work at the Mont St Jean farm, hacking off limbs while Hume was tending
to Gordon.

A mile away, the surgeon of the Coldstream Guards, William Whymper,
operated throughout the ferocious siege at Hougoumont farm with a couple
of assistant surgeons, ignoring the carnage all around them. There were hundreds of casualties lying around the farmyard with horrific injuries, including
many who were burned to the bone when the chateau caught fire, and one
who had a hand cleaved off by a French axe.

On the battlefield, the recently-married wife of Private George Osborne
of the 3rd Foot Guards, was injured while she was acting as a nurse. She was
one of the female camp followers allowed by the army, and tore up her own
clothing for bandages. She was hit in the left arm and breast as she tended to
a wounded officer, Captain Edward Bowater. Mrs Osborne was later awarded
the Queen's Bounty for her bravery. But army surgeons were rarely mentioned in despatches.

The horrific wounds they had to deal with were graphically illustrated by
the Scottish surgeon Sir Charles Bell, who toured the makeshift hospitals in
Brussels where many of the injured were sent to die or recover. He was a
gifted anatomical artist and his archive of watercolours provides an invaluable
medical record, but they are much more – Bell has managed to convey in har-
rowing detail the emotions of the patients.

In one of his sketches after Waterloo, a soldier lies on a bed and lifts up
a white shirt to show his intestines that have tumbled out of his stomach
after being cut open by a sabre. The look on his face is one of horror and
resignation at his own impending death. Bell's skill with the paintbrush was
apparently greater than with a knife: he allegedly had a mortality rate of
90 per cent with amputations.

Dr Hume's handwritten medical notes are an equally vivid reminder that
mingled with the glory that day, there were piles of guts and gore. Army surgeons like Hume carried their own medical kit in a rosewood box with a
red velvet inlay that would be recognisable to surgeons today. A typical set

included knives, saws, a screw tourniquet, ligatures and a tenaculum for securing blood vessels. However, the lack of anaesthetics and the grime of the
battlefield made the field-operating theatre more like a butcher's shop. One
surgeon reported:

> All the decencies of performing surgical operations were soon neglected,
> whilst I amputated one man's thigh there lay at one time 13, all beseeching
> to be taken next. It was strange to feel my clothes stiff with blood and my
> arms powerless with the exertion of using my knife.

Wellington finally climbed out of the saddle at the inn shortly after the village
clock struck 10 p.m., but was too exhausted, physically and mentally, to celebrate the triumph of his victory over Bonaparte. He had ridden out from the
inn after 6 a.m. at the head of forty horsemen, and had returned with no more
than five. All that Wellington wanted was sleep.

He had pursued the French for a time and De Lancey's ADC, Lieutenant
Colonel Jackson, witnessed Wellington's famous meeting with Blücher, the
Prussian field marshal, at La Belle Alliance, although Wellington was later con-
vinced it was at Genappe: 'Mein lieber Kamerad,' said the old Field Marshal.
'Quelle affaire!' Blücher later suffered mad delusions when he got to Paris.
Wellington put it down to a bang on the head Blücher suffered when he was
showing off to some ladies and fell off his horse: 'Poor Blücher went mad for
some time,' the Duke told his astonished dinner guests at Walmer Castle in 1838.
'When I went to take my leave of him he positively told me that he was pregnant! And what do you think he said he was pregnant of? An elephant! And
who do you think he said had produced it? A French soldier! That is the human
mind.' Blücher retired home to Silesia and died in 1819 aged 76. The engineer
George Stephenson later gave Blücher the best memorial – he named a steam
engine after him. Blücher would have liked that. Fire and steam summed him up.

The Duke, like his men, was too tired to go on with the pursuit of the
French Army. He left the fresher Prussians to continue 'hunting by night'. The
Prussians were cock-a-hoop. They captured Napoleon's dark-blue and gilded
carriage, with his travelling case containing nearly 100 pieces in solid gold, and
some diamonds worth an estimated million francs.[5] The emperor had to climb
out of his carriage and escape on a horse with his escort of Red Lancers.[*]
Jardin Aine, Napoleon's equerry, recorded: 'He was at this time extremely pale
and haggard and much changed. He took a small glass of wine and a morsel
of bread which one of his equerries had in his pocket and some moments

---

[*] The carriage was presented to the Prince Regent, but was eventually destroyed in a fire
at Madame Tussaud's in 1925.

later mounted, asking if the horse galloped well …'[6] Blücher's chief of staff, Gneisenau, said it was 'the best night of my life'.

Wellington picked his way on Copenhagen across a landscape lit by moonlight that resembled *Hell* by Hieronymus Bosch. Corpses, some already stripped, lay in heaps; the mutilated bodies of dead horses littered the field; ghostly figures walked through the fields of dead and the dying, firing the occasional shot to deliver the coup de grace; and he had to pick his way through the wreckage of war strewn about the fields and roads – breast plates, broken gun carriages, abandoned muskets, piles of clothes, helmets and shakos and men lying moaning, wanting death. And there was the paper. One of the odder images of Waterloo is that the battlefield was strewn with paper: personal letters and diaries and pay books that were carried by every soldier, cast aside by the looters as they searched for gold. The paper fluttered in the night breeze.

Wellington passed his horse to his groom and went inside the inn. In peacetime, it was chiefly used by wagon drivers carrying goods between France and Belgium. Wellington found it hot and packed with officers, including Dutch and German troops, celebrating their great victory. He went upstairs to see how Sir Alexander Gordon was faring. He had been laid in the Duke's bed, a small wooden cot on the first floor of the inn. Gordon was weak through loss of blood and racked with pain, but raised himself up at the sight of the Duke and whispered: 'Thank God you are safe.' Wellington told Gordon about the great victory that they had secured, and told him he would do well.

Downstairs in the spacious common room, Lieutenant Colonel Jackson found three or four small tables laid for supper and several foreign officers looking hungry and impatient. His friend, Colonel Robert Torrens, a fellow officer on the staff of the Quartermaster General and who was related to the Prince Regent's ADC, Major General Sir Henry Torrens, secured a table and a smoking stew was quickly laid out. A Dutchman bowed and begged to join them. They agreed and he finished up eating their supper; they could not muster an appetite for food.[7]

Jackson had spent the day riding around without orders after De Lancey had been mortally wounded and decided he might as well take De Lancey's bed.* He went upstairs to claim his room, but found it already occupied by a seriously wounded French officer who had a gaping wound from a sabre cut to the back of his head, which went down to the bone of his skull. Jackson washed his enemy's wounds and left him in the bed; he then went back down to the common room to grab some sleep on the floor.

---

*   Frances, Lady Shelley noted in her diary that the door was still marked *quartier general* when she visited Waterloo three months later.

The Duke, leaving Gordon to rest, sat down to a melancholy supper in a private room next door with a few close members of his staff including Álava, who had been with him since the Peninsular campaign. Each time the door opened, the Duke hoped to see more of his young hand-picked staff officers. There were pitifully few to join him. He was in no mood to receive two of Napoleon's senior officers, who had been captured – Marshal Cambronne, who commanded the last of the Imperial Guard and led a rearguard action to protect the emperor at the end of the battle, and Georges Mouton, the Comte de Lobau.

Under the gentlemanly rules of combat, they expected to be invited to join Wellington at supper but the Duke coldly refused. Before Cambronne was captured he is alleged to have said: 'The Guard dies and does not surrender.' He became the butt of barrack room humour: 'Cambronne surrenders, he does not die.' Wellington told one dinner party twenty-four years later he had never heard anything so absurd as his request to join the supper party:

> Why I found him that very evening in my room at Waterloo – him and General Mouton – and I bowed them out! I said to them, 'Messieurs, j'en suis bien fache, mais je ne puis avoir l'honneur de vous recevoir jusqu'a ce que vous ayez fait votre paix avec Sa Majeste Tres Chretienne.' ['Gentlemen, I am very angry, but I cannot have the honour to receive you until you have made your peace with his most Christian Majesty.']
>
> They bowed. I added, 'Ce n'est possible,' and I passed on. I would not let them sup with me that night. I thought they had behaved so very ill to the King of France.[8]

Around midnight, von Müffling, the beefy Prussian[*] who acted as Wellington's go-between with the Prussian marshal, Blücher, sank into his seat at the inn and told the Duke that Blücher wanted to name the victory 'Battle of La Belle Alliance', after their meeting place. Wellington said nothing. The French, with superior local knowledge, still know it as *La Bataille de Mont St Jean*. The Duke had decided to follow military practice by naming it after the place where he began his despatch.

Wellington drank a single glass of wine, toasting 'the Memory of the Peninsular War'. He asked Carlo Pozzo di Borgo to pen an urgent note to Louis XVIII in Ghent, saying he would be restored to the throne in Paris. The French king trusted Pozzo, who – though a Corsican like Napoleon – was Tsar Alexander's ambassador in France and had helped to restore Louis

---

[*]   Wellington complained he had been given the fattest soldier in the Prussian army as a liaison officer and he took thirty hours to go 30 miles with a message.

to the throne in 1814. Pozzo dispatched a Russian officer with his message. Then Wellington went to grab a few hours' sleep on a rough mattress. He was too exhausted and depressed to face writing his official despatch until the morning.

Hume said in his notes that he checked on Gordon after Wellington had retired to sleep:

> He [Gordon] said he felt easier and lay for some time more composed but about one o'clock in the morning, he became restless as before, frequently changing his posture, calling every moment and in this manner he continued till he became perfectly exhausted and expired soon after daylight. I should think [it was] about half past three o'clock in the morning.

Dr Hume woke the Duke with the news of Gordon's death and gave him the list of killed and seriously injured. The dead included Ponsonby, Picton, De Lancey, Canning (his ADC) and now Gordon. Wellington began his despatch at a desk in his private room but the list was too distressing and he could not go on. Wellington scribbled a note for Broke to get the army on the move again and prepared to leave. Jackson, sleeping on the floor downstairs, was roughly shaken and told to take it to the commanders who were still in the field. It said: 'Memorandum – The troops belonging to the allied army will move upon Nivelles at daylight. Wellington.'

Jackson had found it difficult to get to sleep while a group of Dutch soldiers caroused loudly into the early hours of the morning. He drowsily roused up the hostler to prepare his horse and was on the road to the battlefield before daybreak. The Duke needed to replace his staff and decided to ride into Brussels to finish his official despatch for Lord Bathurst, the Secretary of State for War and the Colonies. It would be a story of heroism and sacrifice – he would weep over the losses over dinner weeks later, but the common soldiers who died in their droves were hardly given a mention.

Copenhagen, Wellington's chestnut warhorse, had survived shot and shell without a sign of nerves, and had ridden into one of the British squares as coolly as his rider, but when Wellington got off his horse in Brussels, Copenhagen kicked out. It was the first sign of the stress they had both endured:

'On the Duke dismounting, this noble animal kicked up his heels and scampered half over the town before he was caught,' recorded Lady Shelley.

The Duke sat down in the window of his rented 'billet' 54 rue Royale in the centre of Brussels to complete the despatch he had started in Waterloo, but first he had a few letters to dash off. One of the first was to Lady Frances Webster, the young and beautiful married woman to whom he had sent a note on the morning of the battle. To avoid impropriety, it was drafted as advice to her father, but the fact that the Duke felt it necessary to write to her that morning suggests he was clearly besotted with her:

Bruxelles, 19th June 1815. Half-past 8 in the morning.
My dear Lady Frances,
    Lord Mount-Norris [her father] may remain in Bruxelles in perfect security. I yesterday, after a most severe and bloody contest, gained a complete victory, and pursued the French till after dark. They are in complete confusion; and I have, I believe, 150 pieces of cannon; and Blücher, who continued the pursuit all night, my soldiers being tired to death, sent me word this morning that he had got 60 more. My loss is immense. Lord Uxbridge, Lord FitzRoy Somerset, General Cooke, General Barnes, and Colonel Berkeley are wounded: Colonel De Lancey, Canning, Gordon, General Picton killed. The finger of Providence was upon me, and I escaped unhurt.—Believe me, etc., Wellington.

He put it more bluntly to Frances, Lady Shelley, another of the society ladies in Wellington's 'court', when he told her about his narrow escape at the moment Uxbridge was hit: 'The finger of God was upon me.'[9] He told her:

I hope to God that I have fought my last battle. It is a bad thing to be always fighting. While in the thick of it, I am too much occupied to feel anything, but it is wretched just after. It is quite impossible to think of glory. Both mind and feelings are exhausted. I am wretched even at the moment of victory and I always say that next to a battle lost, the greatest misery is a battle gained.[10]

It was an aphorism that he reworked a number of times.
    The Duke also penned from Brussels a grief-stricken note to Gordon's, brother Lord Aberdeen:

He received the wound which occasioned his death when rallying one of the Brunswick battalions which was shaking a little; and he lived long enough to be informed by myself of the glorious result of our actions, to which he had so much contributed by his active and zealous assistance.

Wellington told him:

I cannot express to you the regret and sorrow with which I look round me, and contemplate the loss which I have sustained, particularly in your brother. The glory resulting from such actions, so dearly bought, is no consolation to me, and I cannot suggest it as any to you and his friends; but

I hope that it may be expected that this last one has been so decisive, as
that no doubt remains that our exertions and our individual losses will be
rewarded by the early attainment of our just object. It is then that the glory
of the actions in which our friends and relations have fallen will be some
consolation for their loss.

It is almost certain that if he had survived, Gordon would have carried
Wellington's Waterloo Despatch back to London, but he entrusted the
honour to the Honourable Henry Percy, because he was one of his few ADCs
to emerge unscathed.

A crowd gathered outside Wellington's rented house to watch the extraordinary historic sight of the Napoleon's nemesis writing his official report. The
curious onlookers included Thomas Creevey, the radical MP who had struck
up an unlikely friendship with the Duke, although they had been political
enemies at Westminster. Wellington saw Creevey and told him to come up.
Creevey noted in his journal Wellington said: 'It has been a damned serious
business. Blücher and I have lost 30,000 men. It has been a damned nice thing
– the nearest run thing you ever saw in your life.' Wellington added: 'By God,
I don't think it would have done if I had not been there.'[11]

The full casualty lists from Waterloo shocked the nation. They included
hundreds of aristocratic fathers and sons, the upper-crust of well-to-do
Georgian society. The foul-mouthed Welshman, Sir Thomas Picton, was the
most senior British officer to be killed at Waterloo and had towns named after
him across the globe.

Wellington also listed De Lancey among the dead, unaware he was still
clinging to life in a hovel in Mont St Jean, as Magdalene, his 22-year-old
wife, agonised about his fate in the safety of Antwerp. First she was told he
was dead, then that he had survived. She eventually found him in a cottage a
few days later. She went by coach with some friends but in Brussels the chaos
on the roads after the battle forced them to abandon it for saddled horses.
She described in her journal how, as they rode near Mont St Jean, the 'horses
screamed at the smell of corruption'.

She had only been married on 4 April 1815 and wrote that she had
expected to live a life of carefree privilege in Regency Britain. Like many
officers' wives, she had gone with her husband to Brussels, little thinking that
their blissful life together would end so suddenly: 'I saw my husband loved
and respected by everyone, my life gliding on, like a gay dream, in his care...'

One of De Lancey's friends, Captain William Hay, paid a visit to De Lancey
and his wife. They were in 'a little wretched cottage at the end of the village
which was pointed out to me as the place where De Lancey was lying mortally wounded,' recalled Captain Hay:

How wholly shocked I was on entering, to find Lady De Lancey seated on the only chair the hovel contained, by the side of her dying husband. I made myself known. She grasped me by the hand, and pointed to poor De Lancey covered with his coat, and with just a spark of life left.

He was strong at first but gradually weakened after several days, until he finally died of his internal injuries. Dr Hume performed a post mortem and found eight ribs had been forced from the spine, one puncturing a lung.

Magdalene wrote an account of his death for her family and it was later published. The painful honesty of her tragic story – *A Week at Waterloo in 1815* – moved Sir Walter Scott and Charles Dickens. She wrote:

> When I went into the room where he lay, he held out his hand and said, 'Come, Magdalene, this is a sad business, is it not?' I could not speak, but sat down by him and took his hand. This was my occupation for six days.

Dickens described in a letter reading Lady De Lancey's account:

> After working at Barnaby [Barnaby Rudge] all day and wandering about the most wretched and distressful streets for a couple of hours in the evening – searching for some pictures I wanted to build upon – I went at it at about 10 o'clock. To say that reading that most astonishing and tremendous account has constituted an epoch in my life – that I shall never forget the lightest word of it … I never saw anything so real, so touching and so actually present before my eyes is nothing. I am husband and wife, dead man and living woman …

The woman who moved Dickens so much in 1819 married another officer, Captain Henry Hervey of the Madras Infantry, but she died young in 1822. Creevey records meeting Wellington on the way to Waterloo in a curicle two days after the battle to see Sir Frederick Cavendish Ponsonby and De Lancey. There were also tens of thousands of common soldiers who were terribly injured – Wellington's 'scum of the earth', who would return to Britain and pass out of history without fanfares.

Officers were given cash rewards from a fund, called His Majesty's Royal Bounty, for serving at Waterloo – £1,274 for generals, £90 for captains, £19 for sergeants and £2 for corporals, drummers and privates. Many had to rely on charity from a public fund called the Waterloo Subscription. For the men in the ranks who lost a leg or arm at Waterloo they had the prospect of a life of poverty and begging, or parish relief when the charity ran out.

The Duke personally interceded on Dr Hume's behalf to make sure he was comfortable in retirement. He persuaded the army in 1819 to give Dr Hume a retirement pension of 30 shillings a day – a large sum when the pay for a soldier in the ranks was a single shilling a day. 'As a mark of special respect to Wellington's recommendation it is resolved that Dr Hume be allowed to retire upon an allowance of 30/- [30s] per diem [per day] …' This was increased to £2 a day in 1821 as a retired inspector of hospitals.

Dr Hume, born in Renfrewshire, remained close to the Duke and his family as a personal physician and trusted friend for the rest of their lives. He was the surgeon at the embassy in Paris while Wellington was there and continued his career as an eminent army surgeon, remaining in the service for a total of thirty-four years. He also became deputy inspector of hospitals and was knighted in 1850. He died of 'cardiac dropsy' in 1857 aged 76 at his home, 9 Curzon Street, Mayfair. He outlived the Duke by five years but after Waterloo, Wellington's surgeon had one more historic service to perform for the Duke. Dr Hume acted as Wellington's second when the Duke felt honour-bound to fight a duel. It was at Battersea Fields at dawn on 21 March 1829 against an obscure peer, Lord Winchelsea. Unbelievably, the Duke was prime minister at the time.

Winchelsea, a fanatical Protestant Loyalist, had accused the Dublin-born[*] Duke of underhand tactics in pursuit of popery after he was forced to cave in to the demands for Catholic Emancipation in his native Ireland. The Duke's second, Sir Henry Hardinge, Secretary of State for War in Wellington's Cabinet who lost his left hand at Ligny, asked Hume to attend a duel but did not say who for. Hume's detailed account of the duel is kept with his medical notes in Edinburgh. He was astonished to see that the rider approaching through the morning light at Battersea Fields was the prime minister, the Duke of Wellington. Hume loaded the two pistols for Hardinge, because he only had one hand. The Duke irritably told Hardinge: 'Look sharp and step out the ground. I have no time to waste.' Hardinge paced out twelve steps, leaving Winchelsea standing with his back to a ditch. The Duke called to Hardinge: 'Damn it! Don't stick him up so near a ditch. If I hit him, he will tumble in.' Wellington planned to shoot Winchelsea in the leg, but not to kill him by drowning in the ditch. Wellington and Winchelsea faced each other. Then Hardinge said: 'Gentlemen, are you ready? Fire!' Wellington clearly trusted his own skill with a pistol, but as a pragmatist he may have felt it wise to have his eminent personal surgeon with him, should the 'finger of providence' have deserted him at last. In the event, Winchelsea wisely kept his pistol clamped to his side and the Duke deliberately missed.

---

[*]   Wellington was reputedly born at Mornington House, Upper Merrion Street, Dublin, now the Merrion Hotel.

Notes

1. Captain W. Siborne, *Waterloo Letters*, p. 257.
2. Medical notes by Dr Hume on the treatment of Sir Alex Gordon, Royal College of Surgeons, Edinburgh, GD1/6.
3. Elizabeth Longford, *Wellington the Years of the Sword* (London: Weidenfeld & Nicolson, 1969), p. 481.
4. Medical notes by Dr Hume, GD1/5.
5. Elizabeth Longford, *Wellington*, p. 482.
6. Jardine Aine, With Napoleon At Waterloo, edited by Macenzie Macbride, Francis Griffiths, London, 1911.
7. Basil Jackson, *Notes and Reminiscences of a Staff Officer* (London: John Murray), p. 42.
8. 5th Earl Stanhope, *Notes of Conversations with the Duke of Wellington*, (London: John Murray, 1888), p. 172.
9. Richard Edgcumbe (ed.), *The Diary of Frances Lady Shelley* (London: John Murray, 1912), p. 103.
10. Ibid., p. 102.
11. Rt Hon. Sir Herbert Maxwell, *The Creevey Papers* (London: John Murray, 1904), p. 142.

7

THE BRAVEST MAN IN ENGLAND

The first tourists arrived on the morning after the battle, Monday, 19 June 1815, as Captain Alexander Cavalié Mercer was sitting on a discarded French breastplate, having breakfast on the slope above Hougoumont with the gunners of G Troop. They stepped down from a carriage, holding perfumed handkerchiefs to their noses. 'As they passed near us, it was amusing to see the horror with which they eyed our frightful figures,' said Mercer.

Their breakfast was a hunk of veal found in a muddy ditch, cooked on the upturned lid of a camp kettle after having the mud scraped off with a sword but the stench came from the bodies. Mercer's troop had killed so many French cuirassiers on the slope above Hougoumont with canister shot from their guns at point-blank range that their position was still marked some days later by the piles of bodies. Mercer and his troop were using their discarded cuirasses for camp chairs. There is a tourist plaque at the spot today.

It is just as well the visitors had not arrived an hour earlier or they would have seen the corpse of one of Mercer's drivers called Crammond lying there too. 'A more hideous sight cannot be imagined,' said Mercer. 'A cannon-shot had carried away the whole head except barely the visage, which still remained attached to the torn and bloody neck.' He made sure he was buried before they had breakfast.

Mercer, who was from a military family in Hull and took the horrors of war in his stride, went for a stroll down to the old chateau but even he was appalled by what he found. Bodies were piled into the ditches:

> The trees all about were most woefully cut and splintered both by cannon-shot and musketry. The courts of the Chateau presented a spectacle more terrible even than any I had yet seen. A large barn had been set on fire and

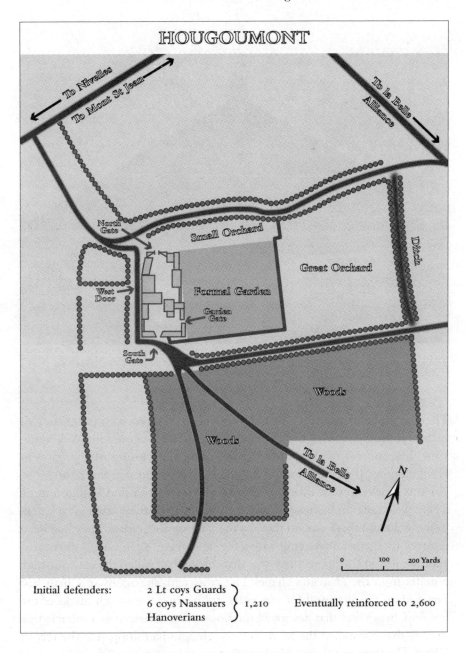

HOUGOUMONT

To Nivelles

To Mont St Jean

To la Belle Alliance

North Gate

Small Orchard

Great Orchard

Ditch

West Door

Formal Garden

Garden Gate

South Gate

Woods

Woods

To la Belle Alliance

N

0   100   200 Yards

Initial defenders: 2 Lt coys Guards   }
                     6 coys Nassauers   } 1,210   Eventually reinforced to 2,600
                     Hanoverians   }

the conflagration had spread to the offices and even to the main building. Here numbers both of French and English had perished in the flames and their blackened swollen remains lay scattered about in all directions. Amongst this heap of ruins and misery many poor devils yet remained alive and were sitting up endeavouring to bandage their wounds. Such a scene of horror, and one so sickening, was surely never witnessed.

The Lion Mound – Wellington was furious it ruined the Mont St Jean ridge. (Author)

There is probably no other British war site so charged with poignancy or such powerful legends as the chateau and farm at Hougoumont. Wellington said, 'The success of the battle turned upon the closing of the gates at Hougoumont.' If so, the future of Europe was also decided at this farm.

I was shocked by its dilapidated state when I first visited Hougoumont. There were holes in the roof, where the rain came in, there were great cracks in the walls and there was no trace of the famous north gates. They had been replaced by chain-link fencing with a big sign saying 'Keep Out'. I discovered later the reason for the security was that thieves had stolen the six-foot-high crucifix from the chateau's chapel. The cross with the agony of Christ had survived on the altar wall for 200 years still bearing the scorch marks of the fire on Christ's feet that destroyed the house. It was viewed as a miracle that the fire that consumed the barns and the chateau had stopped at the feet of Christ. The theft was despicable, but it has since been recovered.

The farm's condition was even worse when I visited Hougoumont again with Barry Sheerman, the Labour MP who took up the campaign to rescue Hougoumont in the House of Commons.[*]

---

[*]   Hougoumont is rising from the ashes thanks to Project Hougoumont, the Walloon authorities and a donation of £1m from the taxpayer by Chancellor George Osborne, who turned out to be a battlefield enthusiast.

Despite the modern fencing, there was still a heavy sadness that hung about the farmyard like a dark cloud, and as he walked through the north gate, Sheerman said: 'I can feel the hairs standing up on the back of my neck.' I knew what he meant. I had also had the 'hairs-on-the-back-of-the-neck' moment the first time I walked into the cobbled yard, where men had died in bitter no-quarter fighting at the gateway. I also felt the tingling sensation down my neck when I looked through a fireloop that had been hacked out of the brick garden walls by the defenders with their bayonets. Looking through the slit, I had the same view as Corporal James Graham when the French infantry attacked the walls. It was easy to imagine the din of battle, the smell of the powder, the yelling of the men and the screams of the dying and the fear that you would die too.

The defence of Hougoumont was one of the most heroic actions in British military history, as valiant as that more famous action at Rorke's Drift in Africa in 1879 where 150 men held out against 4,000 Zulu warriors. Eleven Victoria Crosses were awarded for their action that day, and if VCs had existed in 1815 they would almost certainly have been awarded for the defence of Hougoumont.

The story of Hougoumont has been distilled into one heroic act of bravery – the closing of the north gate. Corporal Graham (later promoted to Lance Sergeant for his heroism) of the Coldstream Guards, an Irish farmer's boy from County Monaghan, became known as the 'Bravest Man in England' for his deeds. However, I discovered when I began to dig deeper into the story of the siege that the truth is far more complicated than that. Hougoumont's walls were breached not once but at least three times, and possibly more, and there were many heroes.

Around 10 o'clock on the morning of the battle, the Duke of Wellington rode with his staff down the slope to the chateau by a dense beech wood to inspect the defences of Hougoumont, because he knew it was of crucial importance to holding his line. He had put Lieutenant Colonel James Macdonell of the Coldstream Guards, the six-foot-tall son of a Scottish highland clan chief, in charge of the defence of Hougoumont.

There had already been one skirmish for the farm before Wellington arrived for a tour of inspection with his staff officers – a party of French cavalry tried to seize it the night before but had been beaten off. Overnight, Macdonell had ordered his men to turn the old farm into a fortress. They had spent the night barricading three of the entrances, hacking out the fireloops in the walls, smashing out roof tiles from the roofs of the barns and the farm buildings so they could fire through them at the French they could see massing across the rolling fields of corn to the south.

There had been a chateau at Goumont for five centuries, before Macdonell and his men arrived in the night. The owner of the chateau, Chevalier de

Louville, was 86 and living in Nivelles but the tenant farmer, Antoine Dumoncea, had fled. So had the gardener's wife, but the gardener, Guillaume van Cutsem, had delayed and was found nervously sheltering in the farm when the Coldstream Guards arrived at nightfall.

The farm buildings and the chateau formed three sides of a square with high walls facing the French. A great barn ran down the west side and a towering gatehouse to the south, with two windows above the huge dark-blue gates to provide elevated shooting positions, and a window in a garret above that. The gatehouse was flanked on the south side by a shed with a steep pantiled roof and on the other side by the gardener's house, with another stable and office building. They were enclosed by an impressive garden wall of red brick, about 8ft high, running along the whole south side of the farm, which shielded the farm from a direct French attack. Behind this wall was a small cottage garden and a formal garden laid out in the Dutch parterre style with an orchard on the north side. Macdonell's men had laid timbers along the base of the wall to provide fire steps so they could fire muskets over the wall at the attackers.

Inside the south gatehouse was an inner courtyard and a door leading into the main cobbled farmyard, with the stables, a circular dovecot and a well for fresh water. The two-storey chateau had a picturesque tower containing a staircase topped by a weather vane. The small family chapel with a spire was attached to the chateau on the south side and a farmer's house attached at the east side with a gate into the formal garden. Three of the gateways had been barricaded with heavy timbers, old carts, slabs of stone – anything the men could lay their hands on. Only the north gate had been left open, to enable the farm's defenders to be resupplied with ammunition and reinforcements during the long hard day ahead. The gate opened into a lane that had been cut down by centuries of cart traffic between two high banks with trees on either side. It was called the 'hollow way' and ran up to the ridge where Wellington's main forces were lined up. It was to prove a vital lifeline.

Hougoumont's defences looked formidable. Macdonell was given four light companies of Maitland's 1st Brigade and Byng's 2nd Brigade of the 1st British Guards Division. The two companies of the 1st Brigade under the command of 30-year-old Lieutenant Colonel Lord Saltoun occupied the front edge of the orchard. The farm and chateau were occupied by the light company of the 2nd Battalion Coldstream Guards commanded by Lieutenant Colonel Henry Wyndham. The garden and ground around the farm was defended by the light company of the 2nd under Lieutenant Colonel Charles Dashwood. They reinforced some crack German troops armed with rifles, including elite Hanoverian Jägers (hunters). Macdonell had deployed them through the orchard, the buildings, the lofts and the wood. But Baron Friedrich von Müffling, the Duke's Prussian liaison officer, was still sceptical. Müffling asked

Wellington whether he really expected to hold Hougoumont with 1,500 men. 'Ah,' said the Duke. 'You don't know Macdonell.'

That was disingenuous. Macdonell was undoubtedly a formidable commander. He was the third son of the Scottish clan chief, Duncan Macdonell, and was born at the clan seat at Glengarry in Inverness. The MacDonell clan – a branch of the Donalds – are proud Highlanders who can trace their roots back to the ancient Picts. But the truth is Wellington committed more than 2,600 men to the defence of Hougoumont and some estimates put the total deployment at over 7,500 men, if you include Byng's men alongside Maitland's guards on the slopes behind Hougoumont.

James Macdonell joined the 78th Highlanders Regiment as a lieutenant in 1794 at the age of 13, when it was routine for young boys to become soldiers. He joined the Coldstream Guards in 1811 and fought in the Peninsular War. He was 34 when he arrived at Hougoumont. There is a portrait of Macdonell in the National Portrait Gallery, which shows him in late middle age wearing the scarlet uniform of a general (which he later became), with a dress sword; he has reddish side-whiskers and he stares out of the portrait with a steady gaze that looks as though he would brook no dissent.

Wellington ordered Macdonell to defend Hougoumont to the 'greatest extremity', by which he meant 'to the death'. If it fell, Napoleon could turn Wellington's right flank. However, it remains unclear whether Napoleon saw its strategic significance. In his general order for the battle issued at 11 a.m., Napoleon gave only a passing reference to Hougoumont, saying the 2nd Corps 'was to support the movement of the 1 Corps covering the left of the Hougoumont wood'. The main attack was to be directed at Wellington's centre on Mont St Jean. This has given the impression that the attack on Hougoumont was a diversion aimed at drawing men away from Wellington's centre. If so, it backfired badly, as more of Napoleon's forces were drawn into the attack on Hougoumont, while Wellington saw that it held with a minimum force. More than 12,000 French troops were committed to the siege and over 6,000 French and allied men were killed or injured around its walls.

Marshal Honoré Reille, commander of the 2nd Corps, entrusted Napoleon's youngest brother, Jérôme Bonaparte, head of the Sixth Division, with leading the siege of Hougoumont, reinforced by Foy's 9th, the 5th under Guilleminot and Joseph Bachelu, and Kellerman's cavalry. Late in the day – far too late – Napoleon pushed forward artillery to pound the walls and buildings with howitzers, which set the barns on fire.

There is still a dispute about when the Battle of Waterloo started – Wellington said 'about ten o'clock'; Lieutenant Colonel G. Gawler said an officer near him pulled out a watch and noted, 'twenty past 11 o'clock' – but there is no dispute that the first shots were fired over Hougoumont and that they came from allied guns.

Wellington, vigilant on the ridge, saw Jérôme's troops advancing towards the wood, and asked Uxbridge to bring Major Robert Bull's troop of howitzers to bear on them. The Royal Horse Artillery troops were intended to be mobile and fast. John Lees, the young wagon driver from Oldham, and his comrades in Major Bull's I Troop had been ordered from their bivouac at 8 a.m. on the morning of the battle and were posted to the left of the road from Waterloo to Charleroi, alongside Lieutenant Colonel William Ponsonby's Heavy Brigade. They had been there for an hour when Bull received the fresh orders from the Earl of Uxbridge to move. Lees and the other drivers urged their horses across the ridge to the right of Wellington's lines and the slopes above Hougoumont. Wellington rode across the slope to Bull and pointed out Jérôme's men as they were advancing through the wood about 1,000yds away. The Duke said he wanted Bull to dislodge them. It was a tricky operation. Bull's six howitzers had to fire shells over the heads of his own troops to explode directly over the French. If they fell short, or were off target, it could be a disaster and sow mayhem among the defenders. The shells, spherical cases carrying metal balls with lit fuses, had been designed by a lieutenant in the British Army artillery called Henry Shrapnel and were still regarded as novel – the French did not use them. The first Shrapnel shell looped over Hougoumont and exploded among the French infantry, killing seventeen men in one blast of red-hot metal. The devastating impact on Jérôme's men was witnessed by Major William Norman Ramsay, who had been given command of H Troop despite incurring Wellington's anger for insubordination at Vitoria. His troop was posted to the left of I Troop and he told Bull that 'the shells opened a perfect lane through them …' Ramsay was later killed by a musket ball, and buried on the field in a lull in the fighting by his friend Sir Augustus Frazer, the commander of the Royal Horse Artillery.[*]

Bull's battery of howitzers was repeatedly overrun by French cavalry in the afternoon and had to retreat inside the nearest hollow squares of infantry. It was also fired on by French artillery, killing men and horses, including the second captain Robert Cairnes.[1] Bull was injured and lost a lot of blood, but after having 'my arm tied up' returned to carry on the battle.

Some of the drivers took their horses and carts into the hollow way on the ridge to escape the worst of the French artillery bombardments, and it is likely Lees would have joined them. But for the rest of the battle Lees was in the thick of the fighting, seeing men and horses killed all around him.

[*]   Ramsay's body was disinterred three weeks later and taken back to his native Scotland
       where he was reburied.

However, after 5 p.m., through loss of men, horses and 'the disabled condition of the guns (through incessant firing) …' Bull's I Troop was forced to retire.

The Duke later praised Bull's dexterity with the Shrapnel shells but Jérôme's men pressed on their attacks. The crackle of muskets became a cacophony of fire as wave after wave of Jérôme's infantry burst through the woods, to be cut down under a hail of rifle and musket balls. 'Soon we had our feet bathed in blood,' said Lerreguy de Civrieux, aged 19, a sergeant major. 'In less than half an hour our ranks were reduced by more than half. Each stoically awaited death or horrible wounds. We were covered in splashes of blood …' The dead included Brigadier General Bauduin but Jérôme pressed on with the attacks, even though his men were being cut down.

Prince Jérôme may have felt he had something to prove to his older brother. Ten years earlier, when he was only 19 and in America, Jérôme enraged Napoleon by falling in love and marrying an American heiress on Christmas Eve 1803. Eighteen-year-old Betsy Patterson was the beautiful, dark-haired daughter of a Baltimore businessman, but she was regarded as unsuitable by Napoleon. He had wanted a European power-match for his brother and ordered the pope to annul the marriage; when the pontiff failed to do so, the emperor did so himself by Imperial decree in March 1805. Jérôme and Betsy sailed to Europe to make an appeal to the emperor; they landed in Portugal and Jérôme went overland to plead with his brother, while his wife went by ship to Amsterdam to travel to Paris, but Napoleon refused to allow her entry to France. Betsy, however, was pregnant, and was forced to sail to England; she gave birth to Jérôme Bonaparte II at 95 Camberwell Grove in leafy South London. The Georgian house is still there in a tree-lined street, but the area, near the Elephant and Castle, is now part of the urban inner city. After the birth of Jérôme II, Prince Jérôme's son and heir, Betsy returned to her family in America with the baby and founded an unlikely American Bonaparte dynasty. The infant Jérôme II – known as 'Bo' – was brought up by his rich mother in Baltimore and married Susan May Williams, daughter of a fabulously wealthy Baltimore rail magnate. They were given the land-mark Montrose Mansion in Maryland as a wedding present and had two sons, firmly establishing the Bonaparte line in the US. Meanwhile, Jérôme meekly bowed to the emperor's wishes. Napoleon married his youngest brother off to a German princess, Catherina of Wurttemberg, and made Jérôme King of Westphalia, a made-up title for a made-up country that only lasted until 1813.

Now at 30, Jérôme (no longer a king, but a mere prince) was clearly determined to show his brother he could take Hougoumont. Jérôme threw more men forward without much of a plan.

Lieutenant Puvis from the 93rd de ligne was told, 'We are going to attack the English lines 'a la baionnette'.' Bayonets were useless against the walls, but

still they went forward and quickly found themselves pinned down behind
a hedge that Ensign George Standen of the Light Company of the 3rd Foot
Guards described as a 'real bullfincher'. It ran parallel to the garden wall, and
gave some protection to the attackers hiding behind it but when they charged
round it, they were caught in the deadly crossfire from the fireloops in the
garden walls. The strip of open land between the hedge and the wall became
a killing zone, piled high with the French dead: 'We tried to get through this
hedge in vain. We suffered enormous casualties; the lieutenant of my company
was killed closed to me. A ball struck the visor of my shako and knocked me
onto my backside …'

A cloud of skirmishers pushed through the cornfield and the wood, forcing
a Nassau battalion and the Jägers through the wood to the rear of the chateau
until a counter-charge by Macdonell forced the French back once more.
General Guilleminot, chef de l'Etat to Jérôme, told the Coldstream Guards
officer Sir Alex Woodford, when they met in Corfu years later, that he advised
Jérôme on the first attack but was against Jérôme's other attacks: 'It always
struck me the subsequent attacks were feeble,' said Woodford.[2]

After nearly two hours of largely futile slaughter, the charismatic French
Colonel Amédée-Louis Despans, the Marquis de Cubières, who already had
one arm in a sling from an injury at Quatre Bras, tried a different approach,
and nearly succeeded.

After 1 p.m., as the battle for the farm raged, a cart of ammunition was
lashed under heavy fire through the north gate by a young wagon driver,
Corporal Joseph Brewer. The men had only time to fill their pouches when
cannon fire 'suddenly burst upon them mingled with the shouts of a column
rushing on to a fresh attack'. Captain Seymour, Lord Uxbridge's ADC was
inadvertently responsible for this show of valour by Brewer. He recalled:

> Late in the day I was called by some officers of the 3rd Guards defending
> Hougoumont to use my best endeavours to send them musket ammunition.
> Soon afterwards I fell in with a private of the Wagon Train in charge of a
> tumbril on the crest of the position. I merely pointed out to him where he
> was wanted when he gallantly started his horses and drove straight down the
> hill to the farm to the gate of which I saw him arrive. He must have lost his
> horses as there was a severe fire kept on him. I feel convinced to that man's
> service the Guards owe their ammunition.

However, it may have given Cubières the clue to the chateau's Achilles heel:
the north gate. He realised that the north gate was not barricaded and was
kept open to admit the supplies of ammunition; he put together a party to
attack it.

Cubières, who had fought in Spain, picked a burly veteran of the Spanish campaign, Lieutenant Bonnet, to lead it and some axe-wielding pioneers to back him up. British accounts say he was called Legros, which literally translated means 'the big'. That certainly describes Bonnet. Around 100 men of the Coldstream Guards were outside the high barn walls on the west side of the farm, including Private Clay of the 3rd Foot Guards, who had tested his musket in the damp dawn. He was kneeling behind a hedge, and poked the muzzle through it to fire at the attackers. Clay and his comrades soon had musket balls zipping around their bodies. Ensign Charles Short of the Coldstream Guards said:

> We were ordered to lie down on the road, the musket shots flying over us like peas – an officer next to me was hit in the cap, but not hurt, as it went through; another next to him was hit also, on the plate of the cap, but it went through also without hurting him. Two sergeants that lay near me were hit in the knapsacks, and were not hurt besides other shots passing as near as possible.

The Guards were forced back into the hollow way by the north corner of the farm. Ensign Standen, a cap in one hand and a sword in the other, ordered some of the men including Clay and Private Robert Gann, a seasoned soldier over 40 years of age, to cover the retreat by attacking the French. Clay and Gann dropped behind the cover of a circular haystack to fire on the attackers but the French set fire to the hay. Clay and Gann were forced back by the heat from the flames, the smoke, and the heavy musket fire to seek whatever cover they could. Cubières spurred his horse towards the gates, and rallied his men with a drummer boy beating out the *pas de charge* to capture the north gate.

As Cubières reached the farm track, he was pulled from his horse by Sergeant Ralph Fraser, a veteran who had fought through the Peninsular campaign, wielding a halberd, an axe on a long pole. Cubières fell to the ground, just below the wall of the west barn. He was about to be shot by the defenders inside the barn, but a Guards officer inside the barn knocked down the rifles of his men to stop the injured Cubières being shot, because he had shown such courage. Lieutenant Colonel Sir Alexander Woodford of the 2nd Battalion Coldstream Guards later said Cubières made a fuss of it every time they met.[3] But there was to be little quarter given after that.

Mackinnon, the historian of the Coldstream Guards, who was posted in the farm's orchard says the 'enemy compelled the few men who remained outside to withdraw into the chateau by the rear gate.' Ensign Standen, Sergeant Fraser and the remaining Third Guards took a lull in the firing to run for their lives inside the north gates, which were slammed shut as soon as they were inside. The defenders rammed ladders, posts, barrows, or whatever was nearest to hand, against the gates to barricade them. But Clay and Gann were cut off from their retreating friends and were stranded, keeping their heads down, outside the farm.

Bonnet grabbed an axe from one of the pioneers and smashed at the lock on the gate* while some powerful *sapeurs* threw themselves at the gates and began hacking at the panels of the doors. Bonnet 'struck with mighty blows the side opening at this entry, threw it down, and penetrated into the court-yard …' The French raiders poured into the cobbled yard, which was puddled with the overnight rain. Bonnet and his men were caught in a hail of musket balls fired into them from the farmer's house and the barns, and the roofs of the farm buildings. Ensign Standen said: 'We flew to the parlour, opened the windows and drove them out, leaving an officer and some men dead within the wall.' A French account said: 'Bonnet and his men were shot down at point-blank range from an elevated platform. All found death there …'[4] The firing died with the last French attacker. Bonnet was left lying dead on the cobbles, still holding his axe. Outside, there were more attackers but they hesi-tated, waiting for reinforcements.

Macdonell, who was across the yard by the gate into the north garden, realised the farm would fall unless the north gates were slammed shut and bar-ricaded again. Macdonell dashed across the yard, shouting at three Coldstream Guards officers to join him in closing the gates. Captain Harry Wyndham, Ensign James Hervey and Ensign Henry Gooch raced across the yard to shut the gates with Macdonnel, and were joined by Corporal James Graham and his brother Joe with four more guardsmen – Sergeants Fraser, McGregor, Joseph Aston and Private Joseph Lester. At that moment, Clay, 20, and Gann, 41, made a run for it. Clay grabbed a discarded musket as he ran – it was still warm from firing – because his own had failed, and scrambled inside the gates with Gann just as they were heaved shut again.

Clay later noted in his pay book, which he used for his journal:

On entering the court-yard, I saw the doors or rather gates were riddled with shot-holes, and it was also very wet and dirty; in its entrance lay many dead bodies of the enemy; one I particularly noticed which appeared to have been a French officer, but they were scarcely distinguishable, being to all appearance as though they had been very much trodden upon, and covered with mud.

On gaining the interior, I saw Lieutenant Colonel Macdonell carrying a large piece of wood or trunk of a tree in his arms (one of his cheeks marked

---

*   The metal lock is on display in the Guards Museum, Bird Cage Walk, London.

'Occupy the ruined walls' was Wellington's order, as Hougoumont chateau was engulfed in flames. Corporal Graham only deserted them to rescue his brother from the flames, which made him a national hero.

with blood, his charger lay bleeding within a short distance) with which he was hastening to secure the gates against the renewed attack of the enemy which was most vigorously repulsed.

Macdonell and his party threw their weight against heavy doors forcing them shut. Immediately they piled stone slabs, broken beams and the remains of broken wagons and farm implements against the gates.

Outside, a French Grenadier was lifted to the top of the wall on the shoulders of the French attackers with a musket. He aimed it at Captain Wyndham, who shouted to Graham: 'Do you see that fellow?' Graham snatched up his musket, took aim and shot the Frenchman dead. No others dared to follow. The French attackers were driven from the gates along the hollow way by four companies of Coldstream Guards under Colonel Alexander Woodford.

Inside the farm, Clay, black-faced from biting the ends off countless musket cartridges, was ordered with others into an upper room of the chateau by Ensign Gooch to prepare for the next attack. They did not have long to wait. They began firing down on the skirmishers through the windows but the French brought up some guns and fired howitzer shells at the building. Suddenly, flames leapt across the roof of the barn. 'Our officer placed himself at the entrance of the room and would not allow anyone to leave his post until our position became hopeless and too perilous to remain,' said Clay.

Burning beams and rafters crashed down, sending red-hot embers flying among the men, as roundshot and flaming missiles smashed into the buildings. Flames burst through the roof and a pall of black smoke filled the air over Hougoumont.

Up on the ridge, the flames and smoke over Hougoumont were immediately spotted by the hawk-eyed Wellington through his telescope. He scribbled a note to Macdonell:

> I see that the fire has communicated from the Hay Stack to the Roof of the Chateau. You must however still keep your men in those parts to which the fire does not reach. Take care that no men are lost by the falling-in of the Roof or floors. After they have both fallen in, occupy the ruined walls inside of the Garden; particularly if it should be possible for the enemy to pass through the Embers in the inside of the house.[*]

Major Macready, of Halkett's brigade, saw the fire:

> Hougoumont and its wood sent up a broad flame through the dark masses of smoke that overhung the field; beneath this cloud the French were indistinctly visible. Here a waving mass of long red feathers could be seen; there, gleams as from a sheet of steel showed that the cuirassiers were moving; 400 cannon were belching forth fire and death on every side; the roaring and shouting were indistinguishably commixed – together they gave me an idea of a labouring volcano.

Manning the garden wall facing the wood at Hougoumont, Corporal Graham asked Macdonell for permission to fall out. Graham had been in the Coldstream Guards for three years and Macdonell knew he did not lack courage; he expressed surprise at his request. Graham said he wanted to save his brother, Joe, who had been injured and was in the blazing barn. James immediately won Macdonell's approval and ran to his brother, dragged him clear and left him in a ditch, to protect him from the shelling, but returned to the walls of the besieged farm. Others who were injured sought refuge in the small chapel, which after the battle was all that remained of the chateau. Many injured men who had been dragged into the barn were not so lucky. Woodford said: 'The heat and smoke of the conflagration were very difficult to bear. Several men were burnt

---

[*]   Wellington's message on a strip of ass's skin is preserved at the Wellington Museum, Apsley House.

as neither Colonel Macdonell nor myself could penetrate the stables where the wounded had been carried.'⁵ Ensign Standen said: 'During the confusion, three or four officers' horses rushed out into the yard from the barn and in a minute or two rushed back into the flames and were burnt.'

The siege was only lifted after 7 p.m., when the allied infantry charged past Hougoumont in pursuit of the retreating Imperial Guard. Captain H.W. Powell of the 1st Foot Guards noted in his journal:

> Lord Saltoun ... holloaed out, 'Now's the time, my boys.' Immediately the brigade sprang forward. La Garde turned and gave us little opportunity of trying the steel. We charged down the hill till we had passed the end of the orchard of Hougoumont ...

It was only then that the defenders of Hougoumont knew, after over eight hours under siege, they had won.

Ensign Short of the Coldstream Guards, who had survived rain, gin and the siege, wrote a boyish summary of the battle to his mother from Nivelles that Monday:

> Dear Mother ... I never saw such luck as we had. The Brigade Major was wounded by a cannon ball, which killed his horse and broke his arm; and General Byng was wounded slightly while standing opposite me about five paces. General Byng did not leave the field. Lord Wellington with his Ball dress was very active indeed, as well as Lord Uxbridge and the Prince of Orange, both severely wounded, the former having lost his leg and the latter being hit in the body. General Cooke, commanding our Division, lost his arm. The battle kept up all day in this wood where our Brigade was stationed. The farm-house was set on fire by shells, however we kept possession of it. The Cavalry came on about five o'clock, and attacked the rest of the line, when the Horse Guards and the other regiments behaved most gallantly. The French charged our hollow squares and were repulsed several times – the Imperial Guards with Napoleon at their head charged the 1st Guards, and the number of killed and wounded is extraordinary – they lie as thick as possible, one on top of the other. They were repulsed in every attack, and about seven o'clock the whole French army made a general attack for their last effort, and we should have had very hard work to repulse them – when 25,000 Prussians came on, and we drove them like chaff before the wind, 20,000 getting into the midst of them played the Devil with them, and they took to flight in the greatest possible hurry. The baggage of Bonaparte was taken by the Prussians, and the last report that has been heard of the French says, that they have

re-passed the frontier and gone by Charleroi hard pressed by the Prussians. The French say that this battle beats Leipsic [sic] hollow in the number of killed and wounded. Our Division suffered exceedingly. We are to follow on Thursday. Today we bivouac at Nivelles. Lord Wellington has thanked our Division through General Byng, and says, 'that he never saw such gallant conduct in his life'.

Bull's howitzer troop stayed close to the battlefield until 3 p.m. on Monday, when they were ordered to move. John Lees whipped his horses in the direction of Paris, but the young wagon driver's role in the turbulent history of his times was not over. He and Byng would be involved in one of the worst atrocities that Britain (see Chapter Ten) has witnessed.

The story of the closing of the gates at Hougoumont captured the imagination of Georgian Britain. It was told as a tale of uniquely British heroism (though German troops were there) and Wellington helped to consolidate that legend, saying over one of his suppers at Deal Castle in 1840: 'You may depend on it – no troops could have held Hougoumont but British, and only the best of them.' Walter Scott was inspired to some bad verse:

Yes – Agincourt may be forgot
And Cressy be an unknown spot
And Blenheim's name be new;
But still in story and in song
For many an aged remember'd long,
Shall live the towers of Hugomont
And field of Waterloo.

Sir Arthur Conan Doyle drew on the heroic wagon driver Brewer, who delivered ammunition to Hougoumont under fire, for a short story, *A Straggler of '15*, although his name was changed to Brewster.

I discovered that the true story of Hougoumont is surrounded by myths. The most persistent myth is that the walls were breached only once. Mackinnon said the French smashed their way through the north gate twice in his official history of the Coldstream Guards in 1833:

The gate was then forced. At this critical moment, Macdonell rushed to the spot with the officers and men nearest at hand and not only expelled the assailants, but reclosed the gate. The enemy from their overwhelming numbers again entered the yard, when the Guards retired to the house and kept up from the windows such a destructive fire, that the French were driven out and the gate once more was closed ...[6]

Gareth Glover, one of the outstanding British experts on Waterloo, told me he believed Mackinnon was confused because he was not in the farmyard at the crucial moment: 'I checked a number of eyewitness accounts, but no one seems to agree with his confused version. The closing of the gate was so famous for its success – this does not make sense if it failed and they broke in again just after!' He believes Mackinnon confused his account with a second break-in through a small gate by the side of the great barn on the west side of the farm. This was described by Lieutenant General Woodford of the 2nd Battalion Coldstream Guards. He said: 'Some few of the enemy penetrated into the yard from the lane on the West, but were speedily driven out, or dispatched.' This is supported by the French versions, which say as many as seventy men tried to get in through this small gate but were repulsed.

Private Clay says the French broke in a third time, through the doors of the great gate house on the south side (which he called the upper gates):

> The enemy's artillery having forced the upper gates, a party of them rushed in who were as quickly driven back, no one being left inside but a drummer boy without his drum, whom I lodged in a stable or outhouse …
>
> A round shot burst them open; stumps intended for firewood laying within were speedily scattered in all directions, the enemy not having succeeded in gaining an entry.
>
> The gates were again secured although much shattered.

Clay's account led to the most famous myth that when the north gate was breached, the only one of the French attackers left alive was the little drummer boy. Clay makes it clear the boy was stranded in the subsequent attack.

A patriotic cleric, the Reverend John Norcross, the curate of Framlingham in Suffolk, was so moved by the stories of heroism at Waterloo that on 19 July 1815, one month after the battle, he wrote to Wellington, who was then in Paris, offering a pension to the man of the Duke's choice who he believed had showed the greatest bravery. Inevitably, the man chosen became known as the 'Bravest Man in England'.

Framlington was one of the richest livings in the country and Norcross, aged 53, offered an annuity to be called the 'Wellington Pension' and paid on Waterloo Day, 18 June, every year for the rest of the curate's life. The current incumbent of the Framlington curacy and his wife showed me a copy of the letter. Reverend Norcross wrote:

> If your Grace will do me the honour to nominate any one of my brave countrymen who have fought under your Grace's banners in the late tremendous but glorious conflict – I shall have great pleasure in settling upon

him for the continuance of my life an annuity of £10 which I humbly request your Grace will permit to be entitled the Wellington Pension.

Norcross said on receipt of the Duke's recommendation, the first payment would be immediately advanced and in future, with his Grace's approbation, paid on each anniversary of the 'memorable' 18 June:

> I will not add more than that, with the exalted sentiments which I entertain of your Grace's transcendent merits and appreciating as I do your splendid and unparalleled achievements, were means commensurate to my inclinations, I would cheerfully centuple the sum I mentioned.

As Norcross hinted, £10 a year – 3s a week – was hardly a prince's ransom even in 1815, but it was a handy sum for a soldier reduced to charity after the war.

Wellington replied in a letter dated Paris, 31 July, promising at the earliest opportunity to make the Reverend Norcross 'acquainted with the name of the soldier, whom, upon enquiry, I shall find most deserving of your bounty'. Wellington added that it was the same 'patriotic spirit' which had induced Norcross to make his financial sacrifice and which so generally prevailed in England that had given so much encouragement to the 'discipline and courage' of his men. It was 'to this spirit that we owe the advantages we have acquired in the field and I beg leave to return you the best thanks in the name of the brave officers and soldiers whom I have had the happiness of commanding.'

On 24 August 1815, Wellington again wrote to Reverend Norcross at Framlingham Rectory from Paris:

> Sir, having made enquiries respecting the soldier to be recommended to you in consequence of your letter of 19th July, to which I wrote an answer on 31st July, I now have leave to recommend to you Lance Sergeant Graham of the Coldstream Regiment of Guards. I have leave to return to you my thanks for your patriotism and your benevolence towards those which have so well deserved the approbation of their country.

Wellington passed Norcross's letter on to Sir John Byng with a request to choose a man from the 2nd Brigade of Guards, which had so highly distinguished itself in the defence of Hougoumont. According to Captain William Siborne, who interviewed Sergeant Graham, it was Byng who picked him, because of the way he rescued his brother from the flames. It was the kind of selfless heroism and human interest story that was certain to capture the hearts of the public in Regency Britain.

John Booth, in his history of Waterloo written only the year after the battle, claimed Norcross had asked for a non-commissioned officer to receive his pension, but Norcross's letter makes no mention of that. There is another myth that Norcross left £500 in his will to Macdonell and the officer split the money with Graham. I have obtained a copy of Norcross's will from 1837 and while he left money to his wife and a number of others, there is no mention in his will of Macdonell, Graham or any others connected with Waterloo.

The Irishman with the curly black hair was given a special bravery medal by his fellow sergeants in addition to his Waterloo Medal. In his Waterloo Despatch, Wellington singled out the saving of Hougoumont for special praise:

> At about ten o'clock he [Napoleon] commenced a furious attack upon our post at Hougoumont. I had occupied that post with a detachment from General Byng's brigade of Guards, which was in position in its rear; and it was for some time under the command of Lieut. Colonel Macdonell, and afterwards of Colonel Home; and I am happy to add that it was maintained throughout the day with the utmost gallantry by these brave troops, not-withstanding the repeated efforts of large bodies of the enemy to obtain possession of it.[7]

Macdonell, who was injured and had to hand over to Home late in the day, was awarded a knighthood by the Prince Regent and made a Knight of Maria Theresa, an Austrian gallantry award that carried a pension. He rose to become a major general and retired to his estates in 1830, where he died in 1859. Sergeant Fraser, who unhorsed Cubières, was discharged two years after Waterloo 'in consequence of long service and being worn out'; he was lucky – he found a post as a Bedesman at Westminster Abbey and died in 1862, aged 80.

Matthew Clay endured terrible poverty in old age. He married his wife Johanna at Stoke Dameral in Devon in 1823; they moved to Bedfordshire and had twelve children, though – in common with mortality rates at the time – only three survived. He spent eleven years after Waterloo as a drill sergeant and after being discharged from the Guards with a pension of 1s 8d, he sup-plemented his income by serving for another twenty years as a sergeant in the Bedfordshire militia. He moved to his birthplace, Blidworth in the Sherwood Forest, in old age. His wife Johanna took in laundry, but she was struck by paralysis and Clay was so poor that he had to sell furniture and other posses-sions to keep them alive and pay the rent.

A family member, Christine Dabbs Clay, who researched her ancestor, said:

> Matthew struggled to make ends meet a few years before he died. The old veteran had denied himself necessities to keep his ailing wife, Johanna, alive

without asking for charity. He had to sell his possessions so that he could pay the rent.

Before the welfare state, there were few options for old soldiers like Clay – poor relief from the parish, begging or the workhouse. The Poor Law Amendment Act of 1834 established 'workhouses', and to cut the cost of poor law provision they had brutal conditions like prisons to deter the poor from turning to them. The regime would have meant the separation of married couples like the Clays. A few of the lucky ones got pensions from the Chelsea Board but few, like Tom Plunkett, who was wounded in the head at Waterloo, passed the interview; he was discharged with just 6*d* a day.

Sergeant Clay's plight was eventually discovered after his wife had died by a General Codrington, who wrote letters to *The Times* that led to a charitable fund for Clay, which soon grew to £100. 'Unfortunately,' said Christine Dabbs Clay:

> the last enemy was too strong and Matthew died on 5 June 1873 aged 78, before he could benefit from the General's kindness.
>
> He died a pauper but was given a hero's funeral and thousands of people came to pay their respects. On the top of his coffin lay his sword and a ring of laurel leaves, because when he was alive, on the anniversary of the Battle of Waterloo, he wore a sprig of laurel leaves to remember that day.[8]

Clay's name appears among the 39,000 who received a Waterloo Medal for their service. The medals were issued to every soldier who had served at Waterloo, Quatre Bras or Ligny – the first time in British history a campaign medal had been issued to everyone who took part, including the 'common soldiers' who were drawn from the 'scum of the earth'. Recipients were credited with two years' extra service and pay, and a holder was known as a 'Waterloo Man'.

The silver medal carried the head of the Prince Regent on the front with the inscription 'GEORGE P. REGENT', while the reverse carried the seated figure of Victory with the words 'WELLINGTON' and 'WATERLOO' below and the date 'JUNE 15 1815'.

There is a portrait of Clay in the Guards Museum in London. He is proudly wearing his scarlet Guards post-Waterloo uniform, with the Waterloo Victory medal, but it is reversed; the side with the Prince Regent's head is turned against his chest. A note by the Guards Museum is quite frank, given their close proximity to royalty (Buckingham Palace is across the road). It says he may have worn it reverse up, because he 'did not like the Prince Regent who was not popular'.

On his discharge papers, Clay was described as 'a very good and efficient soldier, never in hospital, trustworthy and sober.' The Guards Museum note points out this was high praise, given drunkenness was a scourge of the army, 'paralleled by the pox'.

Life for James Graham after Waterloo was bittersweet. James's brother, Joe, died within a week from his injuries, despite James's heroic efforts to save him from the flames. Then after only two years, Norcross stopped paying his pension.

The reason why Norcross withdrew the annuity speaks volumes about the hard times suffered in Suffolk. The Curate's Living at Framlingham was worth £1,300 per annum and, in addition to the Rectory of Framlingham – described as a 'fair mansion house' (now converted into six flats) – there were eighteen pieces of glebe land covering 70 acres, making it the richest of ten benefices in the gift of Pembroke College, apart from the vicarage of Soham in Cambridgeshire. Norcross became a victim of the hard times that hit rural areas after Waterloo, particularly in the Fenland country of Suffolk and Norfolk. Bad weather resulting from the effects of the Tambora volcano led to a huge fall in crop yields and farm incomes in 1816. Wheat yields in England fell from 37 bushels per acre (bpa) in 1815 to 25.3bpa in 1816 (a drop of over 31 per cent). Farmers could no longer afford to pay the tithes – a tenth of their income – that made Framlingham such a rich living or pay their farm workers. The bad weather added to the misery for the 250,000 ex-soldiers looking for work. East Anglia today may seem like a sleepy rural backwater, but it witnessed riots in 1816 at Littleport and Ely over the economic distress.

Former BBC *Newsnight* presenter Jeremy Paxman stumbled across the story of the hardship in Framlingham in his programme for the BBC series *Who Do You Think You Are?* Paxman discovered one of his own ancestors, Thomas Paxman, an impoverished shoemaker in the village, had to turn to parish relief for regular hand-outs of 'dole' money for his family to survive. His ancestor was literally the poor man at the gate. Paxman, noted for his hard interviews, was moved to tears when he found in the parish accounts Thomas Paxman going for regular hand-outs from the dole office at Framlingham Castle – 6s 6d in one week, 7s 10d in another – for months. 'Every week, he is turning up with his hand out,' said Paxman.[9]

Thomas Paxman joined a long-forgotten migration scheme from the Fens to work in the 'satanic mills' of the North of England. It split the Paxman family. A migration agent arranged for Paxman to be transported by canal barge with his wife and four of his seven children, but only those who were over 12 and permitted to work in factories were allowed to go. They were put to work in textile mills in Bradford, while the younger Paxman children were left behind to be looked after by in-laws.

Andrew Phillips, a local historian, told Paxman: 'Anyone who is anybody gets the hell out of Suffolk.'

Poverty and the post-war slump led to a nasty dispute between the tenant farmers and Norcross. The farmers could no longer afford to pay the tithe and Norcross reluctantly stopped paying Sergeant Graham his Waterloo pension after only two years. Graham was told Norcross was 'declared bankrupt' but this is another of the myths surrounding his bequest. Norcross did not go bust. However, he was clearly so upset and embarrassed that he moved with his wife Eleanor to Dawlish in Devon, where he died in obscurity in March 1837 aged 75. While he kept the living at Framlingham, he paid for clergymen to conduct services in his absence.

Graham, like Clay and other old soldiers, faced hardship when his fame faded. His official discharge papers from 1829, which I have obtained, show that within a year of Waterloo the hero of Hougoumont was reduced to the rank of private, no doubt with a cut in his pay. He was discharged by the Coldstream Guards on 24 July 1820 for reasons not given and the next day, 25 July 1820, he was signed on as a private with the 12th Dragoons, who were then in Ireland but later posted to Portugal during a civil war. He clearly had

Discharge papers of Sergeant James Graham.

a rough life, because he was finally invalided out of the army with a severe chest injury, caused when his own horse fell on him, which must have been an occupational hazard for the Dragoons.

His army record says he was discharged 'in consequence of worn out constitution and a severe injury of his chest by his horse falling back with him in Portugal in July 1827'. His conduct was described as 'good', his age was 'about 38', his height 5ft 9¾in, with brown hair, grey eyes and fair complexion. His trade was given as 'weaver', though he had been in the army since 25 March 1812, when he joined the Coldstream Guards at the age of 21. His total service, including two extra years for Waterloo, was 19 years and 294 days. He was given a 'Chelsea' pension of 9*d* a day on 13 January 1830. That is pitiful sum for a national hero.

James Graham was from Clones, County Monaghan – he is said to have been one of three brothers who joined the British Army (possibly including John Graham, the soldier discharged because he was 'undersized'). I could find no contemporary description of James, but there is a crudely drawn pencil portrait of James Graham in the national portrait gallery in Dublin. He has long, jet-black curly sideboards, giving him the dark handsome looks of a gypsy or the singer Tom Jones in his prime. He is wearing his scarlet tunic and a post-Waterloo shako topped by a green plume and a stringed bugle badge, denoting a light company. He is wearing a medal, possibly the Waterloo Medal, but like Clay it appears he wore it reversed as a mute protest to the times. A memorial plaque was put up to his memory at Kilmainham in 1906 saying:

> To the Glory of God and Sergeant James Graham 2nd Btn Coldstream Guards Born 1791–1845: He was one of the five Coldstreamers who successfully defended the main gate ...

However, after the Irish Free State was created, Kilmainham was taken out of the hands of the British and Graham's fame was all but forgotten. An eminent Dublin surgeon, Seton Pringle, who was also a Clones man, arranged in 1929 for the plaque to be put up in the protestant St Tiernach's church that towers over the cobbled square in Clones.

A plaque praising a hero of the British Army may seem incongruous there now. Clones is in the Irish Republic, a strongly Republican area, hard up on the border with County Fermanagh and it has seen its fair share of the Troubles. It was the scene of a bloody shoot-out between the IRA and the special constabulary in 1921, when one IRA man and four constables were killed. A farm in Tirconey with links to the Graham family was firebombed in the 1970s when Billy Fox, an Irish politician, was murdered. I asked one of the locals in Clones whether the 200th anniversary celebrations for this hero of the British Army would be a cause of pride or embarrassment in this strongly republican border area. He told me: 'I don't think there will be any embarrassment – it's just that there aren't many here who know who James Graham was.'

The archives on Sergeant Graham today are surprisingly elusive for someone who was a national hero. His Irish records are thought to have been destroyed by fire at the national archive in Dublin in the Republican uprising of 1922. Graham's army records held by the Coldstream regiment may also have gone up in flames with their other archives in the 1940–41 Blitz.

In 1904, the War Office made a search for his papers after a relative in Toronto, Canada, made some inquiries. They found nothing, because they got his name wrong: they looked for 'John' Graham instead of James. Finally, after months of correspondence, they made inquiries under the right name and his discharge papers were found at Kilmainham Hospital. A set was kept in London (now at the National Archives in Kew)[10] and, with the help of researcher Kevin Asplin, I was able to read them again. They reveal that in July 1835, James Graham – perhaps still suffering with the chest injury – was driven by poverty to appeal to the board of the Chelsea Pensioners' Hospital for 'an augmentation' of his meager army pension.

His letter, in his own spidery handwriting, was sent on 23 July 1835 – after struggling for five years on his army pension of 9*d* per day. It is a poignant and remarkable document. As far as I know, it has not been published before and it speaks volumes of the hardship suffered by some of the heroes of Waterloo, like Graham. He addressed his letter to the Right Honourable Commissioners of Chelsea Hospital:

> Gentlemen,
>
> Having served in the Coldstream Guards for 8 years and in the 12th Dragoons for 9 years and six months, 2 years of Waterloo service, and having been discharged on a pension of 9d per day, I am induced to write to you hoping that you will take my service into consideration and grant me an augmentation of pension. The Rector of Framlingham in Suffolk, soon after the battle of Waterloo, wrote to the Duke of Wellington, stating that in his opinion the non-commissioned officers of the British Army that for their conduct on that day, entitled themselves to some distinct mark of their country's approbation and therefore felt disposed to offer his humble tribute to their merit. In order that this might be properly applied, he requested that his Grace would point out to him the non-commissioned officer whose valorous conduct, from the representations which his Grace had received, appeared the most meritorious to whom the Rector meant to convey in perpetuity a freehold farm value £10 per annum. The Duke set the inquiry immediately on foot through all the commanding officers of the line and

in consequence learned that a Sergeant Graham (the writer of this) of the Coldstream Guards and a corporal of the 1st Regiment of Guards [believed to be Private John Lister of the 3rd Guards] had so distinguished themselves that it was felt difficult to point out the most meritorious. But the Rector having become bankrupt, as I was informed by Colonel Woodford, now Major General, I received the £10 but two years. I had two brothers at the battle of Waterloo, one serving under Colonel [Frederick Cavendish] Ponsonby [of the] 12th Dragoons, the other under Colonel McDonald and Colonel Woodford. What caused more attention to be paid to the humbler writer of this than to almost any other person, was that, having begged permission to retire from the ranks at the battle of Waterloo for a moment, I extricated my wounded brother from the flames of a farmhouse set on fire by the enemy in their retreat and conveyed him away on my shoulders.

As to my character, I can refer you to Sir John Byng, Lieutenant General to Colonel Wyndham. I was informed by Dr McGregor that I was entitled to a rising pension … I was discharged from the 12th Regiment of Dragoons in consequence of an injury of the chest, which I received in Portugal. Your humble servant, James Graham.

He said if they should 'deign to communicate' with him, the commissioners could write to him at 'Captain Buttens, Broomville, near Tullow, County Carlow', which is south of Dublin in the Republic of Ireland. I could find no

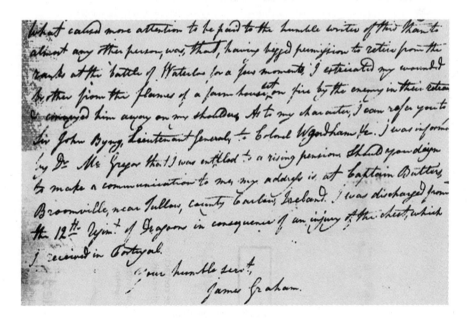

Part of Sergeant James Graham's letter.

record of any additional pension being paid to him, but it seems likely that the Commissioners eventually decided to admit him to Kilmainham on 1 July 1841, where he died four years later at the age of 54 and was buried with full military honours.

And there is no sign of Graham at Kilmainham, modelled on Les Invalides in Paris, which now houses the Irish Museum of Modern Art. I was told 'it does seem that the nineteenth-century headstones for "Rank and File" soldiers buried in the Hospital grounds have all been removed'. As a result, although Sergeant Graham's heroism will be celebrated with the bicentenary of the battle, it is unclear where this national hero was buried.

There was one other intriguing story about Graham I had to track down, however. The *Navy and Military Gazette* edition of May 1845 reported Graham later performed another act of heroism, saving the life of Captain (afterwards Lord Frederick) FitzClarence of the Coldstream Guards and helping to stop a plot to assassinate the Cabinet, including the Duke of Wellington.

Notes

1.   Charles Dalton, *Waterloo Roll Call* (London: Eyre and Spottiswoode, 1904), p. 212.
2.   Major–Gen H.T. Siborne (ed.), *Waterloo Letters*, (London: Cassell and co., 1891), p. 262.
3.   Ibid.
4.   Colonel Petiet, *Memoires du general Auguste Petiet, hussar de l'Empire* (Paris: Kronos Collection, Spm, 1997) p. 443.
5.   Major–Gen H.T. Siborne (ed.), *Waterloo Letters*, p. 256.
6.   Daniel Mackinnon, *The Coldstream Guards* (London: Richard Bentley, 1833), p. 217.
7.   Wellington Despatch to Lord Bathurst, Secretary of State for War, 19 June 1815.
8.   Matthew Clay, note by a family descendant Christine Dabbs Clay, Blidworth and District Historical and Heritage Society.
9.   *Who Do You Think You Are*, Series Two, Acorn Media, 2006.
10. WO 97/55, War Office papers, National Archives, Kew.

8

The Man Who Made a Killing After Waterloo

Major the Honourable Henry Percy, Wellington's ADC, is officially credited with bringing the Waterloo Despatch to London. But the first man in Britain to receive definitive news that Wellington had defeated Napoleon was the financier Nathan Mayer Rothschild.

It was already dusk on Tuesday, 20 June 1815, when a rider clattered into the small cobbled Georgian square at New Court in St Swithin's Lane and rushed inside the counting house in search of the financier to give him the news. It would be another thirty hours before Percy got to London.

Rothschild was perturbed by what he had heard. Rothschild had been banking on a long war. He had bought millions of pounds worth of gold bullion to supply to Wellington to maintain his army on the Continent over the coming months. The last thing he had expected was that it would all be over in a single weekend. The scale and speed of Wellington's great victory had left him facing huge losses.

In the first week of April, Rothschild bought 100,000 guineas in gold, 100,000 Spanish gold dollars and nearly £200,000 in bills of exchange. By 13 June – just five days before the battle – Rothschild had sent £250,000 in gold to Wellington's army. When the tallies were added up on 20 October, he had dispatched 884 boxes and 55 casks of gold coins worth £2.1 million. Now he would be stuck with the gold, and like any commodity in sudden surplus its value was likely to depreciate sharply. He was facing losses, not just for himself, but also for his four brothers, who ran branches of the family finance house in the major capitals of Europe – Amschel in Frankfurt, James in Paris, Carl in Naples and Salomon in Vienna.

An unflattering engraving
of Nathan Mayer
Rothschild – Wellington's
banker and a target for
crude anti-Semitism.
(Mary Evans/Epic/
Tallandier)

What happened next has been the source of controversy for 200 years. Put
bluntly, Rothschild is accused of using his advance news from Waterloo to
make a killing on the Stock Exchange. It is alleged he fed rumours already
circulating in London that Bonaparte had won by dumping government
stocks and then secretly buying them back when the price crashed. It was
said Rothschild made his first million pounds and founded the House of
Rothschild – one of the greatest financial institutions in the world – on the
profits of a Stock Exchange fraud.

I am walking north up one of the small lanes that are the arteries in the heart
of the Square Mile in London to find out the truth about the man who made
a killing on the news from Waterloo. The shiny steel, glass office of Nathan
Mayer Rothschild – ten floors of open-plan offices, a rooftop garden and

a glazed 'sky pavilion' – has been shoe-horned onto the same plot of land at 2 New Court, St Swithin's Lane in the medieval heart of the City, where Rothschild founded his financial empire.

The architects have cleverly created a peek-a-boo entrance, with a space between the two glass entrances framing a view of a Wren gem beyond, the church of St Stephen Walbrook. The Rothschilds are proud of their heritage – there are murals of the family on the wall of the top-floor boardroom and the glass entrance to the Rothschild Archive on the ground floor is dominated by a huge family portrait of Nathan and his family. The canvas is over 3m high and 3.5m wide and shows Nathan and his wife Hannah sitting in an elegant drawing room with their children, Charlotte, Lionel, Anthony, Nathaniel, Hannah Mayer, Mayer Amschel and baby Louise, with the friendly family pet, a Newfoundland dog. The setting is domestic but the room is expensively decorated with a tasteful classical pillar. Nathan sits contentedly on the left on a comfortable red sofa, looking benignly across at the family. It was painted in 1821, barely a decade after Nathan had arrived in London to found the family banking arm by William Armfield Hobday, the son of a wealthy spoon manufacturer from Birmingham who specialised in uninspiring portraits of the newly rich manufacturing middle classes. The most striking feature is the head – Nathan has a great bald dome, like a mini St Paul's, with brown hair at

New Court, St Swithin's Lane – the HQ of NM Rothschild – where first news of Waterloo arrived. (Author)

the sides. Despite its domestic simplicity, it is intended to convey the message that Nathan Mayer Rothschild has made it.

His father, Mayer Amschel Rothschild, began the family banking business almost by accident, trading in antique coins with some of Europe's wealthiest aristocrats. His family rose from the Jewish ghetto in Frankfurt and established its name across Europe in a single generation. Nathan, the third son, left the family business in Frankfurt in 1798 at the age of 21, complaining there was not enough space for him with his four brothers. He sailed to England to set up business as a textile trader in Manchester, exporting cloth from weavers in the north of England to Europe.

He had a natural feel for business and quickly realised there were three ways to make profits from textiles: on the raw material, the dyeing and the manufacturing. He began to supply the material and dye to a manufacturer to produce the finished cloth so that he got three profits instead of one. In six years he made himself a major player in exporting textiles from the mills of Lancashire and Yorkshire to Continental Europe. He boasted how he quickly turned £20,000 into £60,000 – enough to build a substantial town house next to his own warehouse at 25 Mosley Street, Manchester, which is now offices with a tramway in the heart of the city. Nathan's textile export business flourished until Napoleon imposed a blockade on British trade in 1807, leaving Nathan no option but to engage in smuggling textiles to the Continent to turn a profit.

Smuggling was to prove very useful when his business turned to banking during the Napoleonic Wars. He married Hannah Cohen, the daughter of a prominent London Jewish merchant, in 1806 and they had a son, Lionel, born in 1808. The Rothschilds' house was in the commercial centre and just around the corner from St Peter's Field, which was to become infamous in 1819 for the slaughter of protestors demanding Parliamentary reform, including one man who had fought at Waterloo.

Nathan struggled against Napoleon's trade embargo for a couple of years before moving, lock, stock and many barrels, from Manchester to London with his wife and son. Nathan and Hannah brought much of their furniture with them, transporting it to London by canal, though it would not be long before Hannah had the money to replace it with finer things.

Nathan bought the lease on a large house at No. 2 New Court, St Swithin's Lane in the heart of the old city for £750 in 1809. It had three floors, each lit by about nine large sash windows with extensive garrets above; it was modest and slightly shabby, rough stone fronting below and red brick above, with a simple front door onto the square under a plain stone lintel with four steps. It was not elegant but it was all that Nathan needed to run his expanding business with room for his equally rapidly expanding family – Hannah was pregnant with Anthony, born in 1810. Like his property in Manchester, the house had an attached warehouse so that he could continue his business as a merchant. On the south side of the house was a stone colonnade and a stone wall leading up to a large house in soft yellow sandstone, with a third house, also of yellow stone, enclosing the square. There was a fourth house opposite No. 2 in red brick and soon it, along with the other houses, would be filled with Nathan's extended family and business associates. Across the centre of the square was a black iron railing to keep the dogs out. There were familiar faces around Nathan, as many of his household and business staff came with him from Manchester.

The bustling St Swithin's Lane, which had hardly changed since the medieval period, ran along the side of the house with a full complement of tradesmen – a tailor, hairdresser, wine merchant, cheesemonger and general merchants. Behind the house was the churchyard of St Stephen Walbrook, a classical Wren masterpiece with a dome echoing Sir Christopher's design for St Paul's. It was started in 1672 as London was being rebuilt after the Great Fire of 1666. It still stands next to the Mansion House at the east end of Poultry, the site of the City slaughterhouse and pens for the livestock, which had been known since medieval times as the 'Stocks Market'.

The stone colonnade adjoining No. 2 New Court overlooking the little churchyard of St Stephen Walbrook was a place where someone could sit and reflect, but Nathan was not much interested in introspection. His passion was his business. He is reported to have said of his own children:

> I wish them to give mind, and soul, and heart and body and everything to business – that is the way to be happy. It requires a great deal of boldness and a great deal of caution to make a great fortune; and when you have got it, it requires ten times as much wit to keep it.

Victor, the late Lord Rothschild, in his history of N.M. Rothschild, described Nathan as 'short and fat, with blue eyes, reddish hair and a strong German accent'.[1] A silhouette of Nathan produced as a lithograph on his death shows him in a tailcoat and knee-length breeches, standing by his favourite pillar at the Royal Exchange like a corpulent robin in a top hat. He is holding four keys to symbolise the succession of his four sons. It was called *The Shadow of a Great Man*.

Lord Rothschild said it was all the more remarkable that this unprepossessing Jew with a German accent (he could not speak English when he landed) should have made his mark so fast in a hostile city. It was certainly not because of his charm.

Nathan was not interested in titles or high living, although he wished intensely to be accepted by the City of London and was brusque to the point of rudeness. Lord Rothschild said he acquired the 'more abrasive and even churlish side to his character' during those early years when he was struggling to establish himself as a figure to be counted at the Exchange:'Even after he had established himself as a financial potentate both in England and on the Continent of Europe, he remained a master of the wounding phrase.'

Nathan upset his father so much with his angry letters home that the patriarch of the Rothschilds appealed to him:'My dear Nathan you must not be angry with your father …' One of Nathan's brothers-in-law, Myer Davidson, wrote from Amsterdam in 1814 to chide him:

> I was embarrassed for your own brother when I found these serious insults in your letters. Really, you call your brothers nothing but idiots.This, my dear Mr Rothschild, is in all sincerity unjust on your part. It also has a negative effect on the big transactions between the brothers. It makes your brothers completely confused and sad. Now God gave you the good fortune to carry out large scale transactions such as I think no Jew has ever done before …

Solomon wrote in June 1814:'Your letters make me feel ill … To put it quite bluntly, we are neither drunk nor stupid.'

The Rothschilds' arrival was followed by the gradual influx of an entourage of friends and business associates who filled up the adjoining houses in New Court. Nathan acquired the leases of Nos 3 and 4, New Court.The first he sub-let to a succession of merchants. Into No. 4 moved the young Moses and Judith Montefiore, Hannah's sister and her husband (at that time a budding stockbroker, and later to become a noted philanthropist).The close family ties of the Rothschilds – and the secrecy they naturally shared – was an integral part of their business success.

Neighbours noted that the level of activity in the area increased dramatically once Rothschild was in place, with despatch riders charging up the cobbled lane at all hours of the day and night. It was an ideal base for an ambitious young man ready to break into stock broking at the Royal Exchange.

His early will shows he was devoted to his wife, and he was not without, perhaps, a Jewish sense of humour.When a German nobleman was irritated at having to wait while Nathan was working on his accounts, Rothschild said 'Take a seat.'The nobleman said:'I do not think you heard who I am. I am Prince Puckler Muskau.' Rothschild snapped:'Take two seats.'

So how did this tubby Jew with the German accent, who did not suffer fools gladly, make it in the City? Rothschild launched himself in London with a spectacular financial coup, as he told dinner guests at a state banquet with the Lord Mayor of London at Ham House in 1834:

When I was settled in London, the East India Company had £800,000 worth of gold to sell. I went to the sale and bought it all. I knew the Duke of Wellington must have it. I had bought a great many of his bills at a discount. The Government sent for me, and said they must have it. When they had got it, they did not know how to get it to Portugal. I undertook all that and I sent it through France; and that was the best business I ever did.[2]

It was a characteristically bold financial gamble, but it was also a carefully calibrated risk. Napoleon famously said an army marched on its stomach but the emperor generally fed his army on plunder. Wellington, anxious to avoid alienating the people he was liberating, paid locally for supplies of food for his men and fodder for the horses as they marched through Portugal and Spain and to do that he needed gold.

By bringing off that financial coup, Nathan broke into the bullion shipping business. His second big breakthrough came in 1811 when he was 33 – the year before his father died. John Charles Herries, a family friend through a Leipzig connection, was appointed Commissary-in-Chief in charge of pay for the British Army in the Peninsula and became Nathan's key to government business.

Herries, 36, was a rising star in the Treasury and sponsored Nathan's business with the government. It is likely that Nathan paid 'commission' to Herries to secure the business. Commission or bribery – 'our friend Baksheesh' as the Rothschilds described it – is an offence today, but it was common practice in Europe for most of the nineteenth century. That is how a previously obscure German-Jew became Wellington's paymaster. There were other bankers who were more established, not least the Baring brothers, but with his own brothers already in place in key capitals in Europe and with plenty of experience in smuggling, Nathan Mayer Rothschild won Herries' confidence to deliver bullion to Wellington's army. It was a daunting task, which might have put off others – Nathan had to agree to a contract that meant he shouldered the risk for any losses of his precious cargo in transit – but Nathan never lacked self-confidence. Herries gave a glowing account of Nathan's ability to Sir George Burgman, the British paymaster in Amsterdam: 'Rothschild has executed the various services entrusted to him admirably well and, though a Jew, we place a good deal of confidence in him.'

Their business was mutually advantageous, and not merely financially. Herries built a reputation for his own competence, partly thanks to Rothschild's ability to deliver bullion to Wellington's army and Britain's allies, and was later to become Chancellor of the Exchequer. The Duke was haunted by the fear that he would not have enough money to pay his troops and Nathan supplied an answer. Wellington needed £100,000 a month to finance his armies in the Peninsula and pay subsidies to the Portuguese and Spanish. It is largely forgotten now but Britain also paid huge subsidies to the German states, Austria, Russia and Prussia, for sustaining the war against Napoleon, all shipped through N.M. Rothschild. At the end of 1815, N.M. Rothschild's total account with Herries amounted to a colossal £9.7m and two-thirds of it was in subsidies to other countries.

But supplying gold bullion – usually in gold guineas in casks – in war to an army on the move was fraught with dangers and logistical difficulties. As a result, the Commander-in-Chief resorted to issuing bills, like IOUs, which could be cashed at the Bank of England, but by 1812 the market in Portugal was so saturated with his bills that Wellington bitterly lamented the 'patriotic gentlemen at Lisbon will give us no money or very little for the draughts on the Treasury.' Which was also why he complained so petulantly to Bathurst in July 1813 from Huarte near Pamplona in Northern Spain about the 'scum of the earth' in his ranks. He was constantly complaining to Lord Bathurst about his money troubles. In November 1813, he protested to Bathurst in a letter datelined St Jean de Luz, a town on the coast, just over the French border with Spain, south of Biarritz: 'Unless this army should be assisted with a very large sum of money at a very early period, the distress felt by all the troops will be most severe.' He told Lord Bathurst that his success depended on 'moderation and justice and upon the good conduct and discipline of our troops'. The Spaniards were in such a poor state, he said, that it was hardly fair to expect them not to carry out looting as they entered France as conquerors. 'I cannot venture to bring them back into France unless I can feed and pay them.'

In December 1813, as he pursued Napoleon's fleeing army into France, Wellington moaned to Bathurst again:

We are overwhelmed with debts and I can scarcely stir out of my house on account of the public creditors waiting to demand payment of what is due to them. Some of the muleteers are 26 months in arrears, and only yesterday I was obliged to give them bills upon the Treasury for a part of their demands or lose their services ...

The Chancellor, Vansittart, responded by writing to Herries on 11 January 1814 authorising:

that gentleman [N.M. Rothschild] in the most secret and confidential manner to collect in Germany, France and Holland the largest quantity of French gold and silver coins, not exceeding in value £600,000 sterling which he may be able to procure within two months from the present time ...

Vansittart added:

> It will be distinctly understood by Mr Rothschild, not only that he is to take upon himself all risks and losses which may occur prior to the delivery on board His Majesty's ships, but that he will be held responsible for any deficiencies which may be discovered upon the final delivery and inspection of the packages to the consignee ...[3]

In February 1814, Wellington's position, quite suddenly, was transformed by shipments on British warships of bullion by the barrel load. The Duke wrote to Lord Bathurst again, this time saying: 'I am obliged to Your Lordship for the supplies of money which are very ample.'

The big change was that Herries had handed over the entire responsibility for the shipments of Wellington's bullion to Nathan Mayer Rothschild. It is therefore impossible to discuss Wellington's great victories without the man who financed them – N.M. Rothschild. The firm of N.M. Rothschild made money out of the shipments of bullion to Wellington in a number of ways. First, Rothschild was paid a commission of around 2 per cent. Then, in concert with James in Paris and his other brothers, Rothschild bought Wellington's bills of exchange at a discount of up to 25 per cent, smuggled them back to England and cashed them at the Bank of England at a profit. He also made a profit on the fluctuating currency rates.[4] They traded in such large quantities of currency that they were able to influence the exchange rate between the French franc, sterling and other European currencies.

To stay ahead of their rivals, the five Rothschild brothers had developed an intelligence network across Europe to be the first with the news that could move markets. It is hard to imagine in today's world of instant satellite broadcasts and 24/7 news how difficult it was to get reliable news. Nathan Rothschild paid couriers and ships' captains to cross the Channel with reports from his brothers or agents in the other European capitals; he set up agencies in the Channel ports, including Lathom Rice and Co. in Dover and James Leveaux in Calais. He also bought a stud farm, Burmarsh Farm, near Hythe on the coast in Kent, to supply his messengers with a relay of fresh horses at stables along the main routes from the coast to his counting house in St Swithin's Lane. He paid rewards on a fixed tariff to captains of the packet boats and the guards of the Royal Mail coaches to exert themselves in speeding his despatches to his agents.

Nathan was naturally secretive and developed his own system of codes using Yiddish and code words for cities – London was Jerusalem, transfers of bullion were called Rabbi Moses and consignments referred to as children, beer or fish. His messages would have been baffling to the French if they were intercepted.

The end of the war in 1814 put a brake on the big bullion shipments for the Rothschilds. But then Darquin, the clerk to James Leveaux, Rothschild's agent in Calais, brought the first news of Napoleon's escape from Elba to New Court and Nathan assumed it would be back to business as usual. He ordered his brothers to buy gold again. His daily trades in gold would be worth many millions today.

The first inkling of a decisive victory by Wellington may have arrived at New Court as early as Monday night, 19 June. In the weeks before the Battle of Waterloo, Nathan had taken the precaution of sending his brother-in-law, Moses Montefiore, to Dunkirk to organise a fresh news agency there, with an express service from Brussels. The route by road was about 100 miles, slightly longer than to Ostend – the main port for shipping gold bullion to Wellington and British subsidies to Russia and Prussia – but the sea crossing was much shorter and Nathan gambled that this would give him the advantage with news from Brussels.

Bulletins about the progress of the fighting were printed in 'gazettes extraordinary' by the Dutch government in Brussels, where there was a panic at the prospect of Napoleon's forces plundering the city. Four of the bulletins were issued on Sunday 18 June and at 3 a.m. on Monday 19 June, No. 5 reported the injured Prince of Orange had been brought in to Brussels. It referred to the 'victory of yesterday' as having been 'bloody but brilliant', which is thought to have been reported in a bulletin that no longer exists. It is believed a small sheet called *L'Oracle* briefly carried the news at midnight on 18 June in Brussels proclaiming the 'Great Victory of the English'. [5]

According to Leopold de Rothschild, grandson of Nathan Mayer Rothschild, a copy of this gazette was rushed to Captain Cullen, the captain of a small ship, who was another of Rothschild's agents. Cullen weighed anchor for the English coast and a courier raced with the bulletin to New Court, arriving forty-eight hours before Percy delivered the Waterloo Despatch. The next day, N.M. Rothschild had the news confirmed by his intelligence network, direct from the Hotel d'Hane Steenhuyse in Ghent, where the exiled Louis XVIII was staying with his court.

The *London Courier* reported on Wednesday 21 June:

The following is said to have been brought by a gentleman who was at Ghent on Monday at one o'clock. He states 'that a general battle was fought the day before; that he was on Monday at Ghent opposite the hotel of Louis XVIII when at 1 p.m. an officer arrived covered with dust; and as the King receives every despatch openly he instantly entered the hotel with the officer who forthwith congratulated his Majesty on the great victory just gained. 'We have taken all the heavy artillery,' he exclaimed, 'and a great and decisive victory is ours'.

The 'gentleman' who brought the news to London was almost certainly N.M. Rothschild's agent, who may have had special access to the court because, according to an account in the *Daily Graphic* of 1903, Rothschild was also giving financial support to the Bourbon king in exile. Either way, the event was seen from the street. The king was in the habit of relaxing in public view before large bow windows opening onto the street.* A crowd had gathered and witnessed the moment when the Russian messenger handed the Bourbon king the note written by Pozzo di Borgo at Wellington's request the night before. It told the king that Bonaparte had been defeated and his army was in retreat – Louis XVIII could proceed to Paris to reclaim the throne of France. The king's reaction to the news was spontaneous – Louis XVIII kissed everyone in sight. Years later Wellington gave his account of what happened at one of his dinner parties:

> Before that bow-window there happened to be passing an agent of Rothschild – a Jew. He saw the Russian officer enter, and after the letter was read he saw everyone embrace him, and then each other – there was nothing but embracing and kissing in the room. Upon which the Jew concluded that it must be the tidings of joy, and that the fighting which was already known must have ended in a most decisive victory. He said nothing but instantly set off for London. At Ostend, at embarking, he saw Malcolm** to whom he declared that he knew no news – observed strict silence all the way – got to London – went with Rothschild to the Stock Exchange and do his little business there – and when that was done, then Rothschild brought him to Lord Liverpool early in the afternoon.[6]

Wellington was right about the scene in Ghent but he was completely wrong that Rothschild's agent 'happened' to be passing the window. It was no accident. Rothschild had posted the agent outside the hotel. He had raced by post-horse from Ghent to Ostend, then boarded the *Nymph*, one of the many small packet boats that plied their trade across the Channel from the French ports to the English coast. On reaching the safe haven of Dover, the messenger commandeered one of Rothschild's horses and turned towards London, 70 miles away. It was late on Tuesday when the messenger, using horses at staging posts on the route, galloped across Old London Bridge to reach New Court in St Swithin's Lane.

The messenger knew the financier was impatient and told Nathan what he had witnessed. Soon the bells would be ringing throughout most of Europe to herald the victory, but for Nathan Mayer Rothschild, the speed of the

---

*   The hotel has preserved the rooms in their original appearance.
**   Rear Admiral Sir Pulteney Malcolm commanded a Royal Navy squadron in the North Sea during Napoleon's 100 days from his flagship, HMS *Royal Oak*.

victory could turn into a financial disaster unless he handled his affairs very carefully. By the time the messenger arrived at New Court, it was too late to go to the Royal Exchange to act on the news from Waterloo. Nathan spent an anxious night at the counting house with his wife and children, worrying about how it would all play out, before setting out in the morning to rescue what he could from his losses.

6

I followed in Nathan Mayer Rothschild's footsteps along the route he would have taken on Wednesday, 21 June 1815, from New Court to the Royal Exchange, where he did his business. I crossed Lombard Street, went through medieval Pope's Head Alley, where Pepys once bought a catcall from a toy shop run by Adam Chard, and I arrived at the Exchange. The walk took no more than two minutes.

St Swithin's Lane has been at the financial heart of London since the seventeenth century, when the trading of stocks started in the coffee houses of Change Alley. Sir John Soane's pillared Bank of England building, a temple dedicated to money, is in nearby Threadneedle Street. The Exchange, which was rebuilt after a fire in 1838, is now a pillared luxury shopping mall. The trading floor where Rothschild stood is filled with the tables of an expense-account all-day brasserie and surrounded by luxury shops trading in expensive brands such as Tiffany and Hermes for today's bankers. Outside, an equestrian statue of Lord Wellington guards the entrance. It was cast in bronze from Napoleon's cannon captured at Waterloo and was erected by the City merchants for its reopening by Queen Victoria in 1844, as a 'thank you' to the great victor over Napoleon.

There is little doubt that N.M. Rothschild put the information to good use – he did go to the Exchange and do some trading, before going with his messenger to No. 10. Five weeks after Waterloo, John Rowarth, one of Rothschild's most trusted agents based in Paris, who had been at the Battle of Waterloo, sent Nathan a note from Paris saying: 'I am informed by Commissary White you have done well by the early information which you had of the victory gaind [sic] at Waterloo.'[7] It is a tantalising clue. Rowarth's note in the Rothschild Archive suggests that Nathan did make a killing on the news about Waterloo before he went to Downing Street with his exclusive intelligence about the outcome of the battle.

The prime minister, Lord Liverpool, was unsure about the reliability of Rothschild's messenger and sent for John Wilson Croker, the Secretary of the Admiralty, to help him. He told Croker it was difficult to accept the messenger's account as genuine. According to the editor of the Croker Papers,

Croker began to question the man 'with all his legal acumen, but he succeeded no better than Lord Liverpool in making the narrative intelligible'. When about to give it up in despair, as a last resort and by a sudden impulse, Croker questioned the messenger about the French king:

> He asked him how the King was dressed. The messenger replied, 'In his dressing-gown'. Mr Croker then asked him what the King did and said to him, to which the messenger replied: 'His Majesty embraced me, and kissed me'. Mr Croker asked, 'How did the King kiss you?' 'On both cheeks,' replied the messenger upon which Mr Croker emphatically exclaimed: 'My Lord, it is true; his news is genuine.'[8]

Liverpool cautiously decided he would have to wait for Wellington's official despatch from Waterloo. It would take another twelve hours to arrive. It was a tortuous journey for Wellington's ADC, Major Percy.

At the moment Rothschild and his agent were in Downing Street, Wellington's official despatch was still being carried across the Channel by the Honourable Henry Percy of the 14th Light Dragoons, grandson of the first Duke of Northumberland. Incredibly, at that moment, Percy was rowing.

Percy had waited at Wellington's house in Brussels on Monday 19 June for the Duke to produce a 'fair copy' of the despatch he had begun at Waterloo. It was addressed to Lord Bathurst at the Colonial Office in Downing Street. When it was ready, Percy put it for safekeeping in the ladies' purple velvet handkerchief purse he had been given as a keepsake by an unnamed lady at the Duchess of Richmond's Ball on the evening of 15 June. Like many officers who were there, he had rushed off to the battle still wearing his dress uniform, forgetting he had the purse tucked inside.

It was about midday on 19 June that Percy set out from Brussels in a chaise (a small coach) with two battle trophies, the two gold-topped eagle standards captured from Napoleon's 45th and the 105th, which Wellington said in his despatch he had the honour of 'laying at the feet of the Prince Regent'. It took twenty-four hours for Percy to get to Ostend in the coach, according to Percy's own notebook. It was not until after midday on Tuesday, 20 June that Percy boarded HMS *Peruvian*, a 200-ton brig sloop of sixteen guns, skippered by Captain James Kearny White. Percy's arrival was noted by Captain White in his ship's log:

> Tuesday 20 June 1 p.m. Received a Major and Despatches from the Duke of Wellington telling of a desperate action having been fought at Waterloo in which the French retreated with considerable loss. Also a King's Messenger for passage across.

Percy's despatch must have been burning a hole in his purse but they had to wait for the tide and they did not set sail from Ostend until 6.30 p.m. By this time, although Percy did not know it, Rothschild's agent from Ghent had landed in Kent and was riding hard for London. Normally, with a fair wind, the voyage to Dover would have taken six hours but the storms that had lashed Belgium on Saturday had abated and the winds had dropped to no more than a light air across the water. After slipping out of the harbour, HMS *Peruvian* spent all night trying to make progress but by 8 a.m. the log shows they were still becalmed off the English coast. Because of the urgency of Percy's mission, Captain White had no alternative but to get out the ship's gig, the small rowing boat, with four stout sailors to help them row the remaining distance to the shore at Broadstairs.

At 11.50 a.m. on Wednesday 21 June, as Rothschild was taking his agent to Downing Street, it was noted in the ship's log: 'Light airs, made all possible sail – out gig. Captain White and the Major shoved off in the gig with the despatches.' Ten minutes later the noonday watch on board HMS *Peruvian* noted in the log: 'Noon. Bearing and distance at noon. Ramsgate W 4/5 leagues. Light airs, sultry wind …' Four to five leagues is between 15 and 17 miles – a daunting distance to row a boat in a hurry. It was just as well Percy, an Old Etonian, was used to rowing on the Thames. The six rowers, including Percy and Captain White, covered the distance in about three hours, around 5 miles an hour. They shipped the oars and ran up the sandy beach at Broadstairs sometime after 3 p.m.; they must have been exhausted, but Percy could not delay. Percy and Captain White hired a chaise and four and rode to London with the eagles sticking out of the window. They were cheered as they went, and when Percy and Captain White reached Whitehall long after nightfall, large crowds were already following their carriage. Percy had orders to deliver the despatch to Lord Bathurst at the War and Colonial Office in Downing Street.[*]

The Secretary to the Treasury, Charles Arbuthnot, whose wife, Harriet, who was to become a close and respected friend of Wellington, had returned from the Commons and was quietly working at his desk in the old Treasury office (at the back of what is now the Cabinet Office) and went out to see what all the commotion was about. According to Stanhope he thought it was a riot against the Corn Laws: 'He heard a great uproar in Downing Street which he ascribed at first to one of the Corn Laws mobs that were frequent at that time.' He was astonished to see the coach with the eagles, but told Percy that Bathurst was attending the regular Wednesday dinner given by Lord Harrowby, the President of the Council, at his house at Grosvenor Square.

---

[*]   The Colonial Office was on the left at the end of the cul-de-sac. It was later demolished to make way for the Victorian Foreign Office.

He jumped in the coach and they set off again, with Arbuthnot showing the coachman the way.

There were loud cheers in Brooks's club when the carriage with the eagles sticking out of the window went clattering by. Those at Brooks's that night included Thomas Creevey's friend, the Whig MP Henry Grey Bennet. 'When the shouts in the street drew us to the window, we saw the chaise and the eagles,' Bennet wrote to Creevey.

Lord Harrowby's daughter, Mary, who was 14, later recalled peeping over the bannisters and seeing an officer in a scarlet tunic with gold on it, arriving at Lord Harrow's house. He was brandishing the despatch and was followed by two other men crying out 'Victory, Victory, Bonaparte has been beaten.' She noticed how tired and dishevelled Percy looked. He was wearing the ADC's uniform he had worn for the Duchess of Richmond's ball, which was stained with the blood of a fellow officer. At first, Harrowby doubted Percy's account, questioning whether the victory could have been so complete as he said. Percy was adamant. Mary heard bursts of cheering from the dining room and her father went outside to announce the news to the crowd in the square. Then Percy had to climb back into the carriage with Arbuthnot, the despatch and the eagles and race off in search of the Prince Regent, accompanied by the cheering crowds. He found the prince at a ball at Mrs Boehm's, a society hostess at nearby 16 St James's Square, which is today the East India Club, a gentleman's club founded in the middle of the nineteenth century for officers of the East India Company, the army and navy. The music died and Percy went down on bended knee to the Prince Regent, saying 'Victory ... victory, sire.' The prince retreated to a small room to read Wellington's despatch and emerged in tears at the numbers of officers who had been killed. Percy was promoted to the rank of Lieutenant Colonel on the spot by the Prince Regent, and he was later rewarded by Wellington with a gold Breguet watch, which was inscribed on the back. The watch is priceless and is now at Levens Hall in the Lake District, which has a family connection to Percy.

Percy retired on half pay in 1821 and became an MP for the family borough of Bere Alston. He was practically anonymous as an MP and died after a bout of ill health at 8 Portman Square, aged 40. He was a national hero for bringing the news back from Waterloo but today he is virtually forgotten. The scarlet-and-gold ADC's coatee he wore at the ball and through the battle are on display in Percy's other ancestral home, Alnwick Castle in Northumberland, alongside the ladies' deep-purple handkerchief sachet in which he carried the Waterloo Despatch. Today the perfectly preserved medieval castle is more famous as the setting for the opening credits of *Black Adder* or as Harry Potter's school, Hogwart's, in the Hollywood movies than for the long-forgotten hero who brought back Wellington's Waterloo Despatch.

For Mrs Boehm, Percy's historic arrival was a disaster – it wrecked her ball and her husband went bust in 1819. In old age she still complained of 'that dusty figure' Percy arriving with the 'unseasonable news of the Waterloo victory – (surely) it could have been kept until morning?' Not even a gift from the Prince Regent – a solid-gold eagle – could assuage her.

So how did Nathan Mayer Rothschild make his fortune? N.M. Rothschild had quickly made his mark at the Royal Exchange and was followed by other traders, who were keen to cash in on his inside information. He was said to possess 'eyes like shuttered windows' and generally gave nothing away to rival traders who were anxious to use his secret intelligence. It would have been easy for him to engineer a run on government stocks. Regency bucks at Brooks's club in St James's, who would bet on anything, including a peer of the realm having sex in a balloon over 1,000 yards off the ground,* had been betting on a victory by Napoleon for days. That morning, he was said to have looked gloomy as he stood at his favourite pillar to give the false impression that Wellington had been defeated. It is alleged he dumped government stocks, known as Omnium and Consuls, but secretly bought them up when the price went through the floor, knowing they would rise when London learned the truth, that Napoleon had been defeated by Wellington. Rothschild vehemently denied it, but the story of his Stock Exchange coup has persisted for two centuries. One report blamed him for others' losses that day:

> He leaned against 'his' pillar. He did not invest. He sold. He dumped consols. Consols plummeted until, a split second before it was too late, Nathan suddenly bought a giant parcel for a song. Moments afterwards the great news broke, to send consols soaring. We cannot guess the number of hopes and savings wiped out by this engineered panic.

His family took great pains to try to scotch such rumours persisting nearly a century later. It is understandable why: fraud on the Stock Exchange was a serious a crime and it would have damaged the reputation of the financial institution he founded. The punishment for defrauding the Stock Exchange was more severe in 1815 than it is today, for in addition to a fine, miscreants could be pelted in the stocks. Only the year before, in 1814, Rear Admiral Sir Thomas Cochrane, the swashbuckling naval captain and Radical MP on whom the *Captain Jack Aubrey* novels by Patrick O'Brian were based, had been accused of similar fraudulent behaviour when he was found guilty of what became known as 'The Great Stock Exchange Fraud'. Cochrane (like

---

* The bet for 500 guineas between Lord Cholmondeley and Lord Derby is listed in the club's historic betting book for 1785.

Aubrey) was convicted of trying to rig the Stock Exchange on false news that Napoleon had died. The Rear Admiral was fined the large sum, for that time, of £1,000 and, worse, he was ordered to stand in the stocks opposite the Royal Exchange for an hour. Pillorying was not merely humiliating. Victims could have their eyes knocked out of their sockets if organised thugs threw stones at the unfortunates in the stocks. Cochrane had many powerful friends in Parliament and to avoid a riot, the authorities arranged for him to be granted a Royal pardon by the Prince Regent; he escaped the pillory, but the scandal wrecked his Royal Navy career for nearly two decades. He was expelled from the service and not reinstated until a second Royal pardon in 1832.

The allegations against Nathan Mayer Rothschild may have started as grumbles by jealous rival brokers, but they were turned into crude anti-Semitic smears in a pamphlet of 1846 in Paris after a journalist tried to blackmail the Rothschild family. They were picked up and embellished in a Polish account published in East Prussia in 1868 that claimed: 'Nathan rode on an Indian horse at the side of the hero Wellington.' This was nonsense. There is a letter in the Rothschild Archive that was written by Nathan between 16 and 20 June to his brother Carl in Amsterdam that proves he was in London when the battle took place.[9] The Rothschilds tried to stop further publication of the smears in a book called the *Romance of the Rothschilds* as late as 1913. The English courts threw out their case on the grounds that you cannot libel the dead, and Nathan had died in 1836.

The anti-Semitic smears against the Rothschilds were resurrected for Nazi propaganda against the Jews at the start of the Second World War by Nazi spinmeister Joseph Goebbels. In 1940, after the Fall of France when Britain stood alone against the Nazis, Goebbels produced a propaganda film showing Nathan Rothschild bribing a French general to lose the Battle of Waterloo so that the Jewish financier could make his fortune by defrauding the Stock Exchange. It seems incredible that Goebbels would have bothered to recycle the smears about Rothschild at Waterloo for Hitler's Nazis, but he wanted to spread poison about the Rothschilds to stir up hatred in Britain against the many Jews who had escaped from Nazi Germany.

Anti-Semitic conspiracy theories about Rothschild's role in the Battle of Waterloo still circulate on the Internet. One posted on a battle website in 2014 said: 'Napoleon stood in opposition to Rothschild, which is why Wellington was sent to fight him.' That would come as news to Wellington. The conspiracy theorists continue to claim Rothschild rigged the market with news of the battle, and by not prosecuting him the government that he served as its banker was complicit in a cover-up. The truth lies in N.M. Rothschild's own archives, the letters between the brothers, the trading accounts and in the faded newspapers that were his daily life. Far from being delighted by his trading that morning on the Stock Exchange, Nathan and his brothers fell out. Amschel complained he was 'swimming' in gold coins in Frankfurt. Carl stopped payments and found he could not sell the British treasury bills in Amsterdam, even at a bigger discount. John Rowarth, the Rothschild agent in Paris, confirmed that he had been handed back unwanted Prussian specie worth £230,000 when he had reached Dunmore, Wellington's Commissary-General. Rowarth had to go to considerable lengths to get to him – he described walking from Mons to Genappe 'in the midst of a cloud of dust under a burning and scorching sun' (it was hot before the torrential rains) and sleeping 'under the cannon's mouth on the ground' to deliver the bullion, only to be told it was unwanted. Nathan petulantly accused his brothers of failing to follow his orders and frantically set about trying to minimise the damage when he went to the stock exchange.

In its famous edition of 22 June 1815, which carried Wellington's Waterloo Despatch, *The Times* carried a clue to Rothschild's trading on the news of the battle. It reported:

> Those who attended minutely to the operations of the Stock Exchange yesterday were persuaded that the news of the day before would be followed up by something still more brilliant and decisive. Omnium rose in the course of the day to 6 premium, and some houses generally supposed to possess the best information were among the purchasers ...

When it referred to 'some houses', *The Times* clearly meant N.M. Rothschild – and it makes it clear Rothschild was buying stocks, not dumping them. Nathan and his brother-in-law Moses Montefiore bought up government stock 'on a tremendous scale'.

The Course of Exchange, detailing the daily movement of government stocks during the weeks before and after Waterloo, shows the price of government stock did not crash after 18 June; it steadily rose, in response to the news and Rothschild's concerted buying. The records for the Exchange show there was a fall in the value of 4 per cent Consols from 71 on 10 June to 69 on 15 June where they remained until the 17th. Sunday 18 June was not a trading day. When the markets opened on Monday 19 June, the price of Consuls gradually rose to reach over 70 on the 22nd when *The Times* appeared with Wellington's Waterloo Despatch.[10] The daily prices in *The Morning Chronicle* showed 3 per cent Consols at 56 on 21 June rising to 58 on Friday, 23 June. But it was weeks before they spiked – they took off in early October and reached over 61 before falling back slightly.

As rumours of a Wellington victory arrived in the City others followed Nathan's lead and started buying, raising the price of government stocks.

These rises helped N.M. Rothschild cover some of his losses on gold, but they were not enough to make his first million. Victor Rothschild, in his history of his family, estimated that for Nathan to have made £1 million in profits on the news from Waterloo, he would have had to invest over £14 million and he simply did not have that sum available. At the most, he had about £2 million to invest.

The truth is far more complex. The historian Niall Ferguson, who wrote the definitive biography of the Rothschilds, said Nathan made his fortune on a gamble over a much longer period.[11] He used the Rothschilds' gold to invest heavily on the bond market. On 20 July 1815 the *London Courier* reported Nathan had made great purchases of British government bonds, though many thought the price he paid was too high. His gamble was that peace would lead to a sharp reduction in government spending, which would send the price of the government long-term loan stocks up as its requirement for borrowing fell. His brothers had a serious cash-flow crisis and pleaded with him to sell his stocks to refloat their coffers. He flatly refused. Instead, he kept on buying government stocks. Salomon complained: 'Dear Nathan, You write that you have one million or two million over there. Well you really must have, because our brother Amschel is bust. We are bust. Carl is bust. So one of us must have the money.'

The stress was almost unbearable for Nathan, for in the midst of this turmoil his sister Julie died, aged 35. Her death almost stopped him trading. Two weeks after Waterloo, Nathan told his brother Carl:

> I feel my spirits very depressed indeed and by no means able to attend to business as I could wish. The melancholy communication of the death of my sister has entirely unhinged my mind and have done but very little business today on that account.

But Nathan held his nerve. As the price of bonds began to rise over the coming months, he kept on buying. Despite his brothers' desperate entreaties to sell, Nathan continued to hold his nerve for two years.

In July 1817, with bond prices up by 40 per cent, he sold his holdings. Today, his profits on that transaction would be worth an estimated £600 million. It was on that gamble that Nathan built the empire of N.M. Rothschild, not the outcome of the battle at Waterloo. He undoubtedly made a windfall on the news from Waterloo, but the evidence suggests he made his fortune despite the outcome of the Battle of Waterloo, not because of it.

Nathan signed a new twenty-one-year lease on New Court in December 1815 at a rent of £175 per annum. But by 1816 the pressures of a growing business and family, together with a high public profile, led Rothschild – by now he had six children – to move to a more spacious villa at Colberg Place, Stamford Hill (where a number of notable Jewish merchants' families later lived), leaving New Court as the business headquarters of his growing finance house. Nathan bought Gunnersbury Mansion – now a public park – in West London in 1835, the year before he died.

New Court was to become the bustling hub of an international financial empire. In 1824 Nathan and Moses worked together to found the Alliance Assurance (now developed into Royal and Sun Alliance). By 1826 Nathan had made enough to come to the rescue of the Bank of England around the corner when there was a run on the Bank. New Court also was to become the scene of many meetings to secure civil rights including the right to sit in Parliament for the Jewish community won by Catholics in 1829. When he died, a funeral shawl suggests he left around £5 million, as well as a lasting legacy of one of the world's great finance houses in his adopted country. He rose from rags to become the richest man in Britain and possibly the world. Aristocrats such as the Duke of Devonshire earned as much from the land each year as Nathan Mayer Rothschild did from financial deals on the Stock Exchange, but they were heavily in debt to the bankers, having taken out loans to finance their lavish estates. A social reckoning was coming.

In its report of the Battle of Waterloo, *The Times* of 22 June 1815 observed: 'Whoever fell on this glorious day cannot have fallen in vain. The fabric of rebellion is shaken to its base.'[12] That might have been true about the revolution in France but it was wholly wrong about unrest in Britain.

Notes

1.   Lord Rothschild, *The Shadow of a Great Man* (privately printed, 1982; reprinted 1991), p. 2.
2.   Ibid.
3.   Vansittart to J.C. Herries, 11 January 1814, RAL T37/8 (copy).
4.   Lord Rothschild, *The Shadow of a Great Man*, p. 22.
5.   Lucien Wolf, 'Waterloo', *Westminster Gazette*, 26 June, 1909.
6.   5th Earl Stanhope, *Notes of Conversations with the Duke of Wellington* (London: John Murray, 1888), p. 172.
7.   Rowarth, 27 July 1815, Rothschild Archive Library, 112/51 T3/341.
8.   Louise J. Jennings (ed.), *The Croker Papers* (London: J. Murray, 1884, www.openlibrary.org), p. 59.
9.   N.M. Rothschild, letter to Carl Rothschild, 20 June, RAL T5/98.
10. Appendix, *The Waterloo Despatch*, Reginald Colby Monograph 24, (London: Wellington Museum HMSO, 1965), p. 41.
11. Niall Ferguson, *The House of Rothschild Money's Prophets 1798–1848* (London: Penguin).
12. *The Times of London*, 22 June 1815.

The Captive Eagle by James Princep Beadle. Francis Stiles grabs the standard; but was the picture a lie? (Great Yarmouth BC)

Probably the grandest portrait of Napoleon in his pomp, the medal created by Edouard
Gatteaux at the French Academy in Rome. It was not actually struck until 1814 after the
first restoration of Louis XVIII. Gatteaux happily switched his allegiance and his subject
matter to the restored monarchy after 1815 and began a long and illustrious career under
his new masters. (From *Napoleon's Medals* by Richard A. Todd)

Left: Waterloo memorial stone where Picton fell, now rolling farm fields once more. (Author)

Below: Elm trees on the ridge at Mont St Jean, where Wellington stood with his ADCs. (Author)

Gilded eagle standard of Napoleon's 105th claimed by Stiles at the National Army Museum.

Sir Alexander Kennedy Clark-Kennedy in old age; he was officially credited with capturing the eagle. (National Portrait Gallery)

Charles Ewart of the Scots Greys – *The Fight for the Standard* by Richard Ansdell (Crown
Copyright reproduced courtesy of Historic Scotland www.historicscotlandimages.gov.uk)

Ensign Ewart public house, Castle Esplanade, Edinburgh. (Martin Hillman)

Hougoumont South Gate where the French dead were piled up. (Author)

The South Gate visited by Barry Sheerman, MP for Huddersfield. He has been, amongst other things, Labour spokesperson for Disabled People's Rights 1992–1994, a position unavailable in 1815.

Mass burning of the dead, rather than burial, represented at Hougoumont; watercolour engraving and etching by James Rouse after C.C. Hamilton, from *An Historical Account of Campaign in the Netherlands in 1815 …* by W. Mudford. (Musée Wellington, Waterloo)

Hougoumont chateau was burned down in the siege but the chapel miraculously survived. (Author)

Matthew Clay died in poverty – his Waterloo medal is reversed, possibly in protest at the Prince Regent. (The Guards Museum)

In July 1818 the Prince Regent awarded the Waterloo Medal to all combatants in the 1815 campaign in Belgium. The Angel of Victory holds a laurel palm and olive branch.

A fireloop in the garden wall at Hougoumont where many died. (Author)

North gate, Hougoumont, the scene of the most bitter fighting – Wellington said the battle turned here. (Author)

Above: Waterloo souvenirs collected by Lord Byron and sent to his publisher John Murray. (Author)

Left: Steps at Oldham Parish Church. John Lees was buried at this spot – now forgotten. (Author)

Wellington's watch – a gift to Percy – and Napoleon's bee cloak clasps at Levens Hall in South Cumbria.

Marker where the 27th Inniskilling Regiment lay dead in a square. (Author)

Cato Street, off Edgware Road, London – the barn where Davidson and his gang plotted to kill the Cabinet, including Wellington, is hardly changed. (Author)

Apsley House, Wellington's London residence, was attacked by the mob. (Author)

The massacre of Peterloo. 'Give them no quarter, they want to take our beef and pudding from us & remember the more you kill the less poor rates you'll have to pay ...'

Wellington on Copenhagen – far smaller than the statue now largely forgotten in Aldershot. (Author)

9

REGENCY RIOTS

The Regency period has been dubbed the Age of Elegance. It is famous for fine houses on classical lines, flamboyant balls, ladies in elegant dresses, Beau Brummel and, topping it all like a star on a tiered cake, the Prince Regent himself. The Regency was also an age of riots and when Wellington's men returned from the battle to end the Napoleonic Wars they found a country at war with itself.

Just three months before the Battle of Waterloo, Lady Melbourne, one of the fading beauties of the Regency period, wrote to her niece Annabella, Lady Byron, about a mob riot outside her elegant stucco-fronted house overlooking Horse Guards Parade in the heart of Whitehall:

> A Mob having assembled upon the Parade (Horse Guards) to rescue a Man who had been taken up by the constables, it was necessary to have ye assistance of the Military and about a dozen of the Horse Guards galloped at the people and dispersed them. Two Men were rode over but not hurt – and this passing close to my Windows* made it impossible not to leave off writing and it was with great difficulty I could finish my letter … last Night the Mob had many attempts upon different Houses but found them all guarded and no mischief was I believe done.

The mob was protesting against a bill to keep the price of corn artificially high to protect the farmers – including the landowning aristocracy – that also increased the price of bread, the staple food of the poor. Riots caused

---

*   Melbourne House is now the Scotland Office, next to Horse Guards.

panic in the government of Lord Liverpool and redcoats ringed the Houses
of Parliament to protect MPs from the violence of the mobs when they voted
the Corn Laws through. Nicholas Vansittart, the Chancellor, told MPs that if
they voted against the Corn Laws they were giving in to mob rule:

> There would be more real cowardice in giving way to the threatening riots
> which existed, and in transferring the legislative functions from their consti-
> tutional guardians, the King, the Lords, and Commons, to an outrageous mob.

Riots were not new – they had been going on for a generation in protest at
the hardship caused by the social upheaval with a mass population shift from
the country to the factories, as Britain changed from an agricultural society to
the first industrialised nation on earth – but Lady Melbourne noted that the
violence had increased:

> Today it rains hard which will probably prevent their assembling in great
> Numbers and the Town is full of Military so I conclude the Ministers
> think themselves tolerably Safe – they were very much frightened and not
> without reason for this Mob seems to be extremely savage and much more
> in earnest than any I ever remember. They tear up the Iron rails and force
> open the door of the House and if they get in as they did at Mr Robinson's
> (Frederick John Robinson was a vocal advocate of the Corn Laws) they
> throw all the furniture out of the Windows into ye Street where it is broken
> to pieces or carried away …

Elizabeth Milbanke, Lady Melbourne, was remarkable, even in an age of
extraordinary women. She had a string of lovers including the two royal princes,
George and Frederick (Duke of York), both of whom fathered children by her,
but she was far more politically astute than her fashionable friend, Georgiana
Spencer, the Duchess of Devonshire, and just as beautiful in her prime. Lady
Melbourne climbed the social ladder on her back, securing titles and advance-
ment for her family through her lovers while presiding over a Whig salon that
attracted the shining wits[*] of the age, including Charles James Fox and Richard
Brinsley Sheridan, who drew on Georgiana and Lady Melbourne for Lady
Teazle and Lady Sneerwell in his farce *School for Scandal*. In her letter, dated 12
March 1815, Lady Melbourne said someone had tossed a loaf of bread into the
gardens at the Prince Regent's Carlton House as a warning about the Corn
Laws. It had been dunked in blood, she said, and tied up in a black mourning
crape: 'This has caused some mirth as it must have been done by some person

---

[*]   Sheridan was a master at a play on words.

as a Joke but which I have no doubt would be taken very seriously,' she added. Lady Melbourne was hinting at fears there was a darker, more sinister threat to the monarchy from the turmoil on the streets. The French Revolution began with a bread march by women seeking relief from hunger to Versailles, supposedly prompting Marie Antoinette to say: 'Let them eat cake.' The aristocrats of Britain feared the Terror that had gripped Paris was stalking London. It was only three years since Spencer Perceval, the prime minister, was assassinated by John Bellingham. It had nothing to do with revolution – he was a deranged businessman with a grudge against the government – but it unnerved Cabinet ministers. Lady Melbourne had a daily reminder across the road from her front door that King Charles I was beheaded outside the Banqueting House in 1649, long before the French adopted the idea. Bread riots carried real menace in Regency Britain, and the poverty was made worse by the sudden outbreak of peace that left many ex-soldiers destitute. Tens of thousands of men were discharged from the army with little prospect of work.

As N.M. Rothschild predicted, the government adopted austerity with the peace by abolishing income tax and slashing spending. The defence budget was cut by 75 per cent from £43 million in 1815 to £10.7 million in 1820. The army was more than halved over the next decade from 233,000 in 1815 to 92,000. The soldiers – the 'scum of the earth' – had to find a living where they could, mostly in the new factories. Rifleman Benjamin Harris saw:

> thousands of soldiers lining the streets and lounging about the different public houses with every description of wound and casualty incident to modern warfare ... the Irishman shouting and brandishing his crutch; the English soldier reeling with drink; and the Scot with grave and melancholy visage sitting on the steps of the public house amongst the crowd listening to the skirl of his comrades' pipes ...[1]

The Prince Regent seemed impervious to the plight of his people, and came to embody all the grievances of the mob. He had become regent in 1811 to take over the powers of the king from his father, King George III, when he became incapacitated by bouts of 'madness', thought to be a blood disorder called porphyria.* He celebrated with a lavish party at Carlton House terrace – live fish were carried in an ornamental canal on the banquet table and the dinner service cost £60,000 – and he went on a huge palace spending spree to match his new powers. The Prince Regent overspent the £2.8 million (the equivalent purchasing power of £181 million today) he was granted on the

---

* Doubts were cast on the modern porphyria diagnosis in 2013 by more research suggesting he was bipolar.

Civil List over the three years from 1812 to 1815 by a staggering £900,000 (£58m today). Worse, 'Prinny' asked Parliament to advance him a further £100,000 (£6.4m) to celebrate becoming an unrestricted Regent, including a new suit of clothes. He ran up bills all over town – he had a massive credit account of £490 – equivalent to £31,000 today – at his Savile Row tailor Jonathan Meyer (later Meyer and Mortimer) often for letting out his clothes to accommodate his growing girth. They still have the account books in copperplate script for enlarging a jacket in the breast and a yellow waistcoat made higher in the neck with added lace to hide his double chins. He was lampooned as a gluttonous, drunken, womanising, gambling, bloated buffoon, but 'Prinny', like a spoiled child, refused to tighten the royal belt. In 1815 he commissioned his architect John Nash – the architect for his ambitious redesign of central London with Regent Street – to carry out a lavish refurbishment of interiors at Carlton House and turn his classical villa by the sea at Brighton into a Moghul-inspired pleasure palace with domes and fabulously exotic chinoisserie that brought the shock of the Orient to the East Sussex coast. Here he could indulge his twin passions of food and fun. The Whig MP George Tierney successfully demanded a Commons inquiry into the royal expenses after protesting the Prince Regent had run up bills of £260,000 for furniture, upholstery costing £49,000 and plate and jewels costing £23,000 in a single year for Carlton House.

By 1816, even the Tory government of Lord Liverpool had become alarmed at the prince's excesses. In an extraordinary move, the prime minister, the Leader of the Commons Lord Castlereagh and Chancellor Sir Nicholas Vansittart wrote a joint letter to the prince warning him to call a halt to his lavish extravagance or they would not weather the coming storm. They clearly feared the Prince Regent's spending could be the spark that could set off an English revolution. Tom Paine's 1791 *Rights of Man* had proved popular, vastly outselling Edmund Burke's 1790 attack on the revolution, *Reflections on the Revolution in France*. They reminded him the government was having to 'enforce a system of economy and retrenchment' to reduce the debts caused by the Napoleonic Wars and the aftermath of Waterloo. Landowners were 'obliged to submit to losses and privations as well as to retrenchment'. They told him bluntly the only means of 'weathering the impending storm is by stating on the direct authority of Your Royal Highness and by your command … that all new expenses for additions or alterations at Brighton or elsewhere will … be abandoned.'

Their warnings went unheeded. In 1817 a mob attacked the Prince Regent's carriage when he was returning from Parliament after reading the King's Speech. The Lord of the Bedchamber, James Murray, who had been in the carriage with the Prince Regent, was summoned to the Commons to give evidence to MPs about the attack. He said:

On his royal highness's return from the House, between Carleton House Gardens and St. James's gardens, the glass of the carriage on the left side of his royal highness was broken … It seemed to have been produced by two bullets of a small size; about a quarter of an inch apart.

The incident was passed off as an exaggeration by the Prince Regent – many thought the bullets were probably a couple of stones. However, Murray's evidence (two holes were punched in tough glass without smashing it) suggests they may have been bullets fired from an airgun (there was no sound or smell of powder) and two years later there was a serious assassination attempt on the Cabinet.

The unrest was strongest in the burgeoning towns of the newly industrialised Midlands and the North – Manchester, Birmingham, Sheffield, Bradford and Leeds, which were denied representation in Parliament. The new mills with their spinning machines, driven by water or steam, put whole families out of work. One spinning machine operated by a single minder could do the work of over 700 spinners; they brought poverty to entire families who had made a living with their cottage looms and single-spindle spinning wheels. It was little comfort to them to know the factories in the cities would produce more jobs than the fields in the coming decades and drive the British export boom that boosted incomes in the Victorian period.

In their frustration some organised gangs smashed the new weaving and spinning frames in the factories that had taken their jobs. The anonymous gang leaders penned death threats to the magistrates who tried to tackle the lawlessness signed with the nom-de-guerre 'King Lud' and the legend of the Luddites was born. Many were proud artisans whose skills were also lost to machines and new mass manufacture. While the landowning aristocrats remained the ruling elite at Westminster, the factory bosses and the merchants became the new 'aristocrats' of the Midlands and the North, with even less sympathy with the Luddites' demands than the old aristocrats. There was no police force, and the mill owners mobilised volunteer militias, backed by the law through local magistrates, to smash the mobs who had smashed their machines, or make them swing for their crimes on the gibbets.

Lord Byron – a month before he burst onto the literary world with his epic poem *Childe Harold's Pilgrimage* – was so troubled by the plight of some Nottinghamshire weavers who were facing the death penalty that he travelled down from his stately home at Newstead Abbey in Nottinghamshire to the House of Lords to denounce the government in his maiden speech:

These men were willing to dig, but the spade was in other hands; they were not ashamed to beg, but there was none to relieve them. Their own means of subsistence were cut off; all other employments pre-occupied; and their excesses, however to be deplored and condemned, can hardly be the subject of surprise.

The rural poor felt besieged. Not only were their cottage industries under attack from the mill owners, but their ancient rights to graze some sheep or a cow on the commons were taken away by Parliamentary Bills allowing local landowners to enclose their land. A total of 906 enclosure bills were introduced between 1800 and 1810 – nearly double the number in the previous decade. It was little more than legalised land theft, though it replaced the medieval farming system with modern production techniques. The cottage dwellers risked deportation to the colonies if they poached on the land.

The peasant-poet John Clare poured out his heart in his poetry about the loss of his childhood haunts in the flat lands of Northamptonshire:

These paths are stopt – the rude philistine's thrall
Is laid upon them and destroyed them all
Each little tyrant with his little sign
Shows where man claims earth glows no more divine
But paths to freedom and to childhood dear
A board sticks up to notice 'no road here'.

'The Mores', John Clare

Clare shared a two-up-two-down cottage in Helpston with his family of ten, including his father and mother. The cottage is now a museum. Ironically, he was sponsored by the Tory Marquess of Exeter and the Whig, Earl Fitzwilliam, who enclosed his country lanes.

In 1816, Byron was forced into exile because of rumours spread by his ex-lover, Lady Caroline Lamb, Lady Melbourne's daughter-in-law, of his sodomy – then a crime punishable by death. He embarked on a journey to see the Alps, Mont Blanc in Chamonix, and Lake Geneva and visited the battlefield at Waterloo. In a letter from Karlsruhe on 16 May 1816, Byron told his old friend, John Cam Hobhouse, that while a coach wheel was being repaired in Brussels, he:

of course seized the opportunity to visit Mont Saint Jean where I had a gallop over the field on a Cossack horse left by some of the Don gentlemen at Brussels and after a tolerably minute investigation returned by Soignies having purchased a quantity of helmets sabres and all of which are consigned to the care of a Mr Gordon at Brussels (an old acquaintance) who desired to forward them to Mr Murray – in whose keeping I hope to find them safe some day or other …

The helmets and sabres went to Newstead but smaller souvenirs are still held by his publisher, John Murray, in their offices at 50 Albermarle Street, London. Virginia Murray showed me Byron's Waterloo souvenirs. They are wrapped in tissue paper in boxes and include a large ball of canister shot stained red, perhaps by blood, an eagle badge of the 55th, and a couple of leather Napoleonic cockades that had the same shock effect in Regency London as a Nazi swastika still has now. Byron was disappointed to find the fields at Waterloo already under the plough, but was even more disparaging about the battle. He wrote to John Murray saying he had rode across the battlefield with 'pain and pleasure'. 'The Plain at Waterloo is a fine one – but not much after Marathon and Troy – Cheronea and Platea – Perhaps there is something of prejudice in this but – but I detest the cause and the victors – and the victory – including Blücher and the Bourbons.' Byron compared Waterloo unfavourably to the Battle of Marathon in Ancient Greece:

> And Harold stands upon this place of skulls,
> The grave of France, the deadly Waterloo;
> How in an hour the power which gave annuls
> Its gifts, transferring fame as fleeting too!
> In 'pride of place' here last the eagle flew,
> Then tore with bloody talon the rent plain,
> Pierced by the shaft of banded nations through;
> Ambition's life and labours all were vain;
> He wears the shatter'd links of the world's broken chain

More down to earth, Frances, Lady Shelley, on her own tour to Waterloo and Mont Blanc, noted in her diary on 20 July 1816 that Byron was already engaged in another affair: 'Lord Byron is living near here with Percy Shelley or rather with his wife's sister as the *chronique scandalous* says.' She was referring to Claire Clairmont, a starry-eyed 17-year-old who had had an affair with Byron in London and had pursued him to Geneva, where he had taken the handsome Villa Diodati overlooking the lake with his friend and physician John William Polidori. Claire had followed Byron to Lake Geneva with Percy Bysshe Shelley and Shelley's muse, Mary Wollstonecraft Godwin, Claire's step-sister, who stayed at the nearby Maison Chapuis. The weather was atrocious – the lake and the hills echoed to the boom of some spectacular storms of thunder and lightning in the summer of 1816, possibly caused by the after-effects of the Tambora volcano. They were forced to shelter indoors, and passed the time making up ghost stories that would make Mary Wollstonecraft Godwin famous as Mary Shelley. Mary was the daughter of the feminist writer Mary Wollstonecraft and William Godwin, a radical writer and supporter of the Enlightenment. Mary Wollstonecraft had been intoxicated with the Revolution; she had written a feminist response to Burke called *The Rights of Men* (1790) followed by *A Vindication of the Rights of Women* (1792) and arrived in Paris a month before Louis XVI was guillotined.

Villa Diodati is still there today, largely as it was when Byron and the Shelleys were there, though Cologny is a rich and exclusive suburb for the bankers and jewellers who still cluster in the Swiss city. The villa is elevated on a steep grassy hill with airy views over the lake, the marina with its towering fountain and the Jura mountains beyond.

When I visited the villa, a crowd had gathered nearby to watch a couple of vintage biplanes marking the 100th anniversary of the First World War with a dog-fight over the lake. Byron and his friends had a similar grandstand view for the spectacular thunderstorms that inspired Mary Shelley to write *Frankenstein or The Modern Prometheus*:

> A flash of lightning illuminated the object, and discovered its shape plainly to me; its gigantic stature, and the deformity of its aspect more hideous than belongs to humanity, instantly informed me that it was the wretch, the filthy daemon, to whom I had given life.

Mary Shelley's original manuscript in the Bodleian library in Oxford contains Percy Shelley's hand-written annotations in the margins and his personal revolutionary manifesto for Britain:

> The republican institutions of our country (Switzerland) have produced simpler and happier manners than those which prevail in the great monarchies that surround it. Hence there is less distinction between the several classes of its inhabitants; and the lower orders, being neither so poor nor so despised, their manners are more refined and moral. A servant in Geneva does not mean the same thing as a servant in France and England ...

These were views that would strike a chord with the Radicals at home: the monster would soon be on the loose in Britain, and the real storm was about to break.

Notes

1. W.H. Fitchett, *Wellington's Men – Rifleman Harris*, 1900.

10

THE FORGOTTEN HERO
AT PETERLOO

Shortly after 8 a.m. on a warm summer's day in 1819, John Lees stepped out of his family's house in West Street in the centre of Oldham and walked the 100yds to the cotton mill, where he worked as a 'rover' loading yarn onto the cotton bobbins. It was a normal working day for John, who was now a month off his 23rd birthday and had settled down in the town with a job and a girlfriend. But after half an hour he quit the spinning machines, put on his brown coat and hat and left the factory. He was going off to join the thousands walking that day to St Peter's Field in Manchester for an open-air rally. It would end in his death.

John Lees was one of the 'Waterloo Men' – the forgotten heroes – who had served under Wellington. He had joined at 14 or 15 years of age in 1812 as a Royal Artillery Driver. Today, the role he played in the battle is not just forgotten – he is invisible; he does not appear in any of the memoirs, letters or journals concerning the battle. Like tens of thousands of other common soldiers who were there, it is as if he never existed, except for one thing – the list of soldiers who were awarded the Waterloo Medal. I found the name of John Lees listed as number 224 in the *Waterloo Roll Call*, among those in Bull's I troop receiving the Waterloo Medal, and it is possible to piece together where he was on the battlefield as a result of his place on the Muster Roll, which I obtained from the National Archives.

In fine flowing handwriting, it shows he enlisted in Manchester on 23 September as a Royal Artillery Driver. His age is given as 14 (although his birthdate suggests he was 15) and his trade is listed as 'cotton spinner'. He was posted to Major Robert Bull's Royal Horse Artillery I Troop on 1 January 1813 as a driver in time to join it at the end of the Peninsular campaign. It lists his

Memorial plaque to the dead and injured at the Peterloo Massacre on the front of the Radisson Hotel, Peter Street, Manchester. (Author)

height as 5ft 4¼in, his complexion as 'fresh', eyes grey and hair brown. He would have been with Major Robert Bull's troop of 5½-inch howitzers on the slope above Hougoumont when Wellington asked Bull to carry out the delicate task of shelling Jérôme's infantry over the heads of the defending force of Nassauers and Coldstream Guards as the French advanced through the wood. Lees had to keep the guns supplied with powder, shot and shells from a makeshift ammunition depot, riding his wagon behind the lines and back to the guns in the heat of the battle, until the howitzers overheated and could fire no more.

Bull's gunners had been overrun by French cavalry and had to retreat into one of the hollow squares until they could return to their guns. They had to pull out at about 5 p.m., before the fall of La Haye Sainte and the final assault on Wellington's ridge by the Imperial Guard, but they had been in the thick of the action.

John must have come back like a stranger to his family, with some terrible tales of Waterloo. The battle was a long way behind him that Monday morning, 16 August. He did not tell his father Robert Lees where he was going; John knew his father would be against it because his father owned the mill where he worked.

The rally was to make a call for new northern cities such as Manchester to have the right to elect their own MP, but the reason why thousands of mill workers from all over the Oldham area were marching to Manchester was they wanted better pay and conditions in the mills – such as a ten-hour day and an end to child labour. The cotton workers flocking to the meeting wanted their own Member of Parliament to give them a voice at Westminster and represent their demands for relief against the grinding poverty in the Lancashire cotton mills – and that put John Lees at odds with the mill masters, like his father Robert.

The case for electoral reform was clear. The population of Manchester soared in the ten years to 1821 from 409,464 to 526,230 but Manchester had no Member of Parliament for the city, while depopulated medieval villages like Old Sarum on Salisbury Plain had two MPs, including Sir Nicholas Vansittart, the Chancellor of the Exchequer.*

Despite its rapid growth into the biggest cotton town in the world, Manchester was run under a system that had not changed since it was a medieval parish with a court leet, a baronial court and a borough reeve (the chief municipal officer) with parish beadles to keep order. But the Tory grandees such as the Duke of Wellington stoically resisted the demands for change that were being made at gatherings like the one in Manchester that day, because they feared that if they relaxed their grip on power, they would be risking a revolution in England.

Robert Lees was one of the new mill masters of Oldham, who ruled their mills with iron discipline. By going to the rally, John knew he was defying his father. That is why John Lees did not tell his father where he was going. Robert Lees had established the mill on 'The Bent', a road close to the town centre, running into West Street, which adjoined the old market place. The Lees house was just over the road from the mill in West Street, Oldham, where the mill master could watch over it. He had to be vigilant because frame breakers were ready to burn down mills if they could. John lived at the house in West Street with his father, his step-mother, Hannah, her son Thomas Whitaker by an earlier marriage, and three children Robert and Hannah had together – Sarah, James and Benjamin Lees.

Public notices signed by the great orator Henry Hunt had gone up in Oldham and other towns in that part of Lancashire, urging the people to come and hear Hunt speak at the rally. St Peter's Field was not part of the countryside; it was an open space used for such meetings and enclosed on all sides by buildings of the city, including a row of houses at one end and the Quaker Friends Meeting House at the other. Two years earlier, St Peter's Field had been the scene for a huge gathering before a march to London by textile workers, mainly spinners and weavers, carrying blankets over their shoulders to sleep on at night – the 'Blanketeers' meeting was broken up by the King's Dragoon Guards.

---

*   Vansittart was one of the two MPs for the 'rotten borough' from 1802 to 1807. It continued to return two MPs until 1831, although it only had eleven voters.

The magistrates were determined not to allow the troublemakers to gather again. A meeting planned for 9 August had been banned by the magistrates, who were worried about it sparking civil unrest. The Home Secretary, Lord Sidmouth, clearly saw the political danger. He got one of his officials to write on 4 August on Sidmouth's behalf urging the magistrates not to break up the meeting planned for 9 August with violence: 'Reflexion convinces him that more strongly of the inexpediency of attempting forcibly to prevent the meeting on Monday,' he said. Now that meeting had been banned, Sidmouth and the authorities appeared to relax, even after it was announced by Hunt that it was being rescheduled for 16 June. Hunt knew he was taking a risk by calling the meeting a week later in the open space by St Peter's church off Deansgate in Manchester, and he knew the magistrates would be looking for another excuse to break up the meeting.

In the posters, Hunt referred to the authorities' 'victory' with their ban on the earlier meeting:

Fellow Countrymen: our enemies are exulted at the victory they profess to have attained over us.

You will meet on Monday next my friends and by your *steady, firm and temperate* deportment you will convince all your enemies you feel that you have an *important* and an *imperious public duty* to perform and that you will not suffer any private consideration on earth to deter you from exerting every nerve to carry your praiseworthy and patriotic intention into effect. The eyes of all England, nay, of all Europe are fixed upon you …

The italics were his own. His stress on the need for 'steady, firm and temperate deportment' was a warning not to give the magistrates any excuse to resort to violence and for the meeting to turn into a riot as it had at Spa Fields in Clerkenwell, London,* in December 1816.

Hunt, 43, was an unlikely revolutionary. He was a prosperous Wiltshire farmer, who was perhaps the greatest radical speaker of the age – the Tony Benn of the Regency period. He was a colourful 'John Bull' figure who liked to box and wore a trademark white top-hat, but, like Benn, he was a democrat. He was dedicated to the cause of universal men's suffrage and had been touring around the country, drawing huge audiences for his speeches – 80,000 in Birmingham, 40,000 in Blackburn, 20,000 in Nottingham and 10,000 in Macclesfield. Hunt was a moderate, not a revolutionary, but he warned the authorities of revolutionary violence if they did not listen to

---

*   It was around the corner from Gloucester Street where Francis Stiles, the man who claimed he had captured an eagle, went to live. Stiles could have been there. Spa Fields, Skinner Street, is now an urban playground.

their peaceful demands. Another agitator who was at a meeting addressed by Hunt at Spa Fields in Clerkenwell, London, on 2 December 1816 would prove him right.

Arthur Thistlewood, 46, was the illegitimate son of another prosperous farmer but, unlike Hunt, he was an unapologetic revolutionary. He had been to Paris in 1814 to learn about the revolution and was convinced that only bloody revolution and the overthrow of the English ruling elite could bring about change in Britain. He was a member of a group known as the Society of Spencean Philanthropists, followers of Thomas Spence, who believed in equal rights through common ownership of land. Spence had died in 1814 but his followers kept his ideas alive in small cells meeting in pubs. At the first of two meetings at Spa Fields, Hunt had got the support of a crowd of 10,000 to go to the Prince Regent with a petition for reform, but it was rejected out of hand without a meeting with the Prince Regent. Hunt was on his way to a second meeting at Spa Fields when he was told it was too late – the revolution had already started. Thistlewood used the anger of the crowd to launch a naïve plan for the overthrow of the government. Someone was stabbed to death and sailors who had been laid off after the Napoleonic Wars helped the mob to break into a gun shop at Snow Hill to seize weapons. The mob marched with a tricolour to the Royal Exchange to take control of the Bank of England and Thistlewood, showing a childlike conviction that the army was ready to revolt, led another armed mob to the Tower of London. He climbed a wall and called on the soldiers there to surrender the Tower and support the revolution. They did not fire on him but they refused to join Thistlewood's revolution. The rioting was serious – there were pitched battles in Snow Hill and the Minories, an ancient quarter near the Tower, was held for hours by the mob – but the ringleaders were soon disarmed and rounded up. The revolution was put down before it began and Thistlewood, who had tickets to sail to America, was caught trying to board a ship at Gravesend.

Thistlewood did not know that his group had been infiltrated by a group of police spies, including a police agent called John Castle, on the orders of John Stafford, a resourceful spymaster for the police at Bow Street. Stafford ran undercover intelligence agents in a clandestine force that was a forerunner of the Metropolitan Police Special Branch and MI5. Thistlewood and his gang were tried for treason, but despite the damning evidence the jury, possibly sharing sympathy for the defendants, refused to convict them after it heard that the key prosecution witness, Castle, was a criminal and an agent provocateur who had incited the plot – he was a former forger who had once turned evidence against an accomplice who was hanged. Thistlewood and the others were freed. Thistlewood did not learn the lesson from the Spa Fields trial but Stafford did. He would not make the same mistake again.

An investigation was carried out by a secret Parliamentary committee into 'the disturbed state of the country', which was convinced there was a movement seeking to overthrow the government:

Attempts have been made, in various parts of the country, as well as in the metropolis, to take advantage of the distress in which the labouring and manufacturing classes of the community are at present involved, to induce them to look for immediate relief, not only in a reform of Parliament on the plan of universal suffrage and annual election, but in a total overthrow of all existing establishments, and in a division of the landed, and extinction of the funded property of the country.

Lord Sidmouth, the Home Secretary, suspended the ancient right of habeas corpus protecting citizens from unlawful and secret detention. He also introduced the Treason Act 1817 to ensure existing powers remained in force after the death of King George III. The Act made it high treason to imagine, invent, devise or intend the 'death or destruction, or any bodily harm tending to death or destruction, maim or wounding, imprisonment or restraint of the persons of the heirs and successors of George III', starting with the despised Prince Regent. Sidmouth told Parliament there was 'a traitorous conspiracy ... for the purpose of overthrowing ... the established government' and referred to 'a malignant spirit which had brought such disgrace upon the domestic character of the people' and 'had long prevailed in the country, but especially since the commencement of the French Revolution'.

The renewed threat of revolution coincided with an event that further undermined the monarchy – the death of the Prince Regent's daughter Charlotte, during childbirth in November 1817, which caused a national spasm of grief similar to that after the death of Diana, the Princess of Wales, in a car crash in an underpass in Paris on August 1997. The Duke of Wellington was characteristically unmoved: 'The death of Princess Charlotte was probably by no means a misfortune to the nation. I fear she would not have turned out well.'[1]

The poet Shelley was indignant that the country had gone into national mourning for a dead princess but shed no tears for three agitators for reform – Jeremiah Brandreth, a jobless stocking maker from Nottingham, William Turner and Isaac Ludlam, who had just been executed for high treason. These men had carried out a cack-handed uprising in Pentrich, Derbyshire. They were set up by William Oliver, one of the Home Office's paid informants who acted as agent provocateur, and their leader, Francis Bacon, a framework knitter with revolutionary tendencies, was complicit in their prosecution. Bacon got off with transportation to the colonies. His three followers were sentenced to be hanged, drawn and quartered for treason at Nuns Green in front of Friar Gate jail, Derby, shortly after Princess Charlotte's death. The Prince Regent intervened to have their sentence commuted – they were hanged and beheaded but not quartered. That was clemency in Regency England. Shelley wrote: 'Spare no symbol of universal grief. Weep–mourn–lament. Fill the great City – fill the boundless fields, with lamentation and the echo of groans. A beautiful Princess is dead ... But man has murdered Liberty.'[2]

Against that background, with the people and Parliament polarised, it was almost certain that as John Lees set out that morning, the meeting at St Peter's Field would end in violence.

The Manchester magistrates, Hunt warned, were ready to 'put us down by the force of the sword, bayonet and cannon'. Hunt's words were more prophetic than even he realised.

After leaving his father's mill, John Lees joined a gathering of several thousand marchers gathered at Bent Green, near the factory, where they were addressed by Sam Bamford, a grammar-school-educated radical and silk weaver from nearby Middleton. Bamford was another agitator who had been imprisoned in 1817 on charges of high treason for his political activities but had been released after serving a jail sentence. He had marched over from his home town in Rochdale through woods and dingles with thousands of followers with military precision. 'First we selected twelve of the most comely and decent-looking youths, who were placed in two rows of six each, with each a branch of laurel held in his hand, as a token of amity and peace,' said Bamford:

> Then followed the men of several districts in fives; then the band of music
> – an excellent one; then the colours: a blue one of silk with inscriptions in
> golden letters, 'Unity and Strength', 'Liberty and Fraternity', a green one
> of silk with golden letters 'Parliaments Annual', 'Suffrage Universal', and
> betwixt them, on a staff, a handsome cap of crimson velvet with a tuft of
> laurel, and the cap tastefully braided with the words 'Libertas' in front. Next
> were placed the remainder of the men in districts of five. Every hundred
> men had a leader, who was distinguished by a spring of laurel in his hat ...

The military discipline of the marchers was used as a pretext by the magistrates to prove these laurel-carrying radicals were actually a people's army. The military order of the marchers was also used by Lord Liverpool in a Parliamentary debate in 1819 to reject demands by Lord Grey for a public inquiry.

Bamford reminded the men and women who had been gathering since first light not to carry any weapons other than their 'self-approving conscience'. Then a brass band struck up a stirring march, the banners flashed in the sunlight and they moved off to Manchester.

Oldham is 700ft above sea level and John Lees would have been able to see the distant smoke from Manchester almost from the moment he left his father's mill. He walked over the cobbles along Manchester Street and took the dusty road out of Oldham heading west. Today the mills in the centre of Oldham have been swept away to make way for the redevelopment of the town. There is a red-brick shopping centre like a fortress in the centre. The only obvious sign of Oldham's industrial past as a great cotton manufacturing capital is its name: the Spindles.

The houses in West Street where the Lees family lived were cleared to make way for a concrete tower block housing the civic centre. Over the road, roughly where the Robert Lees's mill must have been, is a £2.9m state-of-the-art bus station with an elliptical steel roof that, at night, looks like a starship has landed in the middle of Oldham. Bent Green, a regular meeting place for reformers, was roughly where the road curls round a grassy roundabout with a clump of trees. A town map of the period shows the Bent running into West Street and then the Market Place (now the Spindles shopping centre). There are fields reaching up to Bent Grange and the procession with Bamford at its head would soon have entered countryside along Manchester Street, where the Oldham Way dual carriageway is today.

Oldham had been transformed in a couple of generations from a small wool-weaving village overshadowed by Saddleworth Moor on the edge of the Pennines into one of the cotton capitals of the world. Lees was a common name: the first Oldham cotton mill was opened in 1778 in the district called Lees and by 1819 there were nineteen cotton mills in the town. A few men with enterprise in Oldham like Robert Lees had seen the profits to be made by replacing the inefficient old cottage looms with new mills employing hundreds of men, women and children on their spinning machines. The town's population soared in a century from 12,000 in 1801 to 137,000 in 1901 and more than half of its people in the first half of the century worked on the spinning machines in the big mills. Children were employed fetching the bobbins and picking up rough cotton cast-offs from the floor between the machines as they clattered relentlessly backwards and forwards. It was hard, noisy and dangerous – the suffragette Annie Kenney, who was a cotton worker in Oldham half a century later, had a finger ripped off by a spinning bobbin. Times were also very hard. In 1815, while John Lees was driving his wagon with Bull's troop to Waterloo, the cotton spinners of Oldham went on strike against the attempts of the mill owners to cut their wages. William Rowbottom noted in his diary on 5 June 1815:

> The spinners at most of the factories are now out of employ having refused
> to work at a reduced price. The present price is 2*d* 3 farthings per score for
> 24 hanks and 3*d* per score for finer sorts. The Masters insist on a reduction

of one farthing per score and the spinners refused to comply. And about the middle of July they mostly returned to their employ having subdued their masters by compelling them to give the usual wages.

John Lees was discharged and returned home to Oldham at Christmas, 1818. His father took him in and he was fortunate to be given a job in his mill as a rover, loading cotton yarn onto bobbins and giving the yarn a twist (roving) after the textile had been carded on Arkwright frames to straighten the fibres for spinning and combed. It was deafening, repetitive work, but it was a living. John had to share the same bedroom as Thomas Whitaker, his step-mother's son. They got on and went out drinking together.

Why John, the son of a mill owner, should have turned his back on Oldham and taken the long road to Waterloo with Major Robert Bull's troop will remain a mystery. It could have been the prospect of excitement that drove him to join the army, but he may also have been running away from life in Oldham, for John Lees was born out of wedlock and rebelled against his father. The register of the Oldham St Mary Parish church shows that he was born on 16 September 1796* to Dinah Clough, a spinster at the time of her son's birth, from nearby Lowermoor, Oldham. Robert Lees allowed his name to go on the register as his father, but they were not married. Robert later married Hannah Whitaker who already had a son, Thomas. It is not known what happened to Dinah, John's mother.

The Masters of the Mills like Robert Lees saw Hunt as the enemy. Eleven days before the meeting, an anonymous open letter to Mr Henry Hunt circulated around Oldham. It was a bitter attack on his policies and his personality:

> Infamy seems to accompany your steps as a shadow … Everything which you touch is contaminated and polluted, every cause which you espouse becomes dishonoured and defiled.

The mill masters hated the agitators and there had been a long history of social unrest in Oldham, a Radical town. In the eyes of the mill owners, the crowds converging on Manchester to hear Henry Hunt were dangerous associates of the frame breakers, the followers of Ned Ludd who had tried to wreck their businesses by destroying their mills.

Oldham, like Manchester, was renowned for its high rainfall as the clouds from the Atlantic dump their moisture when they hit the Pennines and the damp air was ideal for cotton spinning because it avoided the threads from breaking. But on that August morning, it was warm and sunny, and there was

---

★   This would have made him 15 when he joined, not 14, as it says on the Muster Roll.

a feeling of optimism in the air. John, dressed in a dark-brown jacket, trousers, a waistcoat, shirt and a hat, was carrying a walking stick for the journey. Perhaps the stick was a clue that he expected trouble. Many were carrying them, although there is no evidence they were used as clubs. The marchers were blissfully unaware as they set off that the magistrates of Manchester were assembling a real army of 1,500 troops with three troops of cavalry and two 6-pounder cannon to preserve the peace.

They were under the overall command of Sir John Byng, who had commanded the guards at Waterloo. After Waterloo, Byng had been put in charge of the military forces for the whole of the north of England. He had his headquarters in Pontefract and would have been at the meeting on 9 August, but he had another pressing engagement on the 16th – he had two horses running in the races at York. He left the Manchester meeting in the capable hands of the commander of the local Manchester District, Lieutenant Colonel Guy L'Estrange, commander of the 15th Dragoons.

The magistrates met at 9 a.m. at the Star Inn on Deansgate near the field where the rally was to be held. At 10.30 a.m. they moved to the house of a prominent Manchester builder to observe events at the meeting place. Edward Buxton's house at 6 Mount Street overlooked St Peter's Field and was about 100yds from where the organisers were putting up the hustings in the form of two flat-bed carts lashed together.

Oldham sent the largest contingent of 10,000 people to the rally and John must have felt the easy comradeship of his fellow cotton workers as they strolled along the dusty main road through the countryside to Manchester to hear Henry Hunt. There was an almost carnival atmosphere, as the procession, with bands playing and banners waving, passed the Werneth Mill and Werneth Hall, the Old Lane Colliery at Little Town and Hollinwood, where the houses spread along the sides of the Oldham road (now the A62) to Newton where the road ran alongside the Rochdale Canal. They met up with spinners from Leeds at Miles Platting, where the outskirts of the town began, and headed for Deansgate. Marchers from Lees, Mosley, Royton and Saddleworth came into the field linking arms, two, three, four and five friends abreast.

The marchers from Oldham arrived around midday and John Lees made for the hustings at Windmill Street. An estimated 5,000 marchers had already arrived from Stockport and more filled the open space as the hour went by. As the crowd steadily grew to around 60,000 – nearly the same as an average Premier League crowd at Old Trafford to watch Manchester United – the chairman and nine magistrates meeting in Buxton's house across the field from the hustings became more nervous.

The magistrates had assembled 600 cavalry from the 15th Hussars, 420 members of the Cheshire Yeomanry Cavalry, with another forty volunteers of the Manchester Yeomanry Cavalry, a troop of the Royal Artillery with two 6-pounders, and 160 soldiers of the 88th Foot, who were ordered to stand with fixed bayonets to block an exit route from the square. The Manchester Yeomanry were mostly mill masters with an axe to grind against the protesting workers and the Radicals. They were essentially amateurs dressed in blue military uniforms.

Lees was not the only veteran of Waterloo at St Peter's Field that day. Some of the men of 15th Hussars had fought at Waterloo. They had been part of the Fifth Brigade of light cavalry under Major General Sir Colquhoun Grant and had been cut up when they failed to break a hollow square of French infantry. Lieutenant Colonel Leighton Dalrymple, the Commander of the 15th Hussars at Waterloo, had been wounded. One of the Hussars' officers, Lieutenant Harry Lane, remarked: 'We did not succeed in breaking it, and, of course, suffered most severely.' Defenceless protesters were easier meat. The 15th Hussars appeared on the streets of Manchester in blue tunics, scarlet facings, and silver lace, and had their swords sharpened, their usual practice before going into action. There was another force that would play an important role that day, the special constables known as Nadin's Runners. Like the Yeomanry, they were drawn from local businessmen, including pub landlords, who were prepared for a fight. Joseph Nadin was a notorious thug who ran the local constabulary before the creation of the official police force. He was 6ft 1in tall, broad-shouldered and a former spinner, who had become a 'thief taker' for the financial rewards and established a corrupt regime of law enforcement backed by brutality. Nadin, the deputy chief of the local police, made sure his men were out in strength.

St Peter's Field was a triangle of ground, bounded by houses in Peter Street, Mount Street and Windmill Street. It is now occupied by the Radisson Hotel, formerly the Free Trade Hall.

I am standing by a taxi rank in Windmill Street at the back of the Radisson Hotel. This is roughly where Hunt stood on the makeshift stage with the two carts lashed together. Across the road, trendy coffee bars have opened where his barouche stopped and the banners were raised. Office workers sit sipping cappuccino at a street cafe, not knowing that it was here among their tables and chairs that an atrocity took place. Over to my right, Buxton's house stood at No. 6 Mount Street, which has been replaced by the corner of The Midland hotel, built at the turn of the nineteenth century for the Midland railway station. Nadin's special constables formed two lines, creating a channel from Buxton's house almost to the right-hand side of the speakers' stage, so that when the time came they could arrest Hunt with ease.

The magistrates watched from the windows to the side of the platform as Hunt's open barouche arrived shortly after a clock struck 1 p.m. It carried Hunt in his distinctive white top hat, John Saxton, the editor of the radical

Manchester Observer, which had invited Hunt to speak at the rally, and several of his fellow speakers including John Knight, who had helped found the *Observer*, Joseph Johnson and Richard Carlile, a publisher of reformist tracts in London. The ladies of the Manchester Female Reform Society, dressed all in white, were to lead the carriage onto the field but owing to the density of the crowds, this proved impractical and the women in white had to follow behind. Their leader Mrs Mary Fildes had been lifted into the carriage to sit alongside Hunt, holding the Female Reformers' colours aloft. The banners at the hustings included 'No Corn Bill', 'Hunt and Liberty' and 'Equal Representation or Death'. The band struck up 'See the Conquering Hero Comes' with a roar from the crowd, and the carriage slowly moved forward with Hunt, his fellow speakers and Mrs Fildes dressed all in white with a straw bonnet. William Harrison, a cotton spinner from Oldham, thought she was the 'most beautiful woman I ever saw in my life'. Before Hunt spoke, the band solemnly played 'God Save the King' to show their loyalty to the Crown but the magistrates had already decided to act.

The magistrates' excuse for deploying such a large force was the interception of a letter by Joe Johnson, a journalist on the *Manchester Observer* and member of the radical Manchester Patriotic Union. It was sent to Henry Hunt saying:

> Nothing but ruin and starvation stare one in the face … the state of this
> district is truly dreadful and I believe nothing but the greatest exertions can
> prevent an insurrection. Oh that you in London were prepared for it.

The word 'insurrection' was enough to give them nightmares.

The Riot Act was read by Reverend Charles Ethelston from Mr Buxton's window, though no one down at the hustings said they heard it. This ordered the crowd to disperse and gave authority to the Yeomanry Cavalry, supported by the Hussars, to act.

Hunt had been speaking for a few minutes, when at 1.30 p.m. the magistrates formally ordered the arrest of Hunt, Knight, Johnson and another speaker called John Moorhouse. Nadin told his Chief Constable, Jonathan Andrews, that despite the double guard of his special constables reaching almost to the hustings, he could not arrest Hunt and the others without military support. When Andrews relayed this to William Hulton, chairman of the magistrates, Hulton replied: 'Then you shall have the military force. For God's sake don't sacrifice the lives of the special constables.' Hulton sent two notes, one to Major Thomas Trafford in charge of the MYC and the other to Lieutenant Colonel L'Estrange commanding the Hussars, who were also waiting in the streets away from the crowd, telling them to proceed immediately to Buxton's house where the magistrates were gathered. He added: 'They consider the Civil Power wholly inadequate to preserve the peace.'

Down at the hustings, Hunt was reinforcing his message to remain peaceful, telling the crowd if any person 'made tumult or attempted disturbance' they should put him down and keep him down and not allow him to rise until the meeting was over. But before he had chance to say more, the Manchester Yeomanry Cavalry, who had been waiting around the corner, rode into the ground to try to arrest Hunt. They came into the square from near the Quaker Friends Meeting House and stood in front of the houses. They had been seen before the rally drinking in a nearby pub and one of them was so drunk he could hardly sit on his horse. He was clinging to it, said William Harrison, 'like a monkey'. Harrison, who described himself as 'real Lancashire blunt', said the cavalryman was 'fuddled'.

The Manchester Yeomanry Cavalry spread out, pushing the crowd back, but could make little headway to the stage. Hunt assumed the magistrates were trying to provoke a riot and shouted: 'Stand firm, my friends. They are in disorder already. This is a trick. Give them three cheers.' Even the magistrates thought the Yeomanry looked incapable of holding their horses steady. The crowd gave the Yeomanry Cavalry three hearty cheers. There are allegations that they threw stones at the volunteers on horseback but most say they remained peaceful because they thought they intended merely to arrest the speakers as many expected. However, the cheerful atmosphere of the crowd changed when the horsemen drew sabres and blades started flashing right and left.

The Yeomanry formed a circle with Nadin's Runners around the hustings, drew their swords and charged into the crowd. Women screamed. Men fended off the blows with their sticks or bare arms. To the magistrates, it looked as though the crowd had turned on the volunteers. The Reverend Edward Stanley, Rector of Alderley, who was in Buxton's house with the magistrates, said for a very few paces the movement of the Yeomanry was not rapid:

> There was some show of an attempt to follow their officer in regular succession, five or six abreast; but they soon increased their speed and with a zeal and ardour which might naturally be expected from men acting with delegated power against a foe by whom it is understood they had long been insulted with taunts of cowardice, continued their course, seeming individually to vie with each other which should be first.

Jonah Andrew, a cotton spinner from Leeds, said, 'They began to cut and hack at the people like butchers.'

Nadin followed behind the Yeomanry with his special constables and arrested Hunt, Johnson and John Tyas, a journalist from *The Times* of London.

Hunt jumped down from the platform and surrendered himself. Although they had got their man, the constables then attacked the colours and the banners around the speakers' platform as vigorously as if they were French eagles at Waterloo. Watching from Buxton's house, Hulton saw the melee around the Yeomanry and ordered L'Estrange to rescue the Manchester Yeomanry Cavalry from the mob. The 15th Hussars formed a line across the eastern end of St Peter's Field and charged into the crowd. Harrison was squeezed against the palisades near the houses. He said: 'The Yeomanry Cavalry began cutting all before them and on each side, and the people began shouting for mercy – they said, "Have mercy, O have mercy".'

John Lees climbed up on the planks of the makeshift stage as the crowd surged forward in panic to get away from the soldiers, but the Yeomanry and the Hussars pursued him. Martha Kearsley from Oldham saw two soldiers striking him and he was warding off their blows with his walking stick as well as he could and a cavalryman fell off his horse. Lees jumped off the hustings and Robert Cooper, a hatter from Oldham, saw one of the 15th Hussars cut him in the right elbow with his sword, as Lees held up his arm to protect his head. Jonah Andrew was close to Lees when the cavalry attacked him; they surrounded him and he saw a Yeoman Cavalryman cutting at him 'with great vengeance'. Andrew said he saw seven of Nadin's special constables round on John Lees, giving him a severe beating with their truncheons all over his back:

Windmill Street, Manchester – site of the Peterloo Massacre. The taxi rank is where John Lees was beaten. (Author)

One of them picked up a staff of a banner that had been cut with a sword and said, 'Damn your bloody eyes, I'll break your back'. And they struck at him for a considerable time with their truncheons and the staff of the banner.

The truncheons carried by Nadin's men were long wooden clubs, with the royal crest on the handle to show they were acting in the name of Prince Regent.

Joseph Wrigley, who met up with John Lees at Oldham on the morning of the meeting, saw him receive the cut on the back of his right arm from a sabre. 'He was parrying off the blows of one of the military and another came up and cut him. He had his right arm up over his head protecting it with a walking-stick.' Wrigley said he could not help Lees because 'everyone had to look to his own life' when the sabres flashed. Wrigley could not tell whether it was Yeomanry or the Hussars who slashed at Lees because they were mixed up.

The Hussars are generally said to have shown greater professional restraint than the volunteers of the Yeomanry, though they were far from blameless. Not all were seeking blood. 'There was an officer who gave me an opportunity of escaping or I should have been left for dead on the field,' said Wrigley. They were under orders to use the flat of their swords – a very difficult manoeuvre for a man holding the reins of his horse. It could explain how John Lees's clothes were slashed on the shoulder, but the skin on his shoulder was not cut.

Lees staggered out of Manchester with his left shoe split open by a cavalry horse that trampled over him. At 5 p.m. he was passing the windows of a pub, the Shears at Newton Heath, on the way back to Oldham when he was spotted by Robert Neald, who had known him for about seven or eight years. Neald called Lees inside: 'He showed me one wound on his right elbow and said he had another on his shoulder ... I thought it was a stab and I saw his shoe was rent.' John pointed out Joseph Wrigley, who said he had seen Lees being cut by the cavalry. John shook hands with Wrigley, who asked him to go to the Woolpack Inn but Lees refused, saying his arm was stiff and he wished to get home. When he got home his stepmother, Hannah Lees, met him at the gate. She was worried – she had been told by her son Thomas that John had been injured in the fracas at Manchester. She gave him some tea and toast and he went to bed. Thomas said:

He looked very pale. I discovered he was wounded. I went up stairs with him. He was very faint when he got to the top and I helped him off with his clothes. I undressed him and pulled his shirt off. He looked very ill and his shirt stuck to his body. He had a severe cut to his right elbow and the flesh was cut to the bone. I saw [it] and I washed it.[3]

John told Thomas the injury to his elbow was not the worst: 'He desired me to look at his shoes, how they were cut off by the horses. I found the left foot [shoe] cut off and the leather torn.'

The next day John went to the factory but was too ill to work. His father, Robert Lees, had little sympathy for his son. He was angry because he had gone to the meeting, and when he saw John standing at the top of the landing at the factory, he bluntly told him that if he could not work he would have to go to the parish for a hand-out because he would give him no money. Hannah Lees advised John to go to the doctor and he went to Mr Earnshaw, a Quaker, who acted as a family doctor, and prescribed him medicines three times a day, which Lees took. One of the odd aspects of his condition is that, despite his injuries, he went out drinking with his half-brother Thomas and his friends and borrowed a couple of shillings from Hannah to pay for the beer.

The following Sunday, 22 August, Thomas and John walked to Widow Wright's, a public house in Oldham, but they had nothing to drink there. At the King's Arms, John had a glass of brandy and water but would drink no more. A week later, on Sunday 29 August, they went to the Dusty Miller with a friend, where they each had a pint of beer at 4*d*, then another pint each at another pub, and later a quart of ale among the three of them at Westwood. John was tipsy but not drunk, said Thomas. John also managed to go with Thomas to Stockport, a distance of about 13 miles, where they spent the night. They left Stockport at six in the morning and stopped at four pubs on the way to Manchester, which they reached at 2 p.m. before they got a cart ride back to Oldham.

But in the third week after he was attacked, John's condition deteriorated and he was no longer able to get about by himself. On Monday, Tuesday and Wednesday of the third week, Thomas and his half-brother James carried John downstairs from his bed to give him company – he hated being left alone. But on Wednesday 1 September, John began retching, being sick and unable to keep his food down.

Thomas Whitaker said:

> As we lay in bed on the Wednesday night he said he had a terrible pain in his shoulders and he could not bear them to be touched. On the Thursday he complained of a pain in his left foot and could not rest at all and he lost the use of his limbs.

He took to his bed on Saturday night and on Sunday he could no longer speak. He also lost the sight in one eye and complained of being cold. He died in the early hours of Tuesday 7 September – twenty-two days after the rally. Two days later, on 9 September, his death was registered in Manchester.

I found entry number 2,350 in the Manchester Death Register. It simply says: 'John Lees of West Street, Age 22.'

John Lees's body was stripped and laid out by Betty Ireland, the wife of a shoemaker in Oldham. She was shocked. She had seen many dead bodies but she had never seen anything like this: there was hardly a place on his back that was not bruised, she said. It looked as though he had been tied to a halberd and flogged and his body was putrefied.

The police summoned a surgeon called John Cox, who carried out a rudimentary post mortem the day after John died. He noted that on the man's elbow there was a cut an inch and a half long, open about an inch at its widest part. The cut had 'taken the extreme point of the bone away – it was a little oblique as if it were done by a sword'. On his left side there was a bruised space as large as his hand over the short ribs. There was a bruise as large as a man's extended hand on the right side of the back, two marks over the hips, which were ulcerous, but he could not find a stab wound on the shoulder. The skin was inflamed and livid all around his neck but there appeared to be no injury to Lees' head. When he moved the body 'much blood gushed from the mouth and nostrils'. After he opened the body, he found the larynx or windpipe and the right lobe of the lungs full of blood.[4]

John Lees was listed among eleven dead in the official report on the massacre as being 'sabred' – suggesting that this veteran of Waterloo had been killed by the men with whom he fought alongside at the battle. The other ten listed in the official report as killed were: John Ashton of Cowhill, Oldham, 'sabred'; John Ashworth, a special constable, of the Bull's Head, Manchester, 'sabred and trampled on'; Thomas Buckley of Baretrees, Chadderton, 'sabred and stabbed'; William Dawson, of Saddleworth, 'sabred and crushed – killed on the spot'; an infant called Fildes of Kennedy Street, Manchester, 'rode over by cavalry'; Arthur O'Neil, No. 3 Pigeon Street, Manchester, 'inwardly crushed'; Martha Partington of Eccles 'thrown into a cellar'; Joseph Whitworth of Hyde, 'shot'; James Crompton of Barton, 'trampled on by the cavalry'; Mary Heys of 8 Rawlinson's Buildings, Oxford Road, Manchester, 'rode over by cavalry'.

The lists of dead and injured graphically illustrate the brutality meted out to the protestors, but all the evidence at the inquest on John Lees suggests that in his case the official report is wrong – John Lees was not killed by a sabre blow either by the Yeoman Cavalry of Manchester or the Hussars.[5] Cox was hesitant about giving a cause of death because he was clearly reluctant to give testimony that would allow a charge of murder to be brought against the cavalry or the police, or the magistrates who ordered them to disperse the crowd; but he was quite clear about one thing – John Lees did not die from a sabre cut. 'The immediate cause [of death] was the suffusion of blood into the lungs,' said Cox. He believed it had been caused by the rupture of a blood vessel. Cox said he carefully put his hand all over Lees' head and saw no injury done to it, but he did not look at the brain, so his evidence does not rule out brain damage.

I asked Dr Julian Burton, clinical lecturer in histopathology at the University of Sheffield, to look at the post mortem evidence from Cox, the police surgeon, to see what a modern pathologist might find. Professor Burton told me that the history of vomiting, loss of sight and loss of the use of his limbs suggests John Lees may have suffered a significant head injury. He was certainly sabred – possibly by his former comrades at Waterloo – but the mortal blows are more likely to have been delivered by Nadin's Runners, who beat him around the head, neck and back. According to Dr Burton:

> This could result in bleeding in, or more likely around, the brain. Such bleeding can occur slowly and it can start, stop and then start again. A bleed inside the cranial cavity would cause vomiting and may account for the loss of sight and the use of limbs, though both together is unusual and hard to reconcile. Raised intracranial pressure can cause inflammation and ulceration of the stomach and can cause vomiting. Recurrent vomiting can cause tears in the lining of the gut at the junction of the gullet and stomach and these can bleed profusely.

This is new evidence and, though speculative, it could explain how John Lees could go on a bender around the pubs of Stockport and Manchester with his half-brother and yet die of his injuries three weeks after he was attacked. Dr Burton believes John Lees almost certainly died from bleeding caused by a stomach ulcer, brought on by a beating that caused a brain injury. And that was almost certainly caused by the pounding he was given by Nadin's Runners. These findings were supported by Paul Johnson, consultant forensic pathologist and Home Office pathologist at the Royal Liverpool University Hospital, who told me:

> A slowly progressive intracranial bleed or re-bleeding into a bleed resulting from the blunt assault could cause subsequent deterioration from raised intracranial pressure in this time frame. However, this is longer than one would usually expect without underlying factors, such as the victim being elderly or alcoholic (with associated clotting abnormalities) …

Dr Johnson suggested another possibility: John Lees was so badly beaten he suffered a broken spine, with possible infection leading to septicaemia (blood poisoning):

I think the possibility that John Lees could have suffered an unstable fracture to his upper posterior neck during the beating should be considered. This would allow for a prolonged period of normal function and then for rapid deterioration if the fractured vertebra moved and caused compression of the spinal cord in the upper neck, which would adequately explain the severe shoulder pain, pain in the leg and loss of all limb function. The compression could also be caused by further bleeding or abscess development at the fracture site.

I also think that sepsis provides a good alternative explanation for his general deterioration, including vomiting, progressive weakness and his death. Since the head, and therefore the deep posterior neck, were not apparently examined during the autopsy, then in addition to a potential neck and/or head injury being missed, a deep source of infection either around the vertebral fracture (or skull fracture – with meningitis) would not be found either ...

The description of reddening and inflammation around the neck could represent spreading infection in the skin and soft tissue – potentially spreading from infection in or around the putative neck fracture site ... Given that the surgeon looked in the wound and described the appearance of the fracture but not any infection, it is unlikely that the sabre injury contributed to the delayed death. This makes it likely, on the available evidence, that the blunt force assault described to the back of John Lees was the central factor.

In all, at least 15 people were killed and 650 were injured in twenty minutes.[*] Over 200 suffered sabre wounds, including 31 women. They included Margaret Downes, who bled to death from a sabre-slash to the breast, and Elizabeth Farren, who was slashed by a sabre twice over the head and almost had her wrist severed defending herself from the blows. Perhaps most shocking of all, they included a mother and child. Ann Fildes (no relation to Mary who carried the flag in Hunt's barouche) was carrying her baby when she was knocked down by a horse ridden by a sergeant major riding after the Yeomanry; the child was thrown out of her arms onto the ground and died at about 10 p.m.

Hunt wrote to Sidmouth to protest his innocence from his cell at the New Bailey prison on 19 August, saying, 'I saw one man with his nose cut off ...' A drill book in use by the Hussars showed how to carry out six cuts across the face, slashing across the nose diagonally and horizontally.

---

[*]   Estimates of the injured vary from 400 (the official figure) to 800 – eight casualty lists were drawn up and some included two men shot in a separate incident at night and a constable killed by a mob in revenge.

Research of the casualty lists shows that, as a proportion of the crowd, women were more likely to be attacked by the Yeomanry Cavalry or beaten up by the Special Constables with truncheons than men. Women demanding political rights offended their idea about how women should behave, but it also seems that, to the marauding Manchester Yeomanry Cavalry and Nadin's Runners, the women in virginal white resembled Marianne, the French symbol of revolution. They had to be struck down. Mary Fildes had her dress slashed open and she was badly injured. Some women were slashed by sabres more than once, even when they were lying on the ground bleeding – the body of Sarah Howarth was cut in twenty places. The greatest number of casualties – 187 men and 31 women – were inflicted by sabre cuts, but nearly as many (136 men and 52 women) were injured by being trampled by horses and some were both slashed and ridden over. A total of 47 men and 23 women were beaten black and blue by truncheons, like John Lees. A volunteer constable was heard gloating at the crowd: 'This is Waterloo for you.' Within a week, the radical *Manchester Observer* coined the title: 'The Peter Loo Massacre.'

It is astonishing that the only inquest that was held was into the death of John Lees. It is often reported that this was because Robert Lees was a magistrate and rich enough to pay for the legal costs. But a careful reading of the evidence suggests the opposite. According to his wife, Robert Lees did not want to pay for the inquest or the fancy lawyer who came up from London to represent the Lees family.

When campaigners called on Hannah Lees to see if she would agree to it she said at first she did not want an inquest. 'I wished him to be buried without any disturbance,' she said. But she told the campaigners she wanted justice for the death of her stepson. They assured her that her husband would not have to bear the cost. 'I did not believe my husband would like to be at any expense on account of law suits. They said, "God forbid".' The campaigners wanted the inquest to highlight the scale of the outrage, while the government wanted it to show evidence of the revolutionary threat facing Britain. The inquest on John Lees therefore was treated as a show trial by both sides.

In the aftermath, on 21 August, Sidmouth wrote again to convey to the magistrates the 'great satisfaction' of the Prince Regent for their 'prompt, decisive and efficient measures for the preservation of the public tranquility …' But the Prince Regent was already in the Isle of Wight, enjoying the sailing at Cowes Week. A cartoon published three days after Peterloo showed a fat Prince Regent being carried by two voluptuous bathing ladies from Brighton to his barge. The message was clear: the monarchy was more interested in having fun than the plight of the people of Manchester.

John Harmer, a skilled London lawyer, travelled up to Oldham to represent the dead man's family. The inquest started on Wednesday, 8 September 1819 at a pub in the town called the Duke of York and the jury were taken to see the body of John Lees before settling down to hear the evidence in a large room at the inn. The inquest makes compulsive reading as a courtroom drama – the coroner's irritation with Harmer, the hotshot lawyer from London, leaps off the pages of the verbatim accounts. There was a row with the lawyers at the outset when the Coroner Thomas Ferrand failed to show up, leaving the inquest in the hands of a deputy, Mr Battye, who angrily told the lawyers: 'If Mr Ferrand were here I am sure he would not allow one of you in the room.' Battye also objected to reporters taking short-hand notes of the proceedings, and tried to throw them out. Battye had been told by the police that Lees had been 'crushed to death' – an obvious cover-up – and even Battye could not allow that to stand because, he said, he had seen that Lees had been cut. But he immediately adjourned the inquest, despite protests by the lawyers, and it was not until 25 September that the inquest got going under Ferrand, this time at the Angel Inn in Oldham, when Robert Lees was called. He recalled seeing his son the next morning after the meeting at Manchester at the top of the landing in his factory and seeing his shirt was bloody. He had his coat and waistcoat off, said the father. 'Did he do any work?', asked the coroner. 'I judged he was unable to work and feeling angry at his having been to the meeting, I told him if he could not work, he must go to the Overseer [of the parish poor relief] for I would not support him.' "What did he say to that?', the Coroner asked. 'He never spoke, and I said no more ...' The next time Robert Lees spoke to his son was 'the Sunday but one following' – thirteen days later – when he was 'very ill'.

Robert Lees admitted he had failed to inquire after his son's health in the coming days. He was questioned about why he had taken so little interest in his son's health. He said he thought his son would get better and left his care to his wife, Hannah, but it sounded less than convincing. The truth is – as Robert Lees told the inquest – he was angry with his son for going to the rally, though he clearly did not know that he was so badly injured.

One of the most telling lines at the inquest came from William Harrison, the blunt-speaking spinner from Oldham, who said he saw Lees some days later 'with a face like a cap'. Asked what he meant by that, Harrison said: 'White as a cap ... He told me he was at the battle of Waterloo but he never was in such danger there as he was at the meeting for at Waterloo it was man to man, but at Manchester it was downright murder.' It is open to question whether a modern inquest jury would bring in a verdict of murder that the campaigners clearly wanted after the Peterloo Massacre.

The inquest lasted about six weeks but Coroner Ferrand adjourned the hearings in October until 1 December before the jury could bring in a verdict of murder, and they were eventually abandoned when the Court of the King's Bench intervened and ruled the inquest proceedings null and void. There were protests in Parliament, accusations of cover-up, countless petitions, and no reform. Sir Francis Burdett presented a petition to Parliament from Robert Lees and Henry Brougham, a lawyer and Radical MP, saying Lees believed 'a verdict of wilful murder must and would have been given against many individuals engaged in the cruel attack [on his son] and that Mr Ferrand, the coroner, stated that he had no doubt such a verdict would be pronounced if he allowed the jury to come to a decision.' It is claimed today that the inquest led to the reforms that Hunt and John Lees wanted. But the shocking truth is that nothing really happened for more than a decade. Most shocking of all, no one was ever tried for murder.

The inquest evidence suggests that the Hussars were not as culpable as the Yeomanry Cavalry and special constables, who seemed determined to ensure the campaigners would never dare hold another protest meeting at St Peter's Field. They were right about that – it still stands out as the worst atrocity of its kind in British history, apart perhaps from Bloody Sunday in Derry. It has been compared to the crushing of the Tiananmen Square protests in China. Percy Bysshe Shelley vented his anger against Castlereagh – who was also Leader of the House of Commons and a symbol of repression – in the *Mask of Anarchy*:

> I met Murder on the way He had a mask like Castlereagh Very smooth he looked, yet grim; Seven blood-hounds followed him:
>   All were fat; and well they might Be in admirable plight, For one by one, and two by two, He tossed them human hearts to chew Which from his wide cloak he drew.

The reform protestors after the 'Peterloo' Massacre adopted the anti-slavery medallion with a twist. Whereas the anti-slavery medal, struck by pottery manufacturer Josiah Wedgwood, depicted a black slave in chains on bended knee posing the question: 'Am I not a Man and a Brother?', the Peterloo medallion depicted a spinner on his knees pleading for his life with a soldier who is about to bring a sabre down on his head.

The Peterloo Massacre and the victims like John Lees became a *cause célèbre* among left-wing activists and was seen as a landmark in the establishment of workers' rights in Britain by historians such as E.P. Thompson in *The Making of the English Working Class*. I researched it at the historic Chetham's Library in Manchester, where Karl Marx met Engels. It would take another decade of repression before the reforms John Lees had given his life for were partially conceded by the government, and a long time after that before the unions that grew up out of the struggles of the Regency period were allowed to organise. Wellington, as Tory prime minister, used the authority he gained from his great victory at Waterloo to hold back the tide of Parliamentary reform until it was unstoppable.

Hulton, the chairman of the Manchester magistrates, was still indignantly justifying his actions as late as 1831 in a letter to Lord Althorp, the Chancellor in Grey's Whig ministry after Wellington had been forced out of office. Althorp was a passionate supporter of the Great Reform Bill and Hulton insisted that only two people were killed at St Peter's Field: 'one a woman who having personated the Goddess of Reason was trampled to death in the crowd; the other a special constable who was cut down unintentionally by a private of a dragoon regiment.' This absurd letter of denial made Hulton a laughing stock, but it underlined the unshakable belief of those involved in the rightness of their action. Hulton pointed out that on the day after the Manchester rally 'a pensioner was beaten to death with portions of his own loom'.

It is one of the great ironies that politicians gather in the autumn each year for party rallies near the site of the massacre at the Manchester Central convention centre (formerly the Central Railway station and G-Mex Centre). They enjoy the free speech that the men and women, gathered to hear Hunt denounce the Corn Laws that day, were denied. The Manchester Free Trade Hall was built on this historic site in 1853 to commemorate the repeal of the hated Corn Laws, but it is probably better known today as the venue for concerts in the 1960s by Pink Floyd, B.B. King and where Bob Dylan went electric. The only sign that the massacre took place here is a red plaque on the front wall of the hotel. The political leaders who come for their annual rallies rarely give the plaque a second glance.

John Lees was buried in the family plot at the parish church of St Mary with St Peter on the hill overlooking Oldham. John's father was to follow him less than six months later, which adds greater poignancy to their role in the Peterloo Massacre. I found the register listing Robert Lees' death in a fine looping hand – 'No 127: Robert Lees of West Street died March 2 aged 54', but it did not give the cause of death. Perhaps it was the stress. The inscription on their headstone read: 'Sacred to the memory of Robert Lees of Bent-Green who died Feby 29 1820 in the 55th year of his age. Also John Lees his son who died Sept 7 1819 in the 22nd year of his age.'[6]

I went to Oldham in search of John Lees's gravestone but it has been cleared away in the landscaping of the grassy knoll around the church. Using the church's burial map, I did locate the place where the grave of John and Robert Lees had been, however. Their plot number is M40 on a parish map. With the help of a church official, I discovered it is roughly where a circle of paving slabs have been laid above a flight of steps on the south side of the church. I was told their remains were moved to another cemetery some years ago, and although John Lees, one of the forgotten heroes of the Battle of Waterloo, has become a working-class hero, he has no marker.

The man in charge of the Hussars, Major General Sir John Byng, is seen by some fair-minded experts on the Peterloo Massacre as a moderate who was in sympathy with the campaigners like John Lees for Parliamentary reform. It is true Byng became a Whig MP and backed reform in 1832, but only four months after the Peterloo Massacre he wrote to Lord Sidmouth, the Home Secretary from Pontefract, on 18 November 1819, warning of more 'seditious and blasphemous tracts' circulating in the North. Byng said he had intelligence that 'simultaneous meetings had been agreed upon to assemble at Newcastle, Carlisle, Leeds, Halifax, Huddersfield and Barnsley in the West Riding of Yorkshire; at Manchester, Bolton, Wigan, Blackburn and Burnley in Lancashire; at Newcastle under Lyme at Nottingham at Leicester and at Coventry …' He gave the impression he was ready to order the army in again to dispurse the protestors. Byng did not know it, but soon the Guards he had commanded at Waterloo would be called out to stop the assassination of the Cabinet. And this time they would be dealing with real revolutionaries.

Notes

1. 5th Earl Stanhope, *Notes of Conversations with the Duke of Wellington*, (London: John Murray, 1888), p. 92.
2. 'An Address to the People on the Death of Princess Charlotte Percy', pamphlet issued to the press by Bysshe Shelley, reprinted (London: Thomas Rodd, circa 1817).
3. *The Whole Proceedings Before the Coroner's Inquest at Oldham on the Body of John Lees, Who Died of Sabre Wounds at Manchester, August 16, 1819* (London: Joseph Augustus Dowling, 1820)
4. 'Report of the Inquest into the death of John Lees', *The Examiner*, 1819.
5. *Official Report into the Peterloo Massacre*, 1820, British Library online.
6. Register of Burials 1820, No. 127, St Mary Parish Church, Oldham.

11

WELLINGTON'S WATERLOO

At 8.30 p.m. on 23 February 1820, a picquet from the 2nd Battalion Coldstream Regiment was ordered to a halt by their commanding officer, Captain Lord Frederick FitzClarence, in a street just off the Edgware Road in north London. They had been called out from their Portman Road barracks to give support to a police operation that was taking place here. It was a ten-minute march through the dark streets in their famous scarlet uniforms, armed with pikes and muskets. Some of the troops were 'Waterloo Men', veterans of the Battle – Sergeant James Lott was in Sir William Gomm's company at Waterloo, Sergeant William Legg was in the company of Colonel Daniel Mackinnon, the Coldstreams' historian, who reinforced Hougoumont during the siege, and Sergeant James Graham, who had been dubbed 'the Bravest Man in England' for his courage in helping to close the north gate at Hougoumont during the siege, allegedly was there.

Captain FitzClarence had been commissioned in 1814 when he was just 14 but he had missed the great victory at Waterloo, possibly for his own safety. He was the third son – one of ten illegitimate children – by the Prince Regent's younger brother, William, the Duke of Clarence, and his mistress, a beautiful Irish actress Dorothea Bland, who was famous under her stage name of 'Mrs Jordan' – a name chosen because she had 'crossed the water' to England. In the days before the contraceptive pill, such affairs with multiple births were tolerated by the aristocratic elite, providing they were carried out with due decorum. William, later crowned as William IV, openly lived with 'Mrs Jordan' for twenty years until 1811 when his brother George became Prince Regent. 'Mrs Jordon' was paid off and William eventually married Princess Adelaide of Saxe-Meiningen in 1818. He recognised his illegitimate offspring but he had no legitimate heirs when he died.

Captain FitzClarence, 20, ordered his men to wait in John Street (now Crawford Place) about 60yds from the entrance to a Mews called Cato Street, where the horses and carriages for the big houses were stabled, while he went to check with a senior police officer who was waiting for them at the Horse and Groom pub. The pub was just across the road from the arched entrance to Cato Street and George Ruthven, an experienced Bow Street undercover police officer, had been keeping the entrance to the Mews under surveillance for several hours. He watched unseen as a gang of men slipped into the Mews carrying sacks. The sacks contained a small arsenal of weapons including knives, swords, nail bombs, fire bombs, pistols and a blunderbuss. The men were members of a desperate gang led by the revolutionary hothead, Arthur Thistlewood, who was bent on the assassination of the Cabinet and the overthrow of the government. As soon as he stepped inside the warmth of the pub, FitzClarence discovered he was too late. A few minutes earlier, the police had gone in.

Ruthven had been joined by Richard Birnie, a Scot who was a hard-headed magistrate in charge of police at Bow Street, with a force of twelve police officers. Birnie was in overall command of the operation and he feared he would miss the chance to grab the gang red-handed.

Birnie decided not to wait any longer for the Coldstream Guards to arrive with FitzClarence. He ordered his men to raid the stables where Thistlewood and his gang were preparing to carry out their attack on the Cabinet.

Birnie had intelligence that Thistlewood, having failed to pull off his plan for an uprising after the Spa Fields Riot, was now planning to start the English Revolution by assassinating the Duke of Wellington and the Cabinet while they sat down to their regular Wednesday night dinner at Lord Harrowby's house at 39 Grosvenor Square. Thistlewood, a down-at-heel former farmer turned revolutionary firebrand, planned to knock on the door of Lord Harrowby's house under the pretence of having a note for Harrowby; the gang would rush into the hall and overpower the servants. Armed with knives, blunderbusses, pistols and hand grenades, Thistlewood and his gang would march into the dining room in which the Cabinet ministers were sitting down to dinner and the bloody executions would begin. It was the same room in which, only five years before, the dust-covered Major Percy had excitedly delivered to the Cabinet the first news of Wellington's great victory at Waterloo with cheering crowds outside.[1]

And it could so easily have worked, but for the undercover intelligence unit at Bow Street police office.

Thistlewood had singled out two members of the Cabinet to be beheaded: Lord Castlereagh, the Leader of the Commons, and Lord Sidmouth, the Home Secretary. He planned to stick their heads on spikes and parade them around the East End of London as trophies. They were hate figures because

they were held personally responsible for a second wave of repressive legislation known as the Six Acts that had been passed by Parliament in response to
the 'Peterloo' outrage. Dismissing calls for a public inquiry into the 'murders'
at Manchester, Sidmouth and Castlereagh had seen the ringleaders jailed and
introduced a series of measure to suppress further civil unrest, including the
Seditious Meetings Prevention Act, banning gatherings of more than fifty
people, and an attack on freedom of speech by imposing punitive taxes to
close down news sheets that called for protests.

Sidmouth had led a crackdown on the campaigners for constitutional
change after Peterloo. The great orator, Henry Hunt, who had addressed the
crowd at Manchester before the Peterloo Massacre, had been imprisoned
for two and a half years; and Richard Carlile, the publisher of cheap tracts,
including Tom Paine's books such as *The Age of Reason* and radical pamphlets
like *Black Dwarf*, was sentenced to over three years in prison. His crime was
publishing another radical sheet, *The Republican*, with calls for the murderers
of the Peterloo victims to be brought to justice. If Britain was going to be
tipped into revolution, Thistlewood believed now was the moment. He was
convinced by taking off the heads of the Cabinet, he would literally decapi-
tate the government. His action would cause chaos and open the way for an
English Revolution. He believed the sight of Castlereagh's aristocratic head
on a spike would make the Irish community in London rise up, because the
Dublin-born Unionist was hated by the Irish for the way, as Secretary of State
for Ireland, he had brutally put down the Irish rebellion in 1798. In a particularly grisly detail, he also planned to cut off Castlereagh's[*] hand, which had
signed the orders for the repressive acts.

The array of weapons that were laid out on a rough carpenter's bench in
the hay loft at Cato Street included the iron spikes on which Thistlewood
planned to fix their heads. The nail bombs were home-made from fist-sized
iron balls containing 3oz of gunpowder and nails used to fix the metal rims to
cartwheels. The firebombs were to be used to set on fire the army barracks to
increase the confusion after the decapitation of the government.

Thistlewood, despite the Spa Fields setback, remained convinced the
disgruntled lower ranks of the army – the men Wellington regarded as the
'scum of the earth' – would join the revolution. Thistlewood felt he would
succeed where he had failed after Spa Fields because at last, the injustice felt
after the Manchester massacre had made the masses ready to rise up for their
rights; England was ripe for revolution. And just as he had after Spa Fields, he
planned to appeal to Wellington's common soldiers to support him and seize

---

[*]   Castlereagh died by his own hand on 12 August 1822, slashing his throat with a
        penknife while he was having a mental breakdown.

some cannon to blow apart any attempt to stop them. He had carefully pulled together a group of up to fifty men who were prepared to risk their lives for their cause in secret meetings in the back rooms of pubs. They waited for orders once the revolution was underway.

The gang that gathered at Cato Street were his most trusted men. They included John Harrison, who had rented the stable with a Jamaican man, William Davidson, three weeks earlier for 5s a week for six months. John Firth, a cow keeper of nearby Bryanston Street, off the Edgware Road, said Harrison told him it was to keep a horse and cart. Harrison was a member of the Marylebone Union Reading Society, where for two-pence a week hard-up would-be revolutionaries could read radical newspapers such as the *Republican* and the *Manchester Observer* and the radical books of Tom Paine, such as the *Rights of Man*. It was at the Marylebone Union that Harrison, a member of the Spencean Philanthropists, who had caused the Spa Fields riot, recruited Davison, the 33-year-old illegitimate son of the Attorney General of Jamaica and a black Jamaican mother. Davidson was educated – he had been sent by his father to Aberdeen to study mathematics – but became a cabinet maker and did some work for Lord Harrowby fitting up his house. He got to know Harrowby's servants and Thistlewood believed his contacts with the servants inside Harrowby's house would be a vital aid to his plan's success. Davidson had become embittered after a love affair with the white daughter of a rich merchant in Lichfield was ended by her father, probably because he was black. He turned to the Wesleyan Methodist Church but was accused of sexual abuse of girls at a Sunday school; he lost his faith in God and embraced revolutionary politics instead of the Bible. Thistlewood was so impressed by Davidson that he appointed him to the Executive of Five who were to organise the assassinations. Davidson was asked by Thistlewood to use his contacts with Harrowby's servants in the Grosvenor-Square house to gain intelligence for their attack.

Another member of the gang was John Adams, who had been a soldier in the Oxford Blues around 1801 and had learned a trade as a shoemaker while he was in the army. He was discharged due to ill health and scratched a living in the shoe trade, but he was heavily in debt. He was introduced to Thistlewood at his lodgings in Stanhope Street, near Clare Market, by two other members of the gang: John Thomas Brunt, 38, also a shoemaker of Fox Court in Gray's Inn Lane, and James Ings, who had been a prosperous butcher in Hampshire until the post-war slump killed his business. Ings was between 30 and 40, rather stout and fierce-looking, with fiery eyes. He had left his family to run a radical coffee shop in Whitechapel, selling political pamphlets for Richard Carlile, who went on the run after the Peterloo Massacre. Thistlewood was interested in Adams's army past. 'I presume you can use a sword?' he asked Adams, who replied, 'I could use it to defend myself if it ever became necessary.'

They kept their weapons at a place Thistlewood called 'the depot'. Adams discovered the 'depot' was the lodgings of another member of the gang called William Tidd, who lived next door to Adams in Hole-in-the-Wall passage. Tidd, a 45-year-old shoemaker born in Grantham, had been a serial deserter from the army, joining for the bounty money and then escaping.

In secret gatherings before the attack, Thistlewood criticised Henry Hunt, the orator who had spoken at Spa Fields, calling him a coward for opposing revolution, and said that he was probably a government spy paid to infiltrate the group. Thistlewood was nearly right – but the spy was not Hunt. George Edwards, whom Thistlewood trusted and had made his ADC, was an undercover agent for John Stafford, the 'spymaster' at Bow Street, who had been trying to catch Thistlewood since he slipped off his hook in the Spa Fields trial.

Thistlewood had been planning to use the funeral of George III, when most of the troops would be drawn out of London to Windsor Castle, as the moment to strike. He planned to attack Parliament and still nursed the ambition of taking over London by seizing the Bank of England and the Tower of London, just as he had at Spa Fields. But at one of their secret planning meetings Edwards said he had seen in the paper that the Cabinet was to meet for dinner at Lord Harrowby's house on 23 February 1820. Thistlewood did not believe him but sent out for the paper and when it was brought to Thistlewood, he confirmed Edwards was right. Brunt jumped around the room shouting for joy, and saying: 'I believe now there is a God.' Ings said, 'Now we shall have an opportunity of cutting off Lord Castlereagh's head.' Thistlewood told Edwards:

> The destruction of the Cabinet ministers would be a most excellent thing and be sure to rouse the whole country. The death of Lord Castlereagh would rouse the Irish and the whole country would be in confusion, the great People would all run away and there would be no-one to give directions. All would be Anarchy and Alarm and Confusion.

The assassination of the Cabinet at Lord Harrowby's house then became the focus for their attack. A watch was kept on Harrowby's house overnight on 22 February and the next afternoon, Wednesday 23 February, they gathered in Brunt's lodgings at Gray's Inn Lane, where they prepared pistols, fixing flints to the firearms. There were cutlasses, pistols and a blunderbuss with a brass barrel. Adams said: 'Edwards was there preparing fuses for hand grenades.'

Thistlewood wrote out some proclamations for the revolution to the people of England. I found copies of the hand-written notes in the Cato Street files at the National Archives: 'Englishmen! Justice is at last triumphant. Your tyrants are destroyed. The friends of liberty are called on to come forward as the provisional government is now sitting. J. Ings, secretary.'

Ings was eager to use his expertise with a butcher's knife to cut off the heads of Castlereagh and Sidmouth. He was busy preparing for action: he put a black belt round his waist, which was to hold two pistols; round his shoulder he had another belt for a cutlass; on each shoulder he had a large bag, in the form of a soldier's haversack, to carry their heads; and he drew a great knife, brandishing it about – this was the knife with which he would cut off their heads.

They arrived in the Edgware Road after 6 p.m. and slipped into Cato Street about an hour after sunset. Cato Street was a twenty-minute walk to Lord Harrowby's house at Grosvenor Square in Mayfair. Sacks had been nailed over the two grimy sash windows looking onto Cato Street to stop prying eyes from the backs of the big houses across the mews from seeing what they were doing. Thistlewood posted Ings and Davidson downstairs as sentries. Davidson was armed with two pistols in a belt, a blunderbuss and a cutlass.

Thistlewood, 46, was a vigorous man, thickset, clean-shaven with long black sideboards and short cropped black hair. He had long nurtured the dream of overthrowing the British Government by beheading its leaders, like the Jacobins, and now, after the Peterloo Massacre, he felt he had his chance to fulfill his ambitions. Unfortunately for Thistlewood and his co-conspirators, he was hopelessly out of touch with reality. The number who supported outright revolution in Britain was small; the vast majority of protestors supported men like Hunt, who believed in peacefully agitating for constitutional reform. Thistlewood had also underestimated the strong popular loyalty of the working classes to the Crown, even one worn by a fourth-generation German prince who was lampooned in the press as a sexually incontinent spendthrift, glutton and buffoon.

Future would-be revolutionaries would be wise to study the files in the National Archives on the Cato Street Conspiracy. They are stuffed with anonymous letters from informers. The notes were written by ordinary members of the public, informing Lord Sidmouth and other ministers about the meetings Thistlewood and members of his gang had been organising in London pubs. The informants had overheard scraps of conversation and had their suspicions raised by meeting in pubs including a room in a yard at the White Hart in Brook's Market and the Scotch Arms, a regular meeting place for agitators in Round Court on the Strand.

A few days before the plot was carried out, a man called Hiden, who kept cows in Manchester Mews, Manchester Street, Marylebone, to supply houses with fresh milk and cream, had written a letter to Castlereagh warning him of the plan but had been unable to deliver it without being seen. He said he was a friend of a man called Wilson, one of the conspirators, who told him the details and tried to recruit him into the plot. On the day before their planned coup, Hiden, desperate to pass on the information, ran in front of Lord Harrowby's horse when he was riding in the park and handed him the letter he had addressed to Castlereagh, warning of the plan to assassinate the Cabinet at Harrowby's home.*

The informers kept writing long after the event, and some were clearly intended to settle private scores. I discovered a note from an informer signing himself 'Veritas' to the Home Secretary saying: 'I have every reason to believe that Bamber Beaumont, a clerk in the county fire office, Regent Street, has long been a supporter of the Cato Street Gang.' It is not known whether the unfortunate Bamber Beaumont was pursued for this smear, but it is likely.

The Cabinet had been having regular dinners at Lord Harrowby's house in Grosvenor Square for years. The dinners had been suspended for some weeks because of the mourning period for the late King George III, so the resumption of the dinners reported in the *Morning Post* was exciting news indeed for Thistlewood. Lord Harrowby, the President of the Council, had put around invitation cards to sixteen members of the Cabinet for supper that night. Those who were to dine at Lord Harrowby's that night included: the Duke of Wellington; Lord Liverpool, the prime minister; Nicholas Vansittart, the Chancellor; Lord Bathurst, the Secretary of State for War and the Colonies; Lord Castlereagh, the Leader of the House and Foreign Secretary; Lord Sidmouth, the Home Secretary; Canning, the future prime minister; and half a dozen others. Thistlewood could have wiped out most of the ruling political elite of Britain. It would have been more shocking than the Brighton bombing by the IRA on Margaret Thatcher and her Cabinet in 1984. But after being tipped off, Harrowby cancelled the dinner and went to Lord Liverpool's Fife House for supper. To avoid tipping off Thistlewood and his co-plotters, Harrowby did not tell his servants and they prepared for the dinner for sixteen, unaware they were about to be attacked by a ruthless armed gang.

Stafford had already set in train his own plan finally to bring Thistlewood to justice and catch his cell red-handed at Cato Street. Birnie was in overall command but it was Stafford who was the instigator. He was going to lead the police raid and had prepared his pistols when, just as he was about to join the officers and proceed to the Cato Street, a message from the Home Office requiring his immediate attendance compelled Stafford to change his plan. He gave his pistols to a policeman, Richard Smithers.[2] Stafford sent

---

*   This doubly historic house was demolished in 1967 despite a building preservation order, and a furious planning row, by the Duke of Westminster's Grosvenor Estates to make way for a block of mansion flats. It is now incorporated in the Millennium Hotel, Mayfair.

George Ruthven, a police constable and former spy who had infiltrated Thistlewood's associates in the Spenceans, to the Horse and Groom pub to keep watch on Thistlewood's gang. When Captain FitzClarence discovered the police had gone in without them, he ran back to his men and ordered them to advance at the double. As they entered the archway in their scarlet uniforms to Cato Street, Sergeant Legg heard a pistol shot. A police constable shouted – 'Soldiers, soldiers – the doorway!' Captain FitzClarence told his men: 'Coldstreams – Do you duty.'

As Sergeant Legg turned to his right inside the gateway leading into Cato Street, he saw a man with his back against the wall and a pistol in his hand. It was levelled straight at Captain FitzClarence. 'I knocked it aside with my pike and seized it on the muzzle with my hand,' said Legg. 'I scuffled with the man for the pistol and he pulled the trigger. The pistol went off and tore my right coat arm. I then secured the man and the pistol with the assistance of the picquet.'[3]

Sergeant James Lott said Davidson fired the first shot: 'The man who stood near the door, a black man (Davidson), fired a pistol, the ball of which passed straight though my cap.' Davidson then slashed at FitzClarence with a sword and ran into the stable. Lott said it was Tidd who then fired at FitzClarence. He said: 'I saw the prisoner Tidd fire another pistol nearly at the same time, the ball of which tore the sleeve of Sergeant Legg's coat. I went for a light and when I returned I found two men secured in the stable.' Sergeant Legg handed Tidd to the police and climbed the ladder to the loft. He found one of the policemen lying on the floor in a pool of blood at the top of the ladder. It was Richard Smithers.

A few moments before, Ruthven had led his team of police officers up the ladder into the loft followed by a police officer called Ellis, then Richard Smithers. They found about twenty-four men in the loft, grouped around the carpenter's bench, where the weapons were laid out. Ruthven shouted: 'We are peace officers. Lay down your arms.' Thistlewood looked up, caught up a sword and backed into a small room to the right of the bench with three or four others. Ruthven knew Thistlewood from the earlier trials and approached him cautiously. Thistlewood began fencing with the sword at him but Smithers, who was on Ruthven's right, rushed forward. Thistlewood lunged with sword, stabbing Smithers in the right side of his chest. Smithers said, 'Oh my God.' Then he staggered back, and collapsed to the floor.

Almost instantly, someone fired a pistol and put out the lights. Then someone shouted: 'Kill the buggers! Throw them down the stairs.' There were flashes in the dark as pistols flared and shots rang out. The gang scattered. There was a rush in the dark for the ladder and the hay shutes downstairs. Thistlewood followed close behind them, fired a pistol as he climbed down,

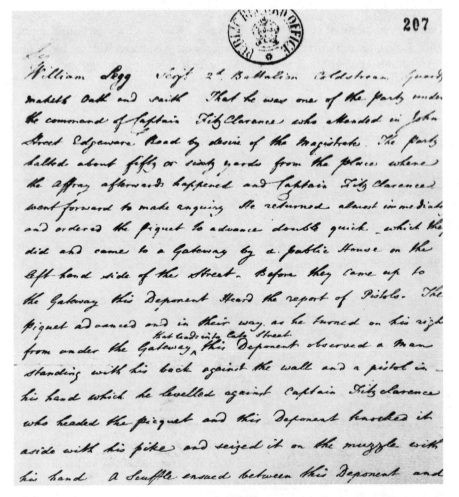

Statement by Sergeant William Legg; he saved the life of Captain FitzClarence. (National Archives)

and then in the darkness ran through the open stable door, past the squad of Coldstream Guards and escaped into the night. Brunt, Adams and Harrison escaped, but the gang leaders were all rounded up in the following days.

Davidson was captured at the stable door. One of the police officers, Benjamin Gill, said he hit Davidson on the wrist with his truncheon and he dropped a blunderbuss before he could fire it.

Ruthven rushed down the stairs – the stable was pitch black – and ran out into John Street, where he met the soldiers. He returned to the stables and saw Tidd coming out of the door; Tidd pulled a pistol on Ruthven, but Ruthven grappled with Tidd and they both fell into a dung-heap. Sergeant Legg pulled them out and took Tidd to the Horse and Groom under guard. A few of the

others were rounded up, including Davidson, who was brought into the pub,
and, according to Ruthven, began to sing, 'Scots wha ha wi Wallace bled'. The
Scottish rebel ballad *March to Bannockburn* by Robbie Burns continues:

> Scots, wham Bruce has aften led,
> Welcome to your gory bed,
> Or to Victorie!
> Now's the day and now's the hour
> See the front o' battle lour;
> See approach proud Edward's power
> Chains and slavery!

Richardson may have learned the ballad written in 1793 when he was in
Aberdeen. He told Ruthven: 'Damn any man that would not die in liberty's cause.'

The Home Secretary Lord Sidmouth offered a £1,000 reward in the
London Gazette for Thistlewood, describing him as:

> about 48 years of age, five feet ten inches high, with a sallow complexion,
> long visage, dark hair (a little grey), dark hazel eyes and arched eye-brows,
> a wide mouth and a good set of teeth, has a scar under his right jaw, and
> slender build.

Thistlewood was captured the next day in bed at the house of a friend called
Harris in a street near Moorfields. He was still partly clothed with his breeches
on and did not put up a fight. It is alleged the police were acting on a tip-off
by Edwards, who claimed the reward.

Today, from the outside, the 'stable' in Cato Street is largely unchanged and
just as Thistlewood would have seen it. The outside is covered by a preservation order and the black stable door is still there, with two windows for the
hayloft above. The only change is that a hay-loft door between the windows
has been bricked up and there is a blue plaque there now to tell tourists this
is where the Cato Street conspiracy took place. Cato Street today is a sought-
after mews where small houses can fetch at least £2.5 million. The owners
kindly allowed me inside the Cato Street 'barn', which has been knocked
through to an adjoining cottage next door. The ladder has gone and the stable
where Tidd fired his pistol at FitzClarence is now a white-walled study with a
partner's desk, where the ladder would have been. The hay loft where Richard
Smithers died has been converted in a bedroom. 'We get groups of tourists
with guides outside, but that's fine,' I was told. 'It's quite nice living in such an
historic place. We haven't noticed any ghosts.'

After the raid, the Coldstreams marched their prisoners to Bow Street, where they made the witness statements that are still in the Cato Street files at the National Archives. Reading them is like touching history. The *United Service Gazette* later said that FitzClarence's life was saved by Sergeant Graham, the hero of Hougoumont:

> He was one of that party of the Guards headed by Lord FitzClarence which attacked the Cato Street gang. On that memorable occasion Graham was one of the instruments by which under Divine Providence, the life of the noble lord was saved. Graham and a brother soldier pulled the noble lord down the ladder at the instant the fellow in the loft had their arms leveled to shoot him. Lord FitzClarence met Graham some time back in Dublin and greeted him most cordially and begged his acceptance of a pension which he has ever since enjoyed.

The raw evidence in the hand-written depositions, however, suggests this is one more of the myths surrounding the hero of Hougoumont. Sergeant Graham may well have been there, but I could find no reference to him in the soldiers' statements. The witness statements I uncovered at the National Archives show it was Sergeant Legg, not Graham, who saved FitzClarence's life. Coldstream Guards including FitzClarence, Legg and Lott were called to give evidence at the trial but Graham was not in the list of witnesses.

The prisoners were held in the Tower of London before being transferred to Newgate prison. In all, eleven men were put on trial for Treason at the Old Bailey. The cases were heard in batches. The trial of Davidson and Richard Tidd was presided over by Baron Garrow, the outstanding criminal lawyer, who was the subject of a BBC series *Garrow's Law*. The Jamaican Davidson complained Garrow in his summing up was 'inveterate against me'. Davidson's pleas were confused – at one moment saying he was a victim of mistaken identity, the next that merely because he was caught with a sword in his hand was not proof he intended to overthrow the government. Davidson told the jury 'you may suppose that because I am a man of colour I am without any understanding or feeling and would act the brute; I am not one of that sort …' Garrow was clearly anxious to deny Davidson's allegation the court was colour-prejudiced against him. Garrow said: 'You may rest most perfectly assured that with respect to the colour of your countenance, no prejudice either has or will exist in any part of this Court against you; a man of colour is entitled to British justice as much as the fairest British subject.' The fact that Davidson was a 'man of colour' has been highlighted by the National Archives as part of their 'Black Presence' theme. There is no evidence that Garrow was prejudiced. It was Garrow who successfully prosecuted, Sir Thomas Picton –

the dead hero of Waterloo – for torturing a young free mulatto girl when he was governor-general of Trinidad.[*] Garrow was a reformer and was credited with the phrase 'innocent until proven guilty', but there was nothing he could do to save Davidson or Tidd.

Davidson, swearing his innocence and claiming that he was set up, said: 'The only regret left is that I have a large family of small children and when I think of that, it unmans me …'

Edwards' lengthy deposition – it is in clear flowing handwriting – is in marked contrast to the soldiers' statements taken down by clerks. The faded pages of Edwards' deposition at the National Archives sent Thistlewood and his cohorts to a bloody end on the gallows. The uncomfortable question remains to what extent Edwards was an *agent provocateur* in the Cato Street conspiracy.

As recent trials have shown, it is a question that is still being asked of under-cover policemen, and it is likely that a court today would seriously question the prosecution case. Indeed, a case could be made that having failed to secure a conviction against Thistlewood in the Spa Fields trial, Stafford used Edwards to pursue Thistlewood to the Old Bailey for a second time as an act of vengeance. Edwards was, by all accounts, little more than a down-and-out when he came under the wing of Stafford, who clearly saw he would be a useful spy in the criminal underworld of Regency London.

The judge at the first hearing, Lord Justice Dallas, said in his summing up it was Edwards who had drawn Thistlewood's attention to the dinner at Lord Harrowby's in *The Morning Post*. This was denied by Edwards in his written evidence. Edwards said it was Thistlewood who had seen the article in *The Morning Post* and told him 'the ministers may then be attacked and murdered while at dinner'. But if Judge Dallas is right, it suggests Edwards was the insti-gator of the plot. Stafford, the Bow Street spymaster, a Londoner hardened to the ways of the criminal world, was clearly determined that after the botched prosecution of Thistlewood in the trial for treason after the Spa Fields riot, he was not going to let Thistlewood off the hook again. To avoid the jury refusing to convict on Edwards' evidence alone, he chose not to call Edwards as the main prosecution witness. Instead, he used Edwards' statement to break the gang by persuading another member to give king's evidence against the others.

Stafford targeted Adams. It was claimed Adams too was one of his agents, but the documents I found in the National Archives do not back that up. I found a short note in the Cato Street files that showed Stafford went to work on Adams shortly after their arrests. He addressed it to 'H Hobhouse' –

---

[*]   There were recent demands for Picton's portrait to be removed from a courthouse
        in his native Carmarthen, Wales, but it is still there. 'I think we have to accept Picton
        warts and all and not judge him by today's standards,' I was told.

Henry Hobhouse, a lawyer and civil servant, and permanent minister of state at the Home Office:

> I saw Adams last night but what he said was not very material. If I find myself equal to it, I will see him again this evening and tomorrow morning you shall have the result. Mr E (Edwards) conjectures that this man, seen near the premises, must have been one of the Marylebone Union.[4]

Stafford got what he wanted. Adams turned against his co-conspirators and gave king's evidence against them, in return for being freed. Once he did so, the result of the trials was a foregone conclusion. Thistlewood did not deny planning to assassinate Wellington and the Cabinet. In a bravura performance at the end of his trial, Thistlewood denounced Edwards, saying he had been the instigator – he claimed Edwards had suggested blowing up Parliament, he proposed assassinating ministers at a fete for the Spanish ambassador, and finally had been behind the attack on the Cabinet dinner. But Thistlewood was not complaining about his own fate. He said he knew he would be walking on the scaffold soon, and appeared to accept it, and said that by holding back Edwards the prosecution prevented Thistlewood from proving he was a spy and that Adams, Hiden and another man called Dwyer were Edwards's agents. Far from denying the plot, Thistlewood justified it: 'With respect to the immorality of our project,' said Thistlewood, 'I will just observe that the assassination of a tyrant has always been deemed meritorious action; Brutus and Cassius were lauded to the very skies for slaying Caesar ...' The judge intervened and told him he could not let him justify murder and high treason, but Thistlewood continued:

> High treason was committed against the people of Manchester ... but the Prince Regent thanked the murderers ... if one spark of honour or inde-pendence still glimmered in the breast of Englishmen, they would have rose to a man; insurrection then became a duty ...

Ings said if Edwards had not befriended him when Ings ran a coffee shop, he would not be in the dock facing death: 'Murdering His Majesty's ministers I admit was a disgrace to nature, but those ministers meet and conspire together and pass laws to starve me and my family and my fellow countrymen ...'

On 28 April 1820 Davidson, Ings, Tidd, Brunt and Thistlewood were found guilty of high treason. The judge said that the newly passed Treason Act applied:

> The judgment is that each of you shall be drawn on a hurdle to the place of execution, and there be hanged by the neck until you be dead; and that

afterwards your heads be severed from your bodies, and your bodies divided into four quarters, be disposed of as His Majesty shall direct ...

Five others were also sentenced to death but their sentences were commuted to transportation for life. Edwards did not appear. Instead, like a modern-day supergrass, he was given a new identity and went into hiding for the rest of his life, first to Guernsey in the Channel Islands and then to South Africa. The new King George IV commuted the sentences of the five who were to die to being hanged and beheaded, saving their corpses the further indignity of being quartered. The death penalty was imposed for over 200 offences in Georgian Britain but beheading was extraordinary. It was clearly intended as a warning to others but the authorities may have been concerned that quartering would cause revulsion and unrest – they made arrangements to read the Riot Act and disperse the crowd if there was any sign of a riot breaking out around the scaffold. The Life Guards were called out, just in case, with six field guns.

On the day of their public execution, 1 May 1820, a great crowd gathered outside the debtors' gate at Newgate Prison at the corner of Newgate Street and the Old Bailey to see the sentence carried out on the men who plotted to murder Wellington and the Cabinet. Graphic accounts of the public execution were published for an avid public and it was witnessed by several writers. Byron's travelling partner for *Childe Harold* and radical writer John Cam Hobhouse wrote: 'The men died like heroes. Ings, perhaps, was too obstreperous in singing "Death or Liberty".' They stepped up onto the scaffold in turn, Thistlewood 'eyes fixed as if in abstract thought', Tidd 'collected, manly', Ings 'laughing without reserve', Brunt 'in fixed and hardened obduracy of mind', Davidson last 'with clasped hands, uplifted eyes, praying most devoutly'. Ings made a show, 'rushed to the platform, leaped and bounded in a most desperate manner'. Turning towards Ludgate Hill, he cried out: 'This is going to be the last remains of James Ings.' Thistlewood told him: 'Don't Ings. There is no use in all this noise. We can die without making a noise.' As the executioner put the rope round his neck, Ings said: 'Do it well – pull it tight!' Then the executioner threw the rope over the scaffold beam above their heads. They were hooded, and 'turned off' together when the executioner dropped the trap door for all five men. Thistlewood 'struggled slightly for a few minutes, but each effort was more faint than that which preceded; and the body soon turned round slowly, as if upon the motion of the hand of death'.[5] Tidd, whose size gave cause to suppose that he would 'pass' with little comparative pain, scarcely moved after the fall. Ings, who was lighter, struggled at the end of the rope. 'The assistants of the executioner pulled his legs with all their might; and even then the reluctance of the soul to part from its native seat was to be observed in the vehement efforts of every part of the body.' Davidson, 'after

The Cato Street plaque.

three or four heaves, became motionless; but Brunt suffered extremely, and considerable exertions were made by the executioners and others to shorten his agonies by pulling and hanging upon his legs. However, in the course of five minutes all was still'.[6]

But that was not the end. Five coffins were laid side by side on the scaffold. Thistlewood's body was cut down and laid on his back in a coffin, with his head extended by the neck onto a block. An executioner wearing a black mask climbed onto the scaffold with a small knife like those used by surgeons in amputations and then severed Thistlewood's head from his body. A cry went up when the crowd saw the blade cutting into Thistlewood's throat. Thistlewood's head was held high by the hair on the Newgate side of the scaffold and the executioner shouted: 'This is the head of Arthur Thistlewood – traitor.'[7]

This performance – for that is what it was – was repeated four more times for Ings, Davidson, Tidd and Brunt. The executioner's assistant had to hold Tidd's head with both hands by the cheeks because he was bald. He dropped Brunt's head with its purple strangled hue on the scaffold, causing 'howlings and groans' from the spectators. Rooms overlooking the gallows were rented out to VIPs to see the spectacle and I think it inconceivable that they did not include some of their intended victims, including Lord Sidmouth and perhaps the Duke of Wellington. Wellington was certainly in London – he later sat for a new Waterloo portrait wearing the cloak he used at Waterloo. There is little doubt he would have felt well-satisfied by the Cato Street trial. Despite the stench of a government conspiracy surrounding the case to get Thistlewood who had escaped the noose once before, the Cato Street Conspiracy put back the cause of reform by years. It demonstrated that some of the radicals like Thistlewood were indeed set on bloody revolution as Sidmouth, Liverpool and Castlereagh claimed. Ministers privately described the discovery of the plot as a 'windfall' for the Tories. They were returned to power in the elections

of March and April 1820 that were called after the death of George III. Lord
Liverpool, who was returned as prime minister, wrote to Canning declaring
that the repressive Six Acts were 'popular' with the public:

> The public feeling has certainly been much more strongly with us than
> at the last general election [1818]. The ... [Six Acts] are decidedly popular
> and scarcely any of the opposition have ventured to bring them forward as
> a ground of attack, whilst they have been most serviceable to many of our
> friends ...[8]

Wellington used his authority, which had never been greater, to dismiss the
calls for reform. The resistance to change was reinforced by many of the
Duke's senior officers who had seats in Parliament, either in the Lords as the
sons of hereditary peers, or in the Commons as local landowners, who held
Parliamentary constituencies in their pockets.

Some estimates suggest that 20 per cent of MPs between 1790 and 1820
had served in the regular army with another 100 in the Royal Navy. In the
period from 1793 to 1815, 135 army officers were elected as MPs. A total of
twenty-five MPs fought at Waterloo and two of Wellington's senior officers,
Ponsonby and Picton, were serving MPs (for Londonderry and Pembroke)
when they were killed. Wellington was surrounded by his most senior former
officers in the House of Lords.

Wellington's former army officers in Parliament undoubtedly helped
Wellington and the Tory government to maintain a substantial blocking
majority against constitutional reform.

One of the rare exceptions was Sir John Byng, commander of the
2nd Brigade of Guards, who stood as a Whig MP in Poole and supported
reform in 1832; he was rewarded by Lord Melbourne – husband of Lady
Caroline Lamb – with an hereditary peerage as Lord Strafford, giving him
a seat in the Lords. More typical was Sir Hussey Vivian, who commanded
the Sixth Brigade of Cavalry at Waterloo and became the MP for Truro –
a seat also held by Lord FitzRoy Somerset, Wellington's military secretary
at Waterloo. On the annual renewal of the Mutiny Bill in 1820, establishing the army strength at 92,000 men, Sir Hussey told the Commons that a
large standing army was necessary to put down insurrection, such as they
had seen at Manchester (Peterloo). Hobhouse, a reforming MP, chided him:
'At Manchester, 100,000 men were put to the rout by 40 flushed, not to say
drunken, yeomen. What then do we want 35,000 soldiers for?' Hobhouse said
the move towards martial law was against Magna Carta. It is a debate that is
still going on today. The summer riots of 2011 that left city centres burning
ruins raised again the question that faced Wellington and his government –

how does the civil power maintain order on the streets if the mobs resort to such violence? At least today, the mobs have the vote. In 1820, the vast majority of Wellington's 'scum of the earth' were disenfranchised.

The case for reform would not go away and public support for change grew as a result of an extraordinary event – the trial of Queen Caroline. Caroline of Brunswick had married George, Prince of Wales, on 8 April 1795 but it was a disaster. He had secretly married the widow, Mrs Maria Fitzherbert in 1785 but as she was a Catholic it was illegal. He openly had a string of mistresses, including Lady Melbourne and Countess Conyngham. When he succeeded his father as king in 1820 as George IV, he sought a divorce from Caroline, and publicly accused her of adultery. A Bill of Pains and Penalties was introduced in the Lords to divorce her on the grounds of her 'licentious, disgraceful and adulterous intercourse' with an Italian servant, Bartolomeo Pergami 'a foreigner of low station'. It began in the House of Lords in August 1820 and turned into a show trial of Caroline's sexual behaviour. Newspapers had a field day, reporting the salacious allegations against the queen while the trial ploughed on, day after scandalous day. There had never been such a public washing of the queen's dirty laundry. The House of Lords had never heard anything like it.

On 25 August, the Attorney General, Robert Gifford, questioned Barbara Kress from the Post-Inn Karlsruhe, where Caroline had stayed with Pergami, in the most intimate, salacious detail: 'Did you at any time see anything on the sheets?' asked the Attorney General. Frau Kress politely replied the sheets were 'wuste'. There was some dispute about the interpretation, but it was agreed she meant 'stained'. The Attorney General would not be deflected from the truth. What sort of stains were they? he demanded. 'White,' said Frau Kress, who broke down in tears at the intimate nature of the questioning. Were they wet or dry? asked the Attorney General. 'Wet,' said the tearful Frau.

The nation was gripped by the trial and Caroline won massive public support as 'the wronged wife'. Thomas Creevey, the Radical MP, compared the great demonstrations in support of the queen to the crowds at 'Peterloo':

> Every Wednesday the scene which caused such alarm at Manchester is repeated under the very nose of Parliament and in a tenfold degree more alarming. A certain number of regiments of the efficient population of the town march on each of those days in a regular lock step, four or five abreast – banners flying – music playing … I should like anyone to tell me what is to come next if this organised army loses its temper.

Wellington drew hisses from the crowds on 17 August as he rode to the opening of the trial on Copenhagen. Creevey noted:

Near the House of Lords there is a fence of railing put across the street from
the Exchequer coffee-house to the enclosed garden ground joining to St
Margaret's churchyard, through which members of both Houses were alone
permitted to pass. A minute after I passed, I heard an uproar, with hissing
and shouting. On turning round, I saw it was Wellington on horseback.
His horse made a little start, and he looked round with some surprise. He
caught my eye as he passed, and nodded, but was evidently annoyed.[9]

The queen arrived in an episcopal black-and-white dress with a white veil
so thick it was difficult to see her face, but Creevey compared her manner to
a toy doll with jerky movements. It was the main subject of conversation at
Brooks's club in St James's Street that was founded by Whigs, and renowned
for gambling. Lord Grey offered odds of 10 to 1 that the bill would be with-
drawn in a fortnight. It is not clear if anyone took him up, but Grey would
have lost his bet. The government persisted with it until 10 November when
on the third reading it could only muster a majority of nine with ninety-nine
peers voting against it, including the Archbishop of York, the Right Reverend
Edward Venables Vernon.

Wellington voted for it, but the prime minister, Lord Liverpool, adjourned
further progress and the government abandoned the measure. Grey said by
introducing the bill, the government 'had betrayed their King, insulted their
Queen, and had given a shock to the morals of society by the promulga-
tion of the detestable and disgusting evidence'. The Radical writer William
Cobbett used the queen's trial to attack the House of Lords in a pamphlet
called *A Peep At The Peers*.

But the government's embarrassment was not over. King George barred
the queen from his side at his Coronation at Westminster Abbey on 19 July
1821. There is a myth that she went to the doors of the Abbey, banged on
the doors and screamed: 'Let me in – I am your Queen.' It is true she was
denied her place by the king's side, but the government was not so stupid
as to shut her out altogether. The authorities had allocated Caroline a place
in the Abbey among the peeresses with instructions for the door-keepers to
let her in and lead her to her place, but she insisted on a place next to the
king as her right as the queen. Wellington said: 'She went to two or three
doors (of the Abbey) and received the same answer at each. This quite dis-
concerted her, and she retired. The mob too, as soon as they found she came
to spoil the ceremony, began hissing and hooting.' She already had one of
the twenty-six tickets issued to the Duke of Wellington as High Constable.
He denied he gave it to the queen and told a dinner party at Walmer Castle
in 1836 that he suspected it was given to Caroline by Lady Jersey, one of her
intimate friends.

Caroline – conveniently for the government and the king – died mysteriously less than a year later on 7 August 1821, aged 53. There were suspicions that she had been poisoned but the symptoms suggested she died from cancer of the stomach. Even in death she proved troublesome. Like the public mood after the death of Diana, Princess of Wales in 1997, the dead queen became a lightning conductor for public anger at the Establishment. Mobs protested that her body was being 'smuggled' out of London via Harwich for burial in her native Brunswick. They wanted to show their support for her – and opposition to George IV – by insisting that her coffin should be put on board a ship in the port of London. There were such violent demonstrations in London when Caroline's body was being carried for embarkation at Harwich that there were scenes reminiscent of the Peterloo Massacre: the Life Guards, who formed an honour guard, fired some rounds, drew sabres, and two members of the public were killed.

Seven years later, the civil unrest was as great as ever when Wellington was called on by George IV to take over as prime minister. The Duke rode Copenhagen to 10 Downing Street to show the smack of firm government. They became a familiar site around Westminster. He was returned as prime minister at the General Election caused by the death of George IV in 1830 and the accession to the throne of George's youngest brother, William (Prince Frederick had died in 1827). But the Duke's popularity had been completely spent, and for Wellington it all went horribly wrong. In the same month he kissed hands with the king, he received a letter posted in Oxford Street saying: 'Parliamentary reform … or death!' The writer added: 'Mark this thou despot.' It was signed 'Swing'. The 'Swing' riots were a protest at the hardship of farm workers. But they need not have threatened murder by the mob. The Duke committed political suicide at the opening of the new Parliament. Wellington utterly dismayed his own side by declaring, at the end of his remarks on the King's Speech opening Parliament in the Lords on 2 November 1830, he would never surrender the vote to the common man. He said Britain had the best Parliamentary system in the world and then in the closing words of speech, he said he would go further:

> Under these circumstances, I am not prepared to bring forward any measure [of Parliamentary reform] … I am not only not prepared to bring forward any measure of this nature but I will at once declare that as long as I hold any station in the government of the country, I shall always feel it my duty to resist such measures when proposed by others.

It was a suicidal comment to make for a prime minister reliant on shifting alliances. Diarist and senior civil servant Charles Greville noted: 'The Duke of Wellington made a violent and uncalled-for declaration against Reform, which has without doubt sealed his fate. Never was there an act of more egregious folly, or one so universally condemned by friends and foes.' A fortnight later, on 16 November, the Duke announced in the Lords he had gone to the king and resigned after losing a vote of no confidence in the Commons.

There are arguments over why he said it. Elizabeth Longford persuasively argues Wellington – though he showed acute imagination on the battlefield – lacked political nous. Others say he was trying to use his authority – enhanced by the memory of his stunning victory at Waterloo – to kill reform stone dead.

In one respect, it was surprising that Wellington stoically refused to budge on the issue of reform. Wellington was not an idealist – he was an arch-pragmatist. He had conceded Irish emancipation when the Catholic Irish nationalist Daniel O'Connell won a Parliamentary by-election for County Clare; an Irish rebellion was threatened if O'Connell was barred from taking his seat in Parliament by the Oath of Supremacy, which was incompatible with his Catholicism. Backed by Robert Peel and reinforced by threats to bring down the government, Wellington persuaded George IV to drop his own personal deep opposition to Catholic Emancipation and allow Irish Catholics to sit in Parliament for the first time (and it led to his duel with Lord Winchelsea). Wellington also showed his pragmatism when he was later used by Peel to persuade the House of Lords to allow the bill to repeal the hated Corn Laws to go through, even though the Duke was against repeal. Croker claims Wellington privately did propose adopting a 'large measure of reform' as a compromise when he tried to form a Cabinet in 1831 and Croker walked out in protest. 'The Duke afterwards sent for me alone and was seriously angry that I was still obstinate,' said Croker.[10]

Having failed to form a Cabinet to offer a compromise, Wellington gave up the effort. From then on, he was vehemently opposed to reform. Elizabeth Longford conceded that his belief that 'the scum of the earth' had to be controlled ultimately by iron discipline, including flogging, was a 'pitifully static view of human nature'. But, she added, that for the Duke, it had a 'superficial realism' which influenced Wellington for many a long year to come. In other words, Wellington believed that 'the scum of the earth' had to be kept in their place or there would be chaos.

Some of the Duke's arguments sound ludicrous today. Wellington argued that if there were elections in Manchester, the mobs would riot and bring pressure to bear on the candidates, whereas under the present system, a Manchester merchant sitting for a county seat would be free to vote as his conscience and judgment dictated because he had so few voters. Charles Lennox, the uncle of Wellington's friend, the 4th Duke of Richmond, put the alternative case perfectly when he introduced a reform bill for universal men's suffrage in 1780: 'The poor man has equal right but more need to have representation than the rich one …' Richmond's reform bill was reprinted as a pamphlet in 1817 by campaigners for reform. However, Wellington appeared as implacable and immovable as if he was being attacked by the Imperial Guard; he went from national hero to hate figure.

Three attempts to pass the Reform Bill were made before it finally went through. The pro-reform Whigs under Earl Grey were returned with a majority in the Commons and a clear mandate to pass the Reform Bill in April 1831, but Wellington led peers in blocking it in the House of Lords. Wellington told the Lords: 'From the period of the adoption of that measure will date the downfall of the Constitution.'

Wellington's refusal to bow to public opinion triggered Reform Riots across England and caused a constitutional crisis. Bristol was occupied by the rioters for three days. Wellington's London home, Apsley House, was attacked by the mob while the body of his wife Kitty lay on her death bed. On 28 April 1831 Wellington wrote to Harriet Arbuthnot: 'I learn from John [his housekeeper] that the mob attacked my house and broke about thirty windows. He fired two blunderbusses in the air from the top of the house, and they went off.' Wellington regarded the London mob as more dangerous than the Paris mob because it was indisciplined: 'Our mob is not trained nor accustomed to regular direction as the French was; once let it loose, and you will see what it will do!' He resorted to putting iron shutters across the windows, and he was ridiculed for it as 'The Iron Duke' – the name by which his troops had proudly known him.

In desperation Prime Minister Grey asked the king, William IV, to create more peers to allow the measure through; when the king refused, Grey resigned as prime minister and the king asked Wellington to form a government. It was then, according to Croker, that the Duke was tempted to dabble in a compromise but with loyal allies like Croker walking out on him, Wellington could never find sufficient support and the king had no option but to summon Grey again. Britain tottered on the brink of anarchy and revolution, the protestors called for a run on the Bank of England and the overthrow of the monarchy. In the midst of a constitutional crisis, William IV secretly wrote to peers without the knowledge of the Cabinet, pleading with them to back down. Erskine May, the constitutional expert, said it was constitutionally highly improper for the king to interfere in this way, but Wellington conceded defeat and the Tory peers relented.

It was not as if the lower classes – the 'scum of the earth' – were being offered the vote as they had in Richmond's bill. The vote was extended merely from 478,000 men to 813,000 men in a population of 24 million, about 4 men in every 100. The vote was limited in the 1832 Reform Act to the new middle classes – the businessmen, professional classes and journalists agitating for change – who were £10 householders in the boroughs and £10 leaseholders in the shires. Even so, when the Bill was presented by Lord John Russell, the Postmaster General, it surprised even its supporters by the sweeping nature of its reform of the rotten boroughs. The 1832 Reform bill marked a watershed that turned Britain from a fundamentally medieval system of privilege for a few aristocrats towards a modern democracy. It abolished 143 smaller borough seats, and replaced them with 130 seats, including two for each of the industrial towns that had led the fight for reform – Birmingham, Manchester, Leeds, Halifax and Bradford and Oldham.

The first MP for Oldham was the veteran campaigner for humble folk in the countryside, William Cobbett, though by then he had returned from America decidedly odd, attacking Jews, rather than the outrage of Peterloo. Hunt became the MP for Preston in 1831 and opposed the Reform Act because it did not go far enough; he lost his seat in 1833 and having turned his back on public life, died in 1835 in Hampshire.

The aristocratic elite held on to most of their 'pocket boroughs'. The Duke of Norfolk still controlled eleven seats – including Creevey's – and the Earl of Lonsdale had nine in his pocket, while the Duke of Devonshire and Lord Darlington each had seven Parliamentary seats in their gift. This not only gave a few aristocratic landowners great influence over the government, but it also gave unelected peers control over the elected Commons until they were swept away in the Reform Act of 1867.

The crisis ended but the campaign for more reform went on. All men over 21 were given a vote in 1918 but it was not until 1928 that women were finally granted equal voting rights with men. The Whig historian Thomas Macaulay was jubilant after the vote on 7 June 1832:

It was like seeing Caesar stabbed in the Senate House, or seeing Oliver [Cromwell] taking the mace from the table ... We set up a shout that you might have heard in Charing Cross - waving our hats – stamping against the floor and clapping our hands. The tellers scarcely got through the crowd. But you might have heard a pin drop as Duncannon read the numbers. Then again the shouts broke out – and many of us shed tears – I could scarcely refrain. And the jaw of Peel fell; and the face of Twiss was as the face of a damned soul. We shook hands and clapped each other on the back, and went out laughing, crying, and huzzaing into the lobby.

A painting of the Commons to celebrate the passage of the Act was started in 1833 by Sir George Hayter (a year before the old chamber in St Stephens Chapel was destroyed by fire). It shows Wellington standing by the opposition benches (as a peer, he could not sit in the Commons) – he is silver-haired and handsome, turning and smiling to his friends as if saying 'they are fools'; and some of the protagonists for reform including Grey, Cobbett, William Lamb the 2nd Viscount Melbourne (who became Queen Victoria's first prime minister) and the Irish nationalist O'Connell. Thomas Creevey saw the Great Reform Act of 1832 as the salvation of the nation:

> The conqueror of Waterloo had great luck on that day; so he had when Marmont made a false move at Salamanca; but at last comes his own false move, which has destroyed himself and his Tory high-flying association for ever, which has passed the Reform Bill without opposition. That has saved the country from confusion and perhaps the monarch and monarchy from destruction.[11]

Wellington's great victory in 1815 was so complete that Waterloo entered the English language as a simile for a crushing defeat. The Great Reform Act of 1832 was Wellington's 'Waterloo'. Wellington lived long enough for the reform battles to be forgotten and for the Duke to be celebrated as the elder statesman of the Victorian Age.

In retirement, Copenhagen was put out to grass at Stratfield Saye, the stately home granted to the Duke by a grateful nation on the Hampshire-Berkshire border, and Copenhagen became a family favourite when old age had dulled his skittishness. Kitty, the Duchess of Wellington, who wore a bracelet of Copenhagen's hair, said: 'He trots after me eating bread out of my hand and wagging his tail like a little dog.' Copenhagen died aged 28 in 1836 and was buried with military honours; he was also honoured with an obituary in *The Times*:

> On the 12th of February died at Stratfield Saye, of old age, Copenhagen, the horse which carried the Duke of Wellington so nobly on the field of Waterloo … He lost an eye some years before his death and has not been used by the noble owner for any purpose during the last ten years. By orders of his grace a salute was fired over his grave and thus he was buried as he had lived, with military honours …

He was buried under the Turkey Oak in the Ice House Paddock at Stratfield Saye, marked by a gravestone put up by the second Duke. The Duke made sure Copenhagen avoided suffering the indignity of Marengo, Napoleon's favourite horse, which had its skeleton mounted after its death in old age. Marengo's bones are still on show at the National Army Museum in London. It was going to be stuffed but the taxidermist lost the hide.

In the outpouring of pride over Waterloo, the Wellington Arch was built at Green Park near Apsley House. It was encouraged by George IV as a triumphal arch as part of a great processional way from Constitution Hill, and in 1848 a giant equestrian statue of the Duke mounted on Copenhagen was commissioned – thanks to a pro-Wellington clique led by his ally John Wilson Croker. It was huge. The equestrian monster weighed 40 tons and was 28 feet high, and immediately became the source of ridicule and acute embarrassment to the government. When the statue of the horse and rider – the biggest equestrian statute ever constructed in Britain – was erected on top of the arch as a trial, it became clear that the scale was far too great for even that grand pedestal. It loomed over Buckingham Palace, upsetting the young Queen Victoria, and caused a row. A campaign was started to remove it before it had settled into place. Wellington wrote to Croker on 19 November 1846 saying: 'My Dear Croker, It appears that the Queen (Victoria) and Prince Albert came to London from Windsor on Saturday morning, the 7th, and her Majesty ordered that it should be removed ...'

It would have been doubly galling to Wellington that Nelson had a vast square and a column dedicated to his memory and the Prince of Orange had the Lion Mound, but the young queen objected to an equestrian statue of Wellington, whose victory was more complete. Because of the Duke's prestige, it was left in place for the next thirty-five years. It was finally taken down in 1883 when the arch was moved and, after an outcry by Waterloo veterans to stop it being melted down, it was removed 41 miles west to the garrison town of Aldershot – probably the longest retreat the Duke had made since the Peninsular War. It now sits largely forgotten by the nation on a grassy knoll by the A325. Instead of towering over Buckingham Palace and the traffic entering London on the Victory Way, Wellington and Copenhagen look down over a suburban roundabout by the Premier Inn.

Notes

1.   *The Trials of Arthur Thistlewood, James Ings, John Thomas Brunt, Richard Tidd, William Davidson and Others* (London: J. Butterworth and Son, 1820), p. 10.
2.   Obituary, John Stafford, *The Times*, September 1837.
3.   HO 44/4 207 Cato Street files, National Archives.
4.   HO 44/4 Cato Street files, National Archives.
5.   George Theodore Wilkinson, *An Authentic History of the Cato Street Conspiracy* <openlibrary.org> (London: Thomas Kelly, 1820), p. 383.
6.   Ibid.
7.   Wilkinson, *An Authentic History*.
8.   Lord Liverpool to Canning, 23 March 1820, Harewood mss. West Yorkshire Archive Service, Leeds.
9.   Rt Hon. Sir Herbert Maxwell, *Creevey Papers*, 17 August 1820 (London: John Murray, 1904), p. 142.
10.   Louise J. Jennings (ed.), *The Croker Papers of John Wilson Croker, Secretary to the Admiralty 1809 to 1830* (London: John Murrary, 1884), p. 137.
11.   Ibid., 26 May 1832.

POSTSCRIPT

Do we treat our veterans any better today? Afghanistan and Iraq have left Britain with a legacy of injured men and women with physical and emotional scars like the veterans of Waterloo. Parish relief has been replaced by charities such as the Royal British Legion, the Not Forgotten Association and Help for Heroes, which was founded in 2007 by Bryn Parry, a former member of the Green Jackets, and his wife Emma after visiting the Selly Oak Hospital in Birmingham and deciding they had to do their bit. The following year David Cameron, then Leader of the Opposition, claimed that the 'military covenant' established by the Labour government in 2000 was 'well and truly broken'.[1] One of the problems highlighted by Cameron stemmed from the phasing out of military hospitals such as the specialist burns unit near Woolwich barracks, London, on the grounds that there were not enough military patients to justify them in the long term. It led to an outcry after reports of soldiers being abused by other patients on NHS wards.

Cameron said injured soldiers should not be treated for their wounds alongside civilian patients in NHS hospitals. He set up a commission under the author Frederick Forsyth to investigate. Forsyth reported there was widespread dissatisfaction over armed forces pensions, widows' pensions and compensation for injury and illness in the act of duty, which was often far less than criminals could claim for injuries. Forsyth's report claimed Labour had failed in a number of respects to match their rhetoric with deeds: the failure to provide Service personnel with appropriate equipment – such as flimsy 'Snatch' Land Rovers that cost lives in Afghanistan – was 'lamentable'. Forsyth's commission also found soldiers were frustrated by 'the onward march of "lawfare"', the legal requirements of the Human Rights courts; this was a problem that never confronted Wellington's men, though they had a strong moral code.

In 2011 the Commons select committee on defence investigated whether the covenant was being upheld any better under the Coalition government. It still found plenty of failures, but its main concern was 'whether the support for personnel when they leave the services will be sustainable …'

Have conditions really changed all that much from the time men like Sergeant Graham, Matthew Clay and John Lees were discarded by the army and made forgotten heroes of Waterloo? The cross-party committee, chaired by a Tory MP James Arbuthnot (whose ancestor Charles Arbuthnot helped to deliver Wellington's Waterloo Despatch to the Cabinet), found many of the same problems that haunted the men when they left the ranks of Wellington's army:

> We are concerned about the number of people who may go on to develop severe and life-limiting mental health, alcohol or neurological problems. We remain to be convinced that the government as a whole fully understands the likely future demands and the related costs.[2]

The committee won a promise from the government that no injured soldiers would be served redundancy notices on their sick beds, but that was little solace to the men and women who knew that when they got better, they could be sacked.

The reduction in the size of the army over the decade to 2020 from 102,000 to 82,000 – and their replacement by 30,000 reservists – is going to be a continuing cause of grievance and strain for the men and women serving in today's armed services.

Wellington's army coped with its bloody victory by enjoying some time in Paris as conquerors. Today, some go through 'decompression' for thirty-six hours in an armed forces 'beach club' in Cyprus after tours in Afghanistan or elsewhere to help them cope with the stress. Many fail to cope. Men like 18-year-old John Bryant, Britain's youngest serving frontline serviceman in Afghanistan in 2010, who broke the rules to get out of the Army and six months later was left homeless.[3]

The MPs returned to the theme of the military covenant in 2013 and recommended that the armed forces should do more to educate its men and women for life outside the forces when they are discharged. Today, after Iraq and Afghanistan, there are nearly 200,000 servicemen and women who depend on the Defence Medical Services, which runs the Defence and National Rehabilitation Centre at Headley Court, Surrey (to be moved to Loughborough in 2018), the NHS, charities and welfare organisations.

The terrible carnage caused on patrols by roadside bombs (they are often so sophisticated that they should no longer be called *Improvised* Explosive Devices) means that Britain is having to get used to the sight of ex-service men and women without limbs, like Regency Britain did in the peace after the Napoleonic Wars.

Historically, Britons have always been wary of a standing army just in case it was used against them. They have always been ambivalent about the problems of the 'Bloody Infantry' until they are needed (as Kipling brilliantly identified in his poem 'Tommy'). The Royal British Legion and Help for Heroes are making a difference to public attitudes. But we still owe it to the men and women of the armed services that they are not forgotten. They deserve better than to be treated like some of Wellington's forgotten heroes, the 'scum of the earth'.

Notes

1. BBC online, 4 March 2008.
2. HC 762, *Armed Forces Covenant in Action?* Commons Select Committee for Defence.
3. *Independent*, 21 February 2013.

SELECT BIBLIOGRAPHY

Manuscript sources

Wellington Archive, Southampton University
Archives of the House of Rothschild, London
National Archives, Kew – for police statements on Cato Street conspiracy

Published Sources

Bush, Michael: *The Casualties of Peterloo* (Lancaster: Carnegie Publishing Ltd, 2005)

Byron, Lord: *Byron's Correspondence* (London: John Murray, 1903)

Cecil, David: *The Young Melbourne and Lord M* (London: Phoenix Press, 1988)

Clare, John: *Poems Chiefly From Manuscript* edited by Edmund Blunden and Alan
   Porter (Project Gutenberg eBook, 2005)

Clay, Matthew: *A Narrative of the Battles of Quatre-Bras and Waterloo; With the Defence
   of Hougoumont*, edited by Garth Glover (UK Ken Trotman Publishing, 2006)

Colby, Reginal: *Waterloo Despatch, The*: (London: HMSO, 1965)

Creevey, Thomas: *The Creevey Papers* (London, John Murray, 1904)

Croker, John Wilson: *The Croker Papers,* (London: John Murray, 1884)

Dalton, Charles: *The Waterloo Roll Call* (London: Eyre and Spottiswood, 1904)

De Lancey: *A Week at Waterloo in 1815. Lady de Lancey's Narrative,* edited by Major B.
   R. Ward (London: John Murray, 1906)

Dowling, Joseph Augustus: *The Whole Proceedings before the Coroner's Inquest at
   Oldham on the Body of John Lees* (London: Joseph Augustus Dowling, 1820)

Ferguson, Niall: *The House of Rothschild – Money's Prophets 1798-1848* (London:
   2000)

Gibson Lockhart, John: *History of Napoleon Buonaparte* (London: J.M. Dent and
   Sons Ltd, 1906)

Gronow, Rees Howell: *The Reminiscences and Recollections of Captain Gronow*
   (London: Smith, Elder and Co, 1862)

Hibbert, Christopher: *George IV* (London: Penguin 1976)

Hibbert, Christopher: *Wellington – A Personal History* (London: HarperCollins, 1997)

Holmes, Richard: *Complete War Walks* (BBC Worldwide, 1997); *Redcoat – The British Soldier in the Age of Horse and Musket* (London: HarperCollins 2001)

Hugo, Victor: *Les Miserables*: (New York: Thomas Y. Crowell and Co, 1887)

Jackson, Lt-Col Basil: *Notes and Reminiscences of a Staff Officer* (London: John Murray, 1903)

Klingaman, William K and Klingaman, Nicholas P: *The Year Without Summer – 1816 And the Volcano That Darkened the World and Changed History* (New York: St Martin's Press, 2013)

Landale, James: *Duel – A true story of death and honour* (Edinburgh: Canongate Books, 2005)

Longford, Elizabeth: *Wellington – the Years of the Sword* (London: Weidenfeld and Nicolson, 1969)

Longford, Elizabeth: *Wellington – Pillar of State* (London: Weidenfeld and Nicolson, 1972)

Macbride, Mackenzie (ed.): *With Napoleon at Waterloo and Other Unpublished Documents of the Waterloo and Peninsular Campaigns* (London: Francis Griffiths, 1911)

Massie, Alan: *Byron's Travels* (London: Sidgwick and Jackson, 1988)

Melbourne, Lady: *Life and Letters, Byron's Corbeau Blanc*, edited by Jonathan David Gross (Liverpool University Press, 1997)

Mercer, General Cavalie: *Journal of the Waterloo Campaign* (London: William Blackwood, 1870)

O'Neil, Charles, *The Recollections of an Irish rogue* (UK: Leonaur, 2007)

Paget, Sir Julian and Saunders, Derek: *Hougoumont The Key to Victory at Waterloo* (Barnsley, South Yorkshire: Leo Cooper, 2001)

Porter, Roy: *English Society in the 18th Century* (London: Penguin 1982)

Roberts, Andrew: *Waterloo - Napoleon's Last Gamble* (London: Harper Perennial, 2005)

Schama, Simon: *A History of Britain V3 – The Fate of Empire 1776-2000* (London: BBC Worldwide, 2002)

Shelley, Lady Frances: *The Diary of Frances Lady Shelley 1787-1817* (London: John Murray, 1913)

Siborne, Captain William: *History of the War in France and Belgium in 1815* (London: T and W Boone, 1848)

Siborne, Maj-Gen. H.T. (ed.): *Waterloo Letters* (London: Cassell and Co., 1891)

Stanhope, 5th Earl: *Notes of Conversations with the Duke of Wellington, 1831-1851* (London: John Murray, 1888)

Summerville, Christopher: *Who Was Who at* Waterloo *– A Biography of the Battle* (London: Routledge, 2013)

Wilson, Harriette: *Harriette Wilson's Memoirs of Herself and Others* (London: Eveleigh Nash, 1909)

INDEX